# Professional Emotions in Court

*Professional Emotions in Court* examines the paramount role of emotions in the legal professions and in the functioning of the democratic judicial system. Based on extensive interview and observation data in Sweden, the authors highlight the silenced background emotions and the tacitly habituated emotion management in the daily work at courts and prosecution offices. Following participants 'backstage' – whether at the office or at lunch – in order to observe preparations for and reflections on the performance in court itself, this book sheds light on the emotionality of courtroom interactions, such as professional collaboration, negotiations, and challenges, with the analysis of micro-interactions being situated in the broader structural regime of the legal system – the emotive-cognitive judicial frame – throughout.

A demonstration of the false dichotomy between emotion and reason that lies behind the assumption of a judicial system that operates rationally and without emotion, *Professional Emotions in Court* reveals how this assumption shapes professionals' perceptions and performance of their work, but hampers emotional reflexivity, and questions whether the judicial system might gain in legitimacy if the role of emotional processes were recognized and reflected upon.

**Stina Bergman Blix** is an Associate Professor in the Department of Sociology at Uppsala University, Sweden.

**Åsa Wettergren** is a Professor of Sociology in the Department of Sociology and Work Science at the University of Gothenburg, Sweden.

# Professional Emotions in Court

A Sociological Perspective

**Stina Bergman Blix and Åsa Wettergren**

Routledge
Taylor & Francis Group

LONDON AND NEW YORK

First published 2018
by Routledge
2 Park Square, Milton Park, Abingdon, Oxon OX14 4RN

and by Routledge
52 Vanderbilt Avenue, New York, NY 10017

*Routledge is an imprint of the Taylor & Francis Group, an informa business*

*British Library Cataloguing-in-Publication Data*
A catalogue record for this book is available from the British Library

*Library of Congress Cataloging-in-Publication Data*
A catalog record has been requested for this book

ISBN: 978-1-138-23450-5 (hbk)
ISBN: 978-1-315-30675-9 (ebk)

Typeset in Times New Roman
by codeMantra

# Contents

# Figures and tables

## Figures

## Tables

# Acknowledgements

Years before we began our research project on emotions in courts, Stina found herself seated next to a judge at a dinner party. When she told him that she did research on emotions in the theatre, he exclaimed: "That sounds just like my work, I work a lot with emotions!" He described an incident when he had "displayed anger" during a hearing with an offensive defendant. He said that he had not at all felt angry; the display of anger was just a tool to move the proceeding forward. Later that day, he was on the train on his way home, reflecting on his workday. When thinking about the disturbing defendant, he suddenly experienced strong irritation: "How rude that defendant was!" The meeting with this judge was surprising both because the judge described himself as doing emotion work and because he described the time-lapse between his expression of anger and his experience of anger as being several hours. At that time, we did not know it, but many more insightful reflections about emotions in court would follow.

This book is deeply indebted to all of the judges and to all of the prosecutors who volunteered to participate in our research project. Forty-three judges from four courts and forty-one prosecutors from four prosecution offices have generously accepted our presence as 'shadows' and spent hours of their precious time in interviews, sharing their thoughts and reflections on emotions in and of their work. Without them, there would be no project and no book. Special thanks goes to the appeals court judge who accepted to be interviewed in the pilot we made for the research application, and who also shared with us invaluable contacts and names of people who might be interested in participating at our first district court. Special thanks also goes to the prosecutor who let us shadow him for two days and who initiated contact with the head of both a prosecution office and a court where we were then allowed to collect data. This judge and this prosecutor paved the way for us, not only in the courts and prosecution offices, but also in getting our research application approved. When proposing previously unresearched topics, it is crucial to show that the topic of study has resonance in the prospected field and that one has already established initial contacts.

In spite of the fact that so many judges and prosecutors recognized that our research was relevant and important, we soon realized that researching legal professional emotions and emotion management was a sensitive topic. We therefore decided that it would be wise to initiate fieldwork at each new location by approaching the chief prosecutors and the presidents of the courts to inform them about the project and our presence in 'their' courts and prosecution offices. We also asked them to let us give a short presentation of the project, so that judges and prosecutors could approach us and volunteer as participants. All of the presidents and chief prosecutors that we contacted not only granted our request but also wholeheartedly endorsed our project. They both literally and symbolically gave us the keys to the courts and prosecution offices, and in some cases even a workspace during our time there. Knowing that the higher up in the hierarchy – especially of judges – we move, the more the management is cautious about new and challenging ideas, we want to express our thanks and our sincere respect for these chief prosecutors and presidents who supported and trusted us. We believe that these times are times of rocking the boat of the legal system's age-old beliefs about positivist objectivity and pure rationality. In this context, all of the participant judges and prosecutors in our project are pioneers on fragile new ground.

The project idea was born in August 2010 when we both met at the midterm conference of the European Sociological Association (ESA) Research Network 11 in Graz. We were familiar with each other's previous research and were both in need of a juicy new project idea with which to apply for research funding, or else we would commit suicide by teaching (Swedish universities do not finance their teachers' research). We read a newspaper notice about a judge and started to talk about the courts as an interesting field. Stina had used dramaturgical theory before and pointed out the performance of justice as an interesting project. Åsa wanted to shift focus from research in the field of migration and asylum, where emotion was overwhelming, to an area where finding out about the emotions would be an empirical challenge in itself. We clicked as partners in research there and then, and eight years later, we are ever so close to finishing the sentence the other begun. Our joint research has benefitted enormously from this collaboration, and the sum of the two, in our case, is certainly more than its parts. Ever since then, the ESA research network has also had emotions and law on its session agenda, in which we have presented numerous ideas and drafts for articles and chapters of this book. We thank the network participants for all of the valuable questions and feedback we have received during these years.

Our close research collaboration has sometimes been taxing for our families in various ways, not to mention the hundreds of hours of overtime that we have spent together working on this book. Both of us are sincerely grateful to our own and each other's families for their understanding and ground-service.

We want to thank the Swedish Research Council for financing the project, Emotions in Court (No. 2011-1553). We also want to thank The Swedish Research Council for Health, Working Life and Welfare, FORTE: (No. 2011-0671) that financed Stina's stay in Adelaide, Australia, kindly invited there by our distinguished colleagues in the field of law and emotions, Professors Sharyn Roach Anleu and Kathy Mack. One of the anonymous reviewers of our research application turned out to be another distinguished colleague Professor Terry Maroney. We did not know her by then, but her appreciative review gave us a serious boost of professional pride that was only reinforced when we half a year later met at a conference and she turned out to be a prominent legal expert and researcher on judges' emotions in the US. Our conversation is ongoing ever since.

Last but not least we thank the colleagues and dear friends who have been reading and commenting on different chapters in this book in their draft versions: Göran Ahrne, Erik Andersson, Moa Bladini, Mary Holmes, Olof Rydén, and Linda Soneryd.

# 1    Why emotions in court?

> The entire courtroom felt like it might burst into tears, the voice of the presiding judge was trembling when we resumed after the father had finished his story; it was, like, so enormously – he explained their whole situation following the incident and you couldn't – the boy was still hospitalized, he could...they could not leave him alone for more than 20 minutes, I mean it was so awful, so terrible, and this was just a small kid – this has followed me for so long [one year].... I remember that trial as if it was yesterday.
>
> (Jonna, court clerk, 25+)

In the above quotation, court clerk Jonna describes what is generally considered an emotional event. She describes it in a way that conveys the density of sadness in the courtroom – it is easy to imagine what it was like and how difficult it must have been to control that sadness and redirect focus to court matters and procedures. These are the kinds of events that court professionals will remember and retell if you ask them to describe the ways in which their job is emotional. Sometimes they will claim this sensitivity to the emotional sides of a case to be, for them, a thing of the past, belonging to a time when they were less experienced and less 'chastened'. In our data, however, there are also numerous examples of experienced judges and prosecutors describing how also they can be deeply emotionally impacted, especially by cases involving children as victims. When that happens, the judge may need to call for a break in the proceedings so that he or she can withdraw backstage and recover before continuing. In this book, we term the kind of strong emotions that may intervene in or disrupt a person's professional performance 'foreground emotions'. Foreground emotions are those "which draw attention not only to objects and events external to the emoting subject but also to the emoting subject's internal states" (Barbalet, 2011: 39). The reason they may disrupt a person's professional performance is, precisely, that they force the subject to reflect upon and regulate his or her own 'internal state'. When judges feel like crying, part of their focus is shifted from overseeing the court proceedings and listening to the parties to making an effort not to cry. This is because a crying judge would be a serious frame break (Goffman, 1974): it would violate the feeling rules of the court.

In this chapter, we first present the background and the overall argument of this book, along with its theoretical problem area – emotion and rationality – that we locate in relation to the developing academic field of law and emotion. Thereafter follows a crash course in the Swedish judicial system, to enable a better understanding of the empirical settings (for a detailed presentation, see Appendix: The Swedish Judicial Procedure). Next, we proceed to explicate the perspectives and key concepts of our sociological approach to emotions. This theoretical section is followed by a discussion of analytical generalization, in general, and of the analytical generalizability of our findings, in particular. While noting certain specificities in different legal systems, we argue for the general relevance, at least in the countries of the Western world, of the analysis and results presented in this book. The chapter ends with an overview of the remaining contents of the book.

In some places in this chapter, the reader will come upon boxes with the heading "How did we do it?" inserted under the text. "How did we do it?" – boxes offer relevant methodological information connected to the theoretical discussions in the paragraph(s) preceding the box. The information on methods conveyed in the boxes is also important to understand the context of the data presented in the rest of the book.

Our interest in studying emotions in court derives from a broader theoretical quest to investigate the role of emotions in rational fields in which they are supposed to be irrelevant, for instance in bureaucratic organizations (Sieben and Wettergren, 2010; Wettergren, 2010). During our first encounters with the courts and prosecution offices, we were careful not to mention the word emotion too often, enquiring rather about legal professionals' thinking about, or experience of, situations in their daily work life. It did not take long, however, before almost everyone we met wanted to talk about emotions and their efforts to manage emotions on an everyday basis: "You should have been there for the hearing I was in today!" The episodes spontaneously recounted to us usually referred to concrete emotional expressions shown by lay or professional actors during hearings. Yet, when probing the issue in interviews, both prosecutors and judges highlighted a whole range of situations and aspects that in their work called for a strategic approach to managing emotions. What was involved in this managing was both other people's emotions ("We meet people in crisis on a daily basis") and one's own ("To some extent I try to present myself as authoritarian, or at least as someone alert, to show that I'm the one in charge of the hearing"). Although not all of the situations described to us were as deeply emotional as the one Jonna recounted in the quote above, all of them provided examples of foreground emotional processes at work.

However, it was not first and foremost foreground emotions that we were after. Our choice of a supposedly hyper-rational context for this study was guided by a wish to unveil emotions and emotional processes that are much less tangible and much more difficult to observe. These emotions are unlikely to leave any strong memories and typically do not disturb one's professional focus. Rather the contrary: they motivate and fuel the latter. As judge Ruth insightfully described it:

> If I weren't genuinely interested I wouldn't continue, since I belong to the 1940s' generation with an obscene pension [laughter] and so I don't have to be in it for the money.... My work as a judge has not been influenced by emotions, except that it's been – that is an emotion of course – to feel *serious* is an emotion ... so in that sense my work's been influenced by emotions.
>
> (Ruth, chief judge, 65+)

Judge Ruth identifies her 'seriousness' at work as an emotion, noting also an 'interest' that motivates her to keep working past the traditional retirement age. In this book, we term the kinds of emotions she speaks of 'background emotions'. These emotions "function by foregrounding external objects of attention while remaining outside the emoting subject's consciousness" (Barbalet, 2011: 36). They form the emotional backdrop needed to perform rational and instrumental action. They are hardly noticed, precisely because they do not occasion any focus shifts. On the contrary, they work with cognition to produce the desired end.

In this book, the concepts of background emotion and foreground emotion provide the central sensitizing and analytical concepts with which to organize our research. While the notion of backgrounded/foregrounded emotion was first coined by Jack Barbalet (1998), in our approach they become key analytical tools enabling us to understand how emotion can be systematically silenced yet influential, and how the management of emotions according to situated feeling rules (i.e. at work) can become routinized and habituated (see the "Theoretical framework and key concepts" section, p. 17). This approach to, and focus on, background emotions is what makes our research unique. Previous research on emotions in court has been limited to foreground emotions and emotion management.

In modern democracies, the legal system revolves around the ideas of pure rationality and positivist objectivity, that is, the assumption that emotion has nothing to do with that system, or, as Max Weber put it in his work on the rationality of bureaucracy, that work in it is carried out "without anger and fondness" (Weber, 1948: 215). It was assumptions of this kind – that there are no emotions at play in legal practice – that made the topic an interesting and challenging one for us to study. Indeed, the role of emotional processes in the production of justice is neither fully recognized nor sufficiently scrutinized. There is therefore a need to open up the black box of emotion in justice and to learn more about how this (tacit) professional competence is applied.

The aim of the project *Emotions in Court* (2012–2016), on which this book is based, was thus to study emotions and emotion management in Swedish courts. Proceeding from the theoretical distinction between background and foreground emotions, we wanted to find out not *whether*, but *in which ways*, emotions were active and acted upon in criminal investigations, court trials, and in the everyday interactions around hearings, and how organizational and structural dimensions, such as power and status, were linked to emotions and emotion management.

---

**How did we do it?**

This book draws upon a multi-sited case study covering four strategically selected Swedish district courts and their respective prosecution offices. The data for it were collected in 2012–2016 using a combination of ethnographic methods: observation, interviews, and shadowing. The shadowing and the interviews (N = 144) involved a total of 100 different legal actors: 43 judges, 41 prosecutors, and 16 defence lawyers.[1] In addition, we observed approximately 300 different hearings. Observations made in connection with the shadowings (e.g. during small talk in the backstage area of the court) were recorded in a separate field diary, along with preliminary analyses and reflections on our own emotions.

   Given our research interest, the study focused on district court (lower court) judges and prosecutors, who are state employees expected to remain objective and, in keeping with the positivist notion of objectivity, unemotional in their work. Defence lawyers, and legal counsels in general, differ from this criterion in that they are privately employed (or self-employed) and partial in their attitude (required to work for their client's interests). It is, furthermore, important to note that though we have strived for our data collection to include roughly the same number of women as men, we have not undertaken a gender analysis of the data. Research on courts in Australia suggests "perhaps a less complete allegiance among women to the cultural script of dispassion in which emotion play no role" (Roach Anleu and Mack, 2017: 67), but the preliminary impression of our findings rather suggests that women and men are as likely to embrace, and to problematize, the ideal of non-emotional justice. To some extent, this may be explained by different gender regimes in Australia and Sweden. We argue, however, that an even more likely explanation for the lack of gender difference in our material is our focus on background emotions. Background emotions – as opposed to foreground emotions – are not conventionally associated with being emotional and are therefore not gender-patterned. The indication of the quoted interviewee's gender (male or female as indicated by the person's fictional name) in this book serves to underscore the point that our emotion analysis is applicable to judges and prosecutors regardless of gender. This is to say that awareness of the relevance of emotions in legal work is not an effect of some increasing 'feminization' of the workplace, nor was it mainly women participants who volunteered to participate in the project.

**Emotion and rationality**

Even though our encounter with the field was predominantly positive and emotions proved to be a topic open for discussion in some respects, in other respects emotions were systematically silenced. This appeared to be due to the dominant notion of positivist objectivity that still reigns in the legal system: one could say that the closer one got to the emotive-cognitive processes surrounding the evaluation of material (facts, evidence, testimonies), the more there was reluctance to consider emotions and emotional processes as useful tools or information carriers. This reluctance became particularly prominent when we asked our respondents about how to evaluate 'trustworthiness', a concept often employed and referred to by defence lawyers, prosecutors, and judges. While there are several methods to evaluate evidence in court (cf. Diesen, 2015; Ekelöf et al., 2009), in the Swedish context, to put it briefly, a statement, according to the country's Supreme Court, is trustworthy if it is coherent, clear, comprehensive, vivid, detailed, stable over time, easy to comprehend, long, spontaneous, and restrained. Reversely, typical of an untrustworthy statement is that it is unclear, poor in details, and/or incomprehensible, and changes over time (see, e.g., NJA, 2009:44: 447, 2010:17: 671). Yet another criterion of trustworthiness is that it "carries the impression of authentic experience", but this characterization has been severely criticized and is disappearing from usage (NJA, 2010:17: 671). In general, research in psychology has demonstrated a very low success rate of such professional criteria for what constitutes a trustworthy/non-trustworthy statement, essentially on the same low level as that of lay people's assessments (Granhag et al., 2005; Strömwall and Granhag, 2003; Vrij et al., 2010). Accordingly, when asked about their notion of trustworthiness, our interviewees either sought to change the subject or embarked on reasoning along the following lines:

> Trustworthiness means that you understand the person to be trying his or her best to give a correct description of what happened, and that you can see that this description of the events squares with what other persons have seen and observed, so you draw the conclusion that this person is trustworthy, reliable. But it's something you have to work out; you can't just, like, say that someone's trustworthy, you first need to hear this person speak, narrate, and then it's about nuances, about details, about the way they narrate, their body language, facial expressions, emotions.... I mean, someone who just straight away talks like this without any emotions: that makes you wonder, of course. At the same time, if someone overacts and shows an awful lot of emotions, that makes you wonder, too ... so that's something you just have to work out for yourself, which is not always that easy. It's a challenge we have, to determine if this person is trustworthy or not. Are there gaps in the story, hesitations? That can be the case even if you're trustworthy...but what it leads to – sometimes in the judgments, you see the judges reason, like, "Well,

there are some contradictions in the victim's story, but they're not so serious as to undermine his or her credibility"....

(Henrik, prosecutor, aged 45+)

Both the above descriptions by the Supreme Court and the reasoning in the quote by the prosecutor Henrik, involve emotions; for any narrative to come across as 'vivid', 'spontaneous', 'restrained', and thus trustworthy, expression of emotion on the part of the narrator is necessary. As we see in the quote by Henrik, the assessment of these qualities also involves emotions, that is, alertness to impressions conveyed by emotional information (nuances, details, the way they narrate, body language, facial expressions, emotions). Yet, because the ideal of pure rationality – that is, rationality 'uncontaminated' by any emotions – forms such a sacred core value of the legal system, openly reflecting on emotions as a source of information would have a disqualifying effect on any legal professional. Nevertheless, in this research, we sometimes came across words that seemed to straddle the line between that which was acceptable and that which was not, such as 'trustworthiness'. Related to this grey zone, the former appeals court judge and current associate professor in procedural law Roberth Nordh discusses the notion of 'intuition':

> It may seem a fragile ground to stand on, but, for the final evaluation and reconciliation against the evidentiary requirement, the most valuable tool is *the judge's intuition*. By that is *not meant the judge's feeling* for the way reality has presented itself. On the contrary, it is important that the judge *frees herself from emotional reactions* and assesses the evidence by way of *objective, rational* considerations. Intuition in this context denotes the judge's *knowledge, experience, wisdom, and sound judgement*.
>
> (Nordh, 2013: our translation, emphasis added)

The quote is full of interesting paradoxes. In order to uphold the ideal of pure rationality, the admission that there is an element of intuition involved in legal assessment processes is immediately countered by a complete disallowance of emotions. To remain objective and rational, the judge must "free herself from emotional reactions". Still, emotions are immediately introduced back again, by defining intuition as 'experience', 'wisdom', and 'sound judgement'. In line with our theoretical framework and the concept of background emotions, what Nordh captures in this quote are the concerted and closely intertwined emotional *and* cognitive background processes that enable the judge to correctly evaluate evidence. Nevertheless, Nordh's habituated professional practice of silencing emotions forces him into a contradictory argument, leading him to try to capture intuition as a merely cognitive assessment, assembling facts and deducing the correct answer in much the same way a computer would (Bladini, 2013: 365; Mellqvist, 2013: 494).

Experience, to begin with, is not an entirely cognitive phenomenon; it is virtually impossible to consciously and cognitively line up everything that we have learnt through all of our experience so far in regard to a specific object – for instance, whether a given person can be trusted or not. Even if this were possible, moreover, it would require an enormous amount of time and effort to present all that accumulated experience in a way that would enable systematic comparison to the actual case at hand. A much faster and more efficient way to access one's memory bank is emotion. According to the neurologist Antonio Damasio (2003), in the decision-making process, an experiential understanding, or a 'feeling' of the consequences of an alternative action, is fundamental to our ability to form rational decisions. Discussing the importance of emotional cues for our ability to draw conclusions from experience, Damasio, when interviewed in a talk show, elaborated the point as follows:

> When we make decisions at any time of the day you do not only remember what the factual result is but also what the emotional result is and that tandem of fact and associated emotion is critical [for making decisions]. Most of what we construct as *wisdom* over time is actually the result of cultivating that knowledge about how our emotions behaved and what we learnt from them.
>
> (Damasio, 2009)

Besides building on experience, wisdom and sound judgement* are concerned with morality: the question of what is good (sound) and what is bad (unsound). Accordingly, wisdom and sound judgement are also concerned with the consequences of a particular decision or assessment, related to a desired, ideally 'good' and 'wise' outcome in the context of a particular frame (Goffman, 1974). In this book, we operate with the term 'emotive-cognitive judicial frame' to conceptualize the specific framing of judicial practice, against which the professional performance, actions, and decisions of judges and prosecutors are measured as 'good' or 'bad'. Good and bad are not solely about cognitive judgement: they are also felt.

Good or bad performance is noticed not only by the professional collective, colleagues, and managements but also by the performing self. The way the self becomes informed about his or her ongoing performance (crucially in the sense of how it is valued by others) is through emotions of pride/satisfaction (good) and shame/embarrassment (bad). Wishing as we do for acceptance and inclusion in the professional world to which we aspire, such emotional clues help us identify and pick up the tacit pieces of knowledge – the 'tricks of the trade' – needed to succeed. One thing that is picked up already at the early stages of law education is the dictum that emotion cannot and should not have anything to do with legal practice (Flower, 2014). The subsequent trick of the trade is to learn to talk about emotions without talking about emotions, as evident also from the examples discussed above.

---

* We use the spelling judgement to refer to 'a sound judgement' in a moral sense (SWE: *omdöme*) and the spelling judgment to refer to legal judgment (SWE: *dom*) issued by the judge. In Sweden, the court decides on the verdict (guilty/not guilty) and the sentence (penalty) during the same hearing and both are announced and explicated in the judgment.

To sum up, the emotive-cognitive judicial frame postulates a disconnect between objectivity and rationality, on the one hand, and emotions, on the other hand. In a broader cultural perspective, this is a profoundly modern Western idea (von Wright, 1986), in line with other dichotomies such as mind vs body, public vs private, culture vs nature, civilized vs wild, and male vs female. Not wanting to stray too far away into a discussion of the dichotomous Western-modernist thinking, suffice it to say here that while intellectual thinking in general is today increasingly involved in undoing these boundaries, with also science questioning the idea of rationality and objectivity as non-emotional, law, as a domain, still seems unwilling to do so. As suggested by Bettina Lange (2002: 199), "emotion is constructed as 'other' to law", and it continues to be so. Terry Maroney (2011: 634) emphasizes this persistence: "the script of judicial dispassion reflects Western jurisprudence's longstanding insistence on a dichotomy between emotion and reason, and therefore between emotion and law".

## Emotion and law: the research field

It is primarily in Anglo-Saxon research and theory that an interest in emotions in court has gained ground over the past two decades. In consequence, most existing research in the area relates to the common-law system that builds on case law, instead of the civil-law system that builds on a code. The overarching ideals of pure rationality, dispassion, and objective justice are the same, however. That said, as will be clear from our analysis in this book, some interesting partial conclusions can be drawn from the fact that, strictly speaking, law is seen as more dynamic in the common-law system, while it is more set in stone and strictly applied in the civil-law system.

### Emotion, law, and morality

The relation between a dynamic and a static system has been discussed by the Swedish sociologist Johan Asplund, who, when describing the historical development of the Swedish judicial system, compares the way law was applied in Scandinavia in the 16th century and in our own time (1992: 46–54). In the 16th century, justice was practised in an 'emerging state', with trials taking place in the village centre, engaging every citizen, and the retributive elements of justice featuring very prominently. Today, justice is practised in a 'mature nation-state', in which the process of making law is left to the politicians and legal experts, leaving its implementation to legal institutions, which are relatively secluded from the rest of society. While this development walks hand in hand with the modern dichotomization of emotion and reason discussed above, Asplund suggests that the modern Swedish judiciary is in essence no less passionate or moralistic than in former times, it is only more controlled in terms of the 'passions' and the retributive elements.

Asplund's discussion of the emergence of modern law has important implications for the topic of law and morality. In our sociological perspective, shared moral consciousness and the associated emotions are the outcome of group interactions (Collins, 2004: see also the "Social interaction, frame, and ritual" section). The basic sociological model to explain this derives from Émile Durkheim who argued that out of religious ceremonies emerged collective effervescence and a collective moral consciousness relating to 'the sacred' and 'the profane' (Durkheim, 2008). The shared moral consciousness achieved social cohesion and integration in traditional and local societies. Building on Durkheim and Erving Goffman (e.g. 1967), Randall Collins asserts the prevalence of myriads of mundane interaction rituals that all give rise to feelings of group solidarity, emotional energy, and shared norms and values on local as well as national level. Emotional energy is the individual experience of belonging, recognition, and confidence, contingent on the extent to which he or she is capable of acting according to the norms and values of the group. High emotional energy entails feelings of pride and confidence (Collins, 1981, 2004). Collective moral values and emotions are thus deeply entwined with individual perceptions of the self, or put the other way around, moral consciousness simultaneously rise out of self-feelings and feelings of group affiliations.

In line with this sociological perspective, we argue that the law can be understood as essentially the codified moral consciousness of secularized society and a trial is the ritualized practice of a society's conceptions of right and wrong and of emotions connected to these conceptions (Dahlberg, 2009). The dislocation of law from the local village centre to the level of the state and its legal institutions does not remove morality from the core of law, but it inserts a distinction between institutionalized morality (the Law) and local or common sense morality/moralities. While the argument that the law rests on collective moral standards is not in itself controversial, it is a problem to the non-emotional image of law that common morality is essentially contingent, perhaps volatile, and deeply emotional. The concept of morality thus runs the risk of being seen, along with the 'passions', as 'other' to law and incompatible with the ideal of objective justice. One effect of this is that participants in our study assert that the law has no relation to morality.

The view on morality seems to be different in the more dynamic North American common-law system. One might speculate that morality in this system becomes of central concern to justice because judges themselves are engaged in the shaping of the law and because, contrary to the civil-law system, judges can be politically elected. The nexus of emotion–justice–morality is theoretically explored in Susan Bandes' collected volume *Passions in Law* (1999), which argues that the judicial system in general not only de facto integrates emotion, but is also morally required to do so in order to maintain its legitimacy. In the US, emotions are considered relevant for the assessments in, for instance, hate crimes, and in the use of shaming penalties. There is, however, also the more general insight that the moral codex does not rest on an exclusively rational basis (Posner, 1999). From a philosophical viewpoint, moral feelings of disgust, vengeance, anger, compassion, sympathy, and mercy saturate the law (Kahan, 1999; Murphy, 1999; Nussbaum, 1999; Solomon, 1999). In this context, it is important to note that Swedish criminal law traditionally rests on norms of restorative rather than retributive justice, making any strong moral emotions (e.g. vengeance) less obvious. Furthermore, in line with the civil-law system, the judiciary is designed to stand outside and above the political sphere; a judge is formally appointed by the state but thereafter untouchable. This focus on the judges' autonomy – lack of bonds and affiliations – thus contributes to the seeming impossible idea of judges as moral beings.

The more law making and the implementation of the law become areas of complex legal expertise, the more there is a risk of an increasing gap between the former and the common moral sense(s) of justice, with the courts seen by citizens as incomprehensible and far removed. The system with lay judges adopted in Sweden (see the "The Swedish judicial system" section) may be one way to keep the law in touch with common-sense morality. Another way is the increased focus on 'good treatment' echoing the ideal of procedural justice. Both 'good treatment' and procedural justice focus on the experienced fairness of the process itself rather than its outcome (Tyler, 2003).

### Morality and objectivity

Judges are removed from the messy reality of a crime and required to be impartial (Roach Anleu and Mack, 2017), which appears as taking a passive role in the adversarial procedure. There is a tension between this passive role and judges' need to be active in their role in presiding over the trial process, in "getting through the list" (Mack and Roach Anleu, 2007), but apart from that they have no concerns with the common-sense morality of justice. In contrast, an overarching predicament of the prosecutor is characterized by the tension between demands for objectivity, on the one hand, and commitment, on the other, where commitment brings forward issues such as loyalty (Bandes, 2006) and morality (Fisher, 1987). It can thus be argued that prosecutors' relative closeness to the victim[2] (sympathy) and the police (loyalty), as combined with the adversarial ideal of two opposing parties, results in an emotive-cognitive orientation towards defending the state/victim, informed by common-sense morality. This orientation may then run into conflict with prosecutors' duty, as state representatives, to pursue objective investigations.

In this context, it is important to underline that in Sweden, prosecutors are responsible for the one and only preliminary investigation of a crime (the defence can, but rarely does, undertake its own investigation), and that they take professional pride in their duty to secure evidence both in favour of and against the accused. Yet, among our study participants, a common reason for not choosing to become a defence lawyer was that one wanted to be on 'the right side'. Katarina Jacobsson's (2008) study of Swedish prosecutors highlights the concerns and adaptations of prosecutors attempting to meet the objectivity demand, showing objectivity not to be a given but a process, accomplished through situated objectivity work of constant reflexivity. We argue that such reflexivity involves negotiation between professional moral standards tacitly inscribed in the emotive-cognitive judicial frame and moral standards of common sense.

### Empathy and emotion management

Considerably more researched than morality by scholars on emotions and law is the topic of empathy (Bandes, 1996; Henderson, 1987). Empathy has been studied in relation to legal professionals' decision-making processes (Abrams, 2010; Bandes, 2009; Brennan, 1988; Mellqvist, 2013; Nussbaum, 1996) and their managing of the parties in court (Darbyshire, 2011; Roach Anleu and Mack, 2013). In our view, empathy is a crucial tool in emotion management. Empathy is the capacity to imagine the situation of others, emotionally tuning in with another person (Wettergren and Bergman Blix, 2016). In the words of Lynne Henderson (1987: 1576): "Empathy aids both processes of discovery [...] and processes of justification [...] in a way that dis-embodied reason simply cannot". To put it differently, in order to both gain relevant information and secure public trust for the legal process, the professional actors need to empathically attend to the emotions of defendants, victims, and witnesses. It has also been shown, moreover, that collaboration between the professional parties in court in showing empathy towards victims facilitates the performance of the legal process (Booth, 2012; Schuster and Propen, 2010). However, as Tracey Booth (2012) found in her study of the Australian Supreme Court, judges tended to display their empathic responses to victims' grief in subtle ways.

Consistent with the findings on empathy, studies have more generally shown judges to take great care to manage their personal emotions in order to display impartiality and fairness/justice before the public (Darbyshire, 2011; Herzog-Evans, 2014; Roach Anleu and Mack, 2005; Scarduzio, 2011). Sharyn Roach Anleu and Kathy Mack (2005), for instance, in their examination of the emotional labour of Australian magistrates found even the magistrates themselves to regard the management of emotions as an essential aspect of their work. Indeed, as also our own findings show (see, e.g., Chapter 4), attending to lay people's emotions is integral to the emotion management of judges, being especially important in situations where the defendant is unrepresented (Darbyshire, 2011; Roach Anleu and Mack, 2005). Judges' style and attitude often differ depending on whether the defendant has a legal representative or not (Hunter, 2005). According to Richard Moorhead (2007), the ideal of an impartial, passive judge presupposes two equal parties, which is never the case when one of the parties is unrepresented. Such cases then warrant more active engagement by the judge. In our research, both Swedish judges and prosecutors were indeed more actively engaged with the defendant when he or she was unrepresented, depending also on the defendant's behaviour in court. Unruly defendants angrily objecting to the claims or loudly demanding their rights received less help and support from the judges, compared to more quiet and collaborative ones.

As found by Sarah Goodrum (2013), rather than undermining the rationality of their courtroom work, prosecutors' empathic approach to victims in fact often helps them to achieve victim satisfaction with the prosecution and, more in general, the judicial system. The emotional attunement worked as a tool for attaining victims' personal goals and prosecutors' organizational goals (Goodrum, 2013: 268). As we have shown elsewhere (Wettergren and Bergman Blix, 2016), this kind of empathy is nonetheless limited by professional emotional orientations such as pride and pleasure taken in one's juridical expertise. Particularly prosecutors, closer than judges to the messy reality of a criminal incident, can avoid getting emotionally involved by focusing on legal encoding (Törnqvist, 2017). As for judges, they have been found to employ various emotion management techniques, such as depersonalization and emotional distancing, to shield themselves from individuals' misery (Roach Anleu and Mack, 2005; Schuster and Propen, 2010). They can, however, also be simply condescending, rude, or harsh towards defendants and other professional actors, or just bored by them (Mack and Roach Anleu, 2010; Ptacek, 1999).

### Power emotions

Emotional displays of anger, contempt, rudeness, boredom, and the like are often associated with power positions: they belong to people in superior positions (cf. Wettergren, 2009). Jennifer Scarduzio (2011) calls such displays and other similar aberrations from the norms of neutrality 'emotional deviance' that judges may be allowed due to their privileged position: their use of humour, expressions of anger and frustration, and rudeness constitute a power device for speeding up the procedure, relieving tension, and steering lay people behaviour. Indeed, as Maroney has shown, anger can be used for the purposes of displaying legitimate power in sentencing when the judge, using her authority, condemns the immoral acts of the defendant. When asserting the judge's dominance, the line between righteous and dehumanizing expressions can, however, be very fine (Maroney, 2012: 1258).

Expressions of the judge's power in court can be interpreted as condescension, indifference, or rudeness, but expressions of power can also be demonstrations of patience and listening (Ptacek, 1999; Roach Anleu and Mack, 2013). In our Swedish case, we found judges to hardly ever openly express such 'power emotions'. This corresponds to the broader understanding that in Swedish courts, it is on the whole very hard to find judges displaying anger in public (Bergman Blix and Wettergren, 2016). Depending on the situation, anger may, however, be sensed in the impenetrable stone face of Swedish judges. The stone face itself – while it is the judge's primary technique to display impartial listening – was sometimes interpreted by lay people in the court as both condescending and rude. The discretionary space to deviate from feeling rules being linked to power means that people in positions of low power need to more strictly conform to the feeling rules (Hochschild, 1983). Studies of paralegals have shown how subordinate legal actors, in particular women, need to manage their own as well as their superior lawyers' emotions, functioning as emotional buffers (Francis, 2006). Power and status positions – especially when these are challenged – are sources of emotional tensions between legal professionals (Kemper, 2011).

Power need not only be related to structural position, but can also be conceived of in a more Foucauldian sense as situated control of knowledge. Deirdre Bowen (2009), for instance, highlights the unequal power balance in plea bargain negotiations. The prosecutors' control of the evidence can give rise to suspicion and irritation from the defence lawyers. In this situation, experienced, high-status defence lawyers could to some degree equalize the power position of the two sides through professional networks and knowledge about how to 'play the rules' (Bowen, 2009: 25). In a similar vein, it is the judge who presides over the court, while prosecutors play the rules by adapting their style and demeanour to those of the judge (Wettergren and Bergman Blix, 2016).

During examinations and cross-examinations, prosecutors strategically expressing frustration, sarcasm, or sympathy can induce victims, defendants, or witnesses to express, for example, sadness or anger (Brannigan and Lynch, 1987; Wettergren and Bergman Blix, 2016). Such strategic use of emotions during hearings was a concern for all prosecutors in our material, although the actual strategies developed to a large extent depended on one's experience. Some of the prosecutors believed that expressing condescending power emotions was a useful way to examine a defendant. Others considered a 'nice', respectful approach to be more efficient, thus attempting to equalize the power asymmetry between prosecutor and defendant.

In summary, previous research has linked emotions to law via morality, suggesting the law to be codified collective moral consciousness. Empathy and emotion management have also been identified by previous research as important tools in legal professionals' interactions with victims, defendants, and witnesses. Legal actors find this task an important aspect of their work, but also take great care in presenting an objective and impartial demeanour in court by managing their own emotions and expressions. Previous studies have also examined some aspects of emotions and power.

Although most previous research is restricted to the common-law system, our research on the Swedish legal system confirms the relevance of previous findings in a civil-law system too. This said, our research takes the field forward by empirically investigating 'background emotions' in naturally occurring situated social interaction relevant to the field of emotions in legal practice. Such a comprehensive empirical approach to the field has not been taken so far. We argue that emotions do not simply enter into specific aspects or tasks of legal professionals' work, but are instead fundamental to it. In this book, we thus pioneer to offer a detailed analysis of background emotional processes in several interconnected dimensions of legal work. Last but not least, in taking the Swedish judicial system as the context of our investigation, we extend the research field of emotions and law to the civil-law system.

*Figure 1.1* Court house of Köping, Sweden. Photo: Helena Björnberg.

## The Swedish judicial system

Scandinavian law in general adheres to the civil-law system, although it shows certain common-law features such as some degree of case law and by adopting an adversarial process where the judge functions as a passive arbitrator. The pretrial features are inquisitorial, while the trial itself is adversarial. In contrast to the more dynamic procedure in common-law systems, judges are not supposed to make their own interpretations, but rather abide by the written law. In the following, key concepts of the Swedish judicial system that will recur also elsewhere in this volume are highlighted in italics. For an expanded presentation of the Swedish judicial system with references, see Appendix.

### Education and the legal professions

Law schools in Sweden take four and a half years to complete, with a degree from a law programme serving as the gateway to a career in the legal profession. Following graduation, the most common next step is to apply to the position of a *court clerk* in one of the country's lower courts. Serving as a court clerk is in principle required to become a judge, a prosecutor, or a defence lawyer. The position of the court clerk is a training position that also involves taking courses, preparing cases, taking notes in court in all matters, and, eventually, presiding in court in minor matters such as traffic offences and shoplifting cases. Court clerks are selected for their position based on their law school grades, which contributes to making the country's law school programmes very competitive. Following clerk service, the training of future prosecutors and judges branches off into its own, separate tracks.

### Prosecutor and prosecution

The prosecutors' main tasks are to lead preliminary investigations, decide about prosecution, and represent the state in court trials. During the preliminary investigations, they are required to act impartially: they have to investigate circumstances both incriminating and exonerating for the defendant. In court, they take the role of the accusing/state party, although they still need to remain objective. New evidence and information coming to light, for instance, must be presented and examined regardless of whether these are incriminating or exonerating for the defendant.

During the preliminary investigation, the prosecutor decides on coercive measures such as arrest and search warrants. When a person has been arrested, the prosecutor can further request that the suspect be detained. The matter will then be decided by the court in *a detention hearing*. At the end of the preliminary investigation, the prosecutor decides on whether to prosecute or drop the case. If there is enough evidence, prosecution is mandatory in most cases. The crime victims themselves cannot affect the decision; it is not possible to drop the charges. Moreover, plea bargains are not permitted in Sweden; if the prosecutor decides to pursue the case, a trial is the only alternative.[3]

Prosecutor training usually starts with a nine-month *prosecutor trainee* period. Trainees follow an experienced prosecutor and also get to observe different police units. Upon the evaluation of the trainee period, one then embarks on a two-year period as *assistant prosecutor*, during which one works as a prosecutor and takes courses. When the training is completed, one is appointed a public *prosecutor*. After a few years of service, one can apply for specialist positions in financial crime, domestic violence, or the like.

### Judge and the court

The district courts are the first-instance courts in the Swedish judicial system. Presiding in district court trials is one professional judge accompanied by three 'lay judges'. The lay judges represent 'the common people' and are appointed by political parties; they come with no legal training. In this book, 'judge' refers to the professional, employed judge.

After the clerk service, one can apply to a training programme for judges. Acceptance depends on the recommendations given by the judges the clerk has served for. The training starts with a year in an appeals court, where the judge trainees prepare cases for decision. Thereafter, they move on to lower courts to work in them for two years as 'associate judges', followed by another year in the appeals court. The training also includes participation in courses spread out over the programme years. When the training has been completed, the successful judge trainees are awarded the title of assessor and are now formally eligible to apply for permanent positions, although it is common to serve at the Ministry of Justice or the Supreme Court for a few years first. An alternative career path is to be appointed judge directly based on one's work experience as, for instance, a prosecutor or a lawyer. This career path is not very common, although there were a few examples of judges appointed this way in our study. Unlike the case with prosecutors, who may specialize, there are no specialized courts and no specialization in the courts; all judges handle all types of cases, both criminal and civil.

### Defence and victim counsels

In Sweden, public defence lawyers are usually members of the Swedish Bar Association. They are assigned to a case by the court, either from a list of available lawyers or based on a specific request by the defendant. The defendants have the right to have a defence lawyer when they are detained; if, for the crime in question, there is a mandatory sentence of imprisonment for a minimum of six months; or if there are any special reasons. Defence lawyer's fees are reviewed and ruled on by the court, and they are paid by the state if the defendant lacks the means to pay.

In contrast to common-law contexts, in Sweden the victim has a relatively strong position and takes part in the trial. During the 1980s and the 1990s, several changes were made to strengthen victims' rights in the criminal process, introducing, among other things, the right to *legal counsel* in violent-abuse proceedings (see further Enarsson, 2009). This counsel does not need to be a member of the Swedish Bar Association, and in practice those serving as one tend to be recent law school graduates, who need more experience before being able to enter the Bar Association.

### The trial

There are two central principles guiding the criminal proceedings: first, that the evidence should be presented orally, which means that parties should in general talk freely; and, second, that the judgement should be based on facts presented orally during the trial, which entails that the judge does not read the case files before the trial. In court, the judge's main task, besides listening to the parties and evaluating the presented evidence, is to ensure that the court procedure is followed and the case properly clarified. The judge can ask clarifying questions during the examination in court, but should refrain from questions resulting in the defendant being convicted.

In Sweden, the legal actors do not wear robes or wigs in court; they dress in an ordinary suit instead. At the start of the hearing, the legally trained presiding judge establishes that there is nothing to prevent the hearing from taking place, and then asks the prosecutor and, if applicable, the legal counsel to present their claims. The judge then asks the defendant about his or her plea to the charges as presented. Thereafter, the prosecutor develops the facts of the case, describing the circumstances and presenting the evidence, with the defence then given an opportunity to respond.

In most cases, the prosecutor first asks the victim to give a full account of the event and then probes into details. This is followed by the defence's cross-examination of the victim. Next, the judge asks the defendant to provide his or her description of the event or, as in some cases, leaves the questioning to the prosecutor. After the examination by the prosecutor, the defence lawyer can put complementary questions to the defendant. Witnesses are then called in one at a time. The examination of witnesses begins with the prosecution/victim calling their witnesses first. Unless they are related to the defendant, the witnesses have to take the oath before giving evidence.

Towards the end of the trial, the chair gives an account of the defendant's personal matters, such as previous convictions and financial situation. The last part of the trial consists of the closing statements by the prosecution and the defence, summing up their arguments including their suggestion for sanction. After the trial, the judge and the lay judges deliberate, with the deliberations and the discussions kept confidential. The verdict is by majority vote. The professional judge delivers the judgment, sometimes orally in the courtroom, yet always also in written form, with the document delivered to the parties by mail.

## Theoretical framework and key concepts

In this section, we introduce our emotion-sociological framework and some fundamental concepts used in our analysis: background/foreground emotions, emotion management, habituation, ritual, front stage/backstage, the emotive-cognitive judicial frame, emotional profiles, power, and status.

### *Emotion, emotion management, habituation*

Emotional processes continuously monitor and orient our actions and interactions in the social world. Most of the time, however, these processes are backgrounded and unarticulated; in that sense, they are subconscious. 'Emotional processes' generally refer here to the unarticulated and unbound character of emotion prior to cognitive reflection: emotional processes are bundles of emotion, not yet disentangled discrete emotions. Departing from Thoits' (1989) comprehensive definition (but see also Feldman Barrett, 2013), we may consider the essential elements of a discrete 'emotion', looking at the example of a judge's experience of anger. What we may call an anger-sequence begins with an appraisal of a situation that builds on simultaneous social and physiological cues. Facing the judge in court, there is an ill-prepared lawyer, representing a breach of professional norms. This understanding – though not necessarily conscious – of the situation is, for the judge, entwined with an emotional reaction (e.g. anger) involving physiological changes (e.g. blood rush). Her feeling angry is an assessment composed of both the experience of the situation and the experienced physiological change. Because the feeling rules of the judge's behaviour in the courtroom postulate non-expression, she becomes aware of her emotion *as* an emotion of anger *and* as 'problematic' – it becomes foregrounded. In Barbalet's (2011: 39) words, the judge's attention is drawn "not only to objects and events external to the emoting subject but also to the emoting subject's internal states". Her emotional expression can thus be more or less congruent with her experience; if she keeps her expressionless stone face, it amounts to 'surface acting' (Hochschild, 1983) in which the expression of the emotion is decoupled from the experience (Bergman Blix, 2015). For Swedish judges, putting on the stone face represents a kind of surface-acting emotion management technique that helps them conform to the feeling rules of the courtroom. If our judge instead expresses her anger, the expression would be congruent with the experience. In our observations, angry encounters between judges and other court professionals were frequently solved by toning down the expression to such a subtle level that it still did not breach the feeling rules of the courtroom. A judge could, for example, cross her arms, lean back in her chair, and just look at the lawyer stone-faced. In the world of the legal professionals, this expression is congruent with the feeling of anger, and depending on the particular context and the topic of the interaction at hand, it is also received and understood as such: the judge is angry. Importantly, the judge's anger management momentarily turns her attention away from her work in presiding over the proceedings. 'Foreground emotions' require the subject's attention and involvement, and they are therefore often experienced as disruptive of focused attention on a specific task or course of action external to oneself.

Consider, in contrast, a situation in which the judge, instead of having to deal with a poorly prepared lawyer, has a new case file dropped on her desk. Here her appraisal of the simultaneous external and physiological internal cues is likely less dramatic. She might feel curiosity, interest, and other similar emotions that orient and support her focused attention on the documents in question. Were someone to ask her about it, she would probably say that she is curious about this new case; yet, unlike when she became angry with the lawyer, she does not reflect on, nor labels, the emotion, unless it is deliberately brought to her attention. It remains backgrounded because it is continuous with the feeling rules governing her work, and because her work is propelled by it. 'Background emotions' "typically have relatively low expressivity and weak physiological correlates, [and] function by giving attention to external but not internal objects of emotional apprehension" (Barbalet, 2011: 39). They may thus facilitate and enhance involvement in a desired course of action, instead of being experienced as disruptive. This is important, because background emotions may still, from an external point of view, be 'disruptive' in the sense that they motivate bad decisions based on the subject's profession-specific wisdom (cf. Nordh, 2013). As we saw earlier (p. 7), wisdom is always relative to experience and knowledge and therefore embodied and situated (Damasio, 2009). Thus, while background emotions help to sustain focus and enable discrimination between matters deemed relevant and matters deemed irrelevant, this orienting function – when it remains backgrounded – may still be flawed. In other words, especially when we encounter unfamiliar situations or people whose experiences and worldviews differ from our own, we may not be well served by background emotions guiding our interactions (Morton, 2013; Zaki, 2014).

We are taught in primary and secondary socialization to understand and discriminate between our emotions and express them in accordance with situated feeling rules (Hochschild, 1983).[4] To emphasize the embodied aspects of socialization processes, in this book we use the concept of 'habituation' as developed by Stina Bergman Blix (2015) in her study of stage actors. Habituation is the outcome of repeated emotional expressions turning emotion management, which at first was foregrounded and required active involvement, into backgrounded emotion management performed without conscious effort. While, in other words, adapting to the feeling rules in a situation initially requires active involvement in both the emotions themselves and their management, the process becomes habituated and backgrounded through repetition, experience, and routinization (Scheer, 2012). The clerk presiding in court needs to remind herself of the feeling rules of the court, while the experienced judge has already habituated these rules and needs no longer do so. The clerk's emotion management is active and foregrounded, and thus interferes to a degree in the task of presiding in court, even where the action is highly routinized and basic. In contrast, the experienced judge's emotion management is habituated and backgrounded for as long as the proceedings appear routine to her ('routine' for an experienced judge covers more than that of a clerk). Successful habituation results in less accentuated emotional experiences (i.e. fewer foreground emotions), but it also provides a sense of security in terms of 'knowing how to behave', paving the way for 'emotional presence'. Experienced judges in our material sometimes engaged in emotional improvisation deviating from the stone-faced norm, without nevertheless considering themselves as transgressing the feeling rules of the courtroom. As Bergman Blix explains it:

> Habituation would then be the underlying mechanism behind two opposite scenarios, routinisation that leads to emotional distancing and the emotional presence that actors need to be able to maintain on stage without becoming overwhelmed by emotions. Both scenarios seem to provide some professional shield.
>
> (Bergman Blix, 2015: 8)

Both 'emotional distance', such as when reading witness narratives as material for judicial encoding, and emotional presence, needed, for instance, for court interactions, become habituated in professional court work.

---

### How did we do it?

The method of shadowing (McDonald, 2005) has proved highly successful for uncovering legal professionals' background emotions. Following judges and prosecutors through their workday, we variously engaged them in small talk encouraging reflection about the situations faced. This manner of information gathering was combined with formal follow-up interviews, for which we used our court observation notes to help us focus on courtroom situations often observed just a few hours earlier. Centred on concrete and temporally close events, both the small talk and the formal interviews were geared to elicit reflection on background emotional processes. When one prosecutor, for example, was asked why she had kept avoiding the gaze of the defence lawyer in a court session that had just concluded, she replied that:

> I think one of the reasons I do that – I am looking for the right formulation here, as, talking to you, I sometimes get insights into why I do things – yes, here we go: I do that because it's the most neutral way I can be. When I sit and look down, it's not because I want to make them feel that I'm not listening to them – I don't look up at the ceiling and look like I'm bored – but this way, me sitting like that, I do that regardless of whether the defendant is [likely to be] convicted or acquitted, because that way the defence can't get hold of me, so to speak, they can't play me. I decide how I react, and my reaction doesn't show, unless I think that "that's enough"; I don't want to appear easily flattered or easily offended.
>
> (Faida, prosecutor, 45+)

In this quote, Faida speaks of background strategic emotion management, describing how she braces herself against attacks by the defence. Indirectly, however, her account is also one about the discomfort prosecutors often feel due to their exposure in court (see Chapter 2).

The small talk and the follow-up interviews enabled continuous resolutions of questions encountered in the observations and validation of the researcher's interpretations (Agar, 1986). Noteworthy here is that even front-stage emotions of legal professionals and their congruent expressions in court were predominantly subtle and low key, making them difficult for the researcher to register. Again, shadowing proved vital for capturing not only the experience of the shadowed participants but also their interpretation of the other legal profession-als' subtle emotional expressions. The judges' typical use of their pen to express annoyance in court, for instance, was only registered after being pointed out by one study participant: "Did you see how angry the judge was, he put down his pen!"

To be able to better focus our attention and follow the fluctuation of emotional intensity, we also employed 'emotional participation', a method in which our own emotions were used as a tool to generate reflections and insights relative to the situations and persons observed (Bergman Blix, 2009; Wettergren, 2015). A critical aspect of this method is that the researcher's emotional understanding of the observed situ-ation can be either more or less accurate (as would, in our case, be-come clear in the small-talk settings and the follow-up interviews): in both cases, however, it can be used as an information source to enable insights into the emotional processes in the field. Such insights were, again, drawn upon in the interviews to arrive at a more nuanced and tangible interpretation of both foreground and background emotions.

### *Social interaction, frame, and ritual*

Our sociological approach to the study of emotions in this book entails a fo-cus on the social aspects of emotions. As should be clear from the discussion of emotion thus far, what we are interested in is how social situations evoke emotion and how emotion orients and informs social action. Accordingly, we look at emotion as something originating in social interaction among peo-ple, or between people and their social environment (see, e.g., Wettergren, 2013). What this means in the context of this study is that the performance of 'objective', emotionless justice in Swedish courts is examined as a joint interactional achievement of the different legal professionals acting in court.

Our analysis of the social interaction and the situated feeling rules builds on Erving Goffman's (1974) work on 'frames'. In his early work of social interaction, Goffman employed the metaphor of the theatre stage to show how interactions can be interpreted as 'rituals' with specific structures, and how people move between front-stage areas where performances occur and related backstage areas where preparations, venting of thoughts and feel-ings, and the like are handled (Goffman, 1959). Accordingly, front stage and backstage need to be understood in relation to each other: the backstage, such as the courthouse canteen, always exists in relation to a particular front stage, such as the courtroom, and there can be several backstages and several front stages. In his later writings, Goffman developed the concept of frame (of reference) to incorporate this multiple and continuous moving between different stages (Collins, 1988), and how these stages/frames organ-ize and structure our experiences (Goffman, 1974: 13). Frames provide the background or the context within which we interpret "What is it that's going on here?" (Goffman, 1974: 8), and they are taken for granted as long as the interaction that takes place fits with our interpretations; the ritualized inter-actions of a court hearing, for instance, seem perfectly normal and natural to a professional legal actor who knows what to expect. In this way, follow-ing our discussion of morality earlier in this chapter, frames are connected to moral evaluations:

> Social constraints are not encoded in the form of verbal prescriptions, but are something deeper. These are not rules that people have learned to carry around in their heads, but are ways in which situations unfold, so that participants feel they have to behave in a certain way, or make amends for not doing so. It is the frames that are the constraints. Even when they are broken, the situation that emerges remains constraining in a predictable transformed way.
>
> (Collins, 1988: 57)

In other words, a judge can remain stone-faced and even reproach a de-fendant for a joke attempted in court, while laugh at the same joke in the canteen (Bergman Blix and Wettergren, 2018). Although a person usually moves between multiple frames in the course of a day, some of these frames bear more weight and thus serve as more encompassing definitional refer-ences. As Goffman (1974: 27) himself puts it, "the primary frameworks of a particular social group constitute a central element of its culture".

The "emotive-cognitive judicial frame" constitutes one such primary frame-work, or a restricted behavioural script, for law professionals (Wettergren and Bergman Blix, 2016). By terming it emotive-cognitive, we want to stress the way the emotional *and* cognitive constraints of the frame are entwined and the fact that emotions and emotion management are vital for learning the behavioural script and for orienting behaviour when the constraints of the frame become habituated and non-reflected. As will be seen throughout this book, the emotive-cognitive judicial frame seals off certain emotions while motivating or orienting towards others, thereby guiding routine profes-sional work. It provides background emotional rewards of pride and pleasure when the frame's requirement to perform rationality by silencing emotions is satisfied, while producing shame and embarrassment when the expectation is violated (see also Wettergren, 2010). It is, however, rare that situations of full-blown shame emerge; our use of the term 'trigger warning' in this con-text pertains to how background anticipation of shame alerts the subject to steer away from potentially bad courses of action. This is in line with Arlie Hochschild's (1983) argument about "the signal function of emotions" albeit emphasizing that this signal function mostly works in the background.

That said, within this primary frame, there are also other frames function-ing as sanctuaries and free zones where the requirement of non-emotionality is relaxed. In the course of our research, we noticed that the emotive-cognitive judicial frame worked differently for prosecutors and judges. This we attributed to their differently organized work tasks and differing positioning in webs of professional interactions and dependencies. To conceptualize these differences, we adopted the term 'professional emotional profiles' (Chapter 2).

While 'backstage' and 'front stage' refer to the delineated arenas of in-court (courtroom) interaction and out-of-court interaction (e.g. in the waiting room), on the one hand, we employ the concept of emotive-cognitive judicial frame (primary framework) to show how this primary framework operates across these different arenas. On the other hand, in this book, we reserve the notion of ritual to describe the highly formalized nature of the court proceedings, although, in its classical sociological sense (including that of Goffman), the term also denotes the structured nature of everyday interactions (cf. Collins, 2004).

---

**How did we do it?**

We developed the concept of emotive-cognitive judicial frame during the fieldwork phase of our research, albeit it was also inspired by our initial aim to understand how emotions play out in an apparently emotionless field in which emotion and reason are traditionally understood as conceptual opposites. Our selection of courts and study participants was important here. We selected courts and prosecution offices of various sizes and with different catchment areas to strengthen our case for any cross-case patterns identified, and we shadowed, observed, and interviewed participants representing varying experience levels and positions, to be able to factor in degrees of professional development. When engaged in observation, we looked at the different actors' body language, facial expressions, gestures, glances, and gazes, along with their use of explicit emotion words. In the interviews, we asked respondents to, among other things, reflect upon the connection between emotion management and role performance, situations where emotions are legitimate or illegitimate, the significance of education/work experience, their use of tacit codes, and so forth. Importantly, one of us began collecting data in a court, while the other started in a prosecution office. When exchanging information about our respective understanding of the emotive-cognitive behaviour in these two different environments (a court and a prosecution office), we soon noticed that this behaviour was differently patterned. This was because prosecutors' and judges' work is structured differently and their roles and work tasks in the overall organization of the legal system differ. When we switched places (e.g. moved from the courthouse to the prosecution office and the other way around), our respective experiences of the emotive-cognitive behaviour switched accordingly. This led us to adopt the term 'professional emotional profile' to describe the specific characteristics of each particular legal profession. In other words, the professional emotional profiles differ, but the emotive-cognitive judicial frame governing these profiles remains the same.

## Power and status

As pointed out by previous research (see the "Emotion and law" section), attention to power and status appears to be an inherent characteristic of any study of judges and prosecutors in their capacity as elite professionals. An analytical interest in power and status positions, however, also follows logically on our sociological approach, which assumes social interactions to always be structured (framed). In sociology, power and status positions are inherent to social interaction; they are part and parcel of how interactions develop and evolve, either through the effect of formal positions that structure the emerging interactions from the start or in the form of subsequent interactions that revolve around relational power and status negotiations. In the power and status theory of emotions (Kemper, 2011), it is usually the latter kind of cases that are subject to analysis, looking at how the negotiations then give rise to, but are also informed by, discrete emotions. As will be shown in Chapter 5, shifts in the power balance give rise to emotion that motivates action, with experiences of power shaping the subject's professional role.

The classical concept of power has been thoroughly treated in social science and philosophy (e.g. Arendt, 1998; Foucault, 1995; Kemper, 2011; Lukes, 2005; Weber, 1978). For the purposes of this book, we use the notion of power in two senses. First of all, in its traditional Weberian sense, in which it is conceptualized as describing an asymmetrical relation (Weber, 1978). Power belongs to an individual or group who through their position are granted the resources to command others: to get what they want even against others' opposition. Such power is connected to security, guilt, and fear (Kemper, 2011): guilt is evoked when power has been used wrongfully or excessively, fear when one's own power is reduced in relation to that of another's. Second, however, we also employ the Foucauldian notion of productive power. Power relations shape subjectivity through emotions. Judges' habituation of power, for instance, has consequences for their sense of self. In our view, power is a dimension of social relations that is only rarely either repressive or productive; usually, it is inherently both of these, although to a variable degree.

The concept of 'status' is often associated with a profession's social recognition (Abbott, 1981). Our focus in this book, however, is on how intra-professional, inter-professional, as well as situated status (Kemper, 2011) influence relations of professional power. Situated status comes about as an interactional accomplishment, in which a person is recognized – for instance, as a competent judge – and thereby achieves the goal of a smooth court procedure without the use of power. For, as Theodore Kemper (2011: 13) has defined it, the relationship between the effect of status and power is one between, respectively, voluntary and non-voluntary compliance. In other words, a person or a group with a higher status can make another with a lower status to act in accordance with its purposes without needing to resort to the use of naked power. What is noteworthy, however, is that actually ending up using one's power to achieve one's aims reduces one's status (Abbott, 1981).

In the sociology of emotion, status is linked to emotions in a somewhat similar way as power is, meaning that status relations embed and produce emotions. For instance, a person who accords status to another may be 'liked' by that other, a person who claims more status than he or she is due may evoke contempt, and the one who refuses to accord status to others, or withdraws it from them, may be disliked (Kemper, 2011). Collin's (2004) theory of interaction ritual chains elaborates on the emotional energy of status positions in group interactions, claiming that high status in an interaction ritual evokes high emotional energy including confidence, pride, and the like. Low status is, instead, associated with low emotional energy including low confidence and shame.

Looking closer at the relation between power and status, we suggest that accorded status brings power through the emotional resources of self-confidence, trust, and pride. In this way, power is productive rather than oppressive. Status thus gives power to act to achieve one's goals. To be sure, power can also be enacted without status, but then it is repressive and likely to result in resentment, perhaps even contempt, in the subordinate person or group (Barbalet, 1998). Accordingly, power may also involve a strive to gain status in order to legitimize power and/or prevent resentment and resistance. In society, being a prosecutor and being a judge are both structurally high-status professions; both also act as representatives of the state and thus use coercive power as part of their daily work, exercising it through their decisions that have far-reaching consequences for lay people's lives. The potential of abusing or misusing this power equals the risk of experiencing feelings of guilt. Also inter-professional mutual recognitions of, and challenges to, status function as a source of emotions in judges' and prosecutors' work. In court, the collective achievement of the performance of objective (non-emotional) justice requires ritual deference to, and support for, the judge's power as chair (see Chapter 5).

---

**How did we do it?**

What interested us here were not only the judges' and prosecutors' reflections on their position of power but also their inter-professional relations and situated negotiations of power and status. When conducting observations, we focused, in particular, on professional actors' tone of voice, speech interruptions, and expressions of sympathy/ shaming, along with the way they managed open transgressions. In the interviews, we asked the participants to reflect on their position of power and also on their feelings of loyalty/disagreement with other professionals and clients. Through the shadowings, we then gained an opportunity to develop a deeper understanding of the complexity of power and status as an interplay of mutual dependencies. We noted how legal professionals showed ritual deference to judges in order to support the judges' status in court. We also observed how the prosecutors' power over the police was negotiated by establishing situated status, in order to manage potential emotions of resistance among the police. From the interactions between lay judges and professional judges, we realized how such situated status negotiations may fail, warranting the explicit use of power resources (Chapter 5).

## Our findings in an international perspective

The ability to generalize from qualitative findings has been discussed in terms of analytical generalizability (Alvesson and Sköldberg, 2009; Kvale and Brinkmann, 2014). Analytical or theoretical generalizations aim at producing 'context-bound typicalities' (Halkier, 2011: 788). Such typicalities refer to emerging patterns in the data, and in the analysis, they are usually translated, for instance, into ideal-typologies or theoretical concepts. Although there may be local context-specific variations, such theory-building presumes that the overall patterns identified are similar across cases, given that the cases are socially structured in similar ways. Whether this is true or not is of course an empirical question. We therefore argue that the empirically derived analytical concepts presented in this book can be applied to any legal system that, like the Swedish one, builds on the premises that emotion and reason are mutually exclusive phenomena and that the legal system epitomizes the ideal of pure reason. In this section, we discuss how some context-specific variations may be understood.

As already noted, the Swedish judicial system is hybrid in nature. It mixes elements of the adversarial process built around antagonistic parties and a passive, non-interfering judge with an inquisitorial process centred on a single (impartial) investigation, undertaken by the prosecutor. In which way, then, are our findings regarding emotions and emotion work in Swedish courts relevant to either civil-law or common-law systems, or both?

Theoretically, apart from our case being marked by the hyper-rationalist script of judicial dispassion, the sociological emotion theory that we engage in our analyses carries general claims. The same structural circumstances that were encountered in our case, such as, for instance, power and status positions (Kemper, 2011) triggering emotions in the interaction among legal professionals, can be found in all legal systems, albeit with local variations in terms of the exact power/status position of the prosecutor vs the judge, and so on. Structural theories of emotion provide a helpful analytical toolkit, allowing one to roughly predict what emotions to expect when power/status relations are observed to shift to the advantage or disadvantage of the individuals involved. This, however, is not the same as *knowing* that the predicted emotions will occur, which is why empirical research is needed. In this volume, we present empirical findings from Swedish courts that either corroborate or nuance those theories, depending on the situations. To the extent that power/status relations of the kind that we explore in this book exist in other judicial settings, we may expect there to be emotional outcomes similar to those found in our study. Finally, leaning on previous research, we put forward the general claim that feeling and display rules similar to the ones identified here as characteristic of Swedish courts are also at work in other Western courts operating under the ideal of non-emotional (pure) rationality.

There are always domestic nuances involved, however. To begin with, Sweden stands out in comparative studies as a high-trust society, one in which there is generalized trust in the impartiality of the executive functions of the state, such as the courts and the police (Rothstein and Stolle, 2008). This quality, combined with a tradition of public consensus (Daun, 1996), corresponds to the model of the inquisitorial system and its legal code, and might explain the subtle antagonism typically seen between the parties in court in the country. However, even where the court process is adversarial, the objectivity of the investigation and presentation of factual evidence is not supposed to ever be questioned. What these particularly Swedish features entail is that the emotional displays by, and the open antagonistic element between, parties engaged in an adversarial trial process in Swedish courts are likely to be much more subtle than, for instance, those in US American cases. Nevertheless, Swedish judges, just like their US American counterparts, also do get angry sometimes, and they become angry for similar reasons. This pattern of angry judges thus remains the same even in a comparative perspective.

Of interest in this regard is the fact that in spite of the demonstrated outbursts and (compared to their Swedish colleagues) forceful expressions of anger by judges in the US, one can still claim also the American courts follow a 'script of judicial dispassion' (Maroney, 2011: 634). In other words, it is not necessarily the absence of visible emotional expressions that sustains the idea of non-emotional law. In the US American system, when legal professionals express emotions in line with the rationalist emotional regime of judicial dispassion, these are interpreted as instrumental and rational and thereby supposedly not contradicting the regime's rules. This much appears evident also from the high level of antagonism, imbued with emotions, that is allowed between parties in the adversarial US American court process. At the same time, however, the courts in question profess dispassion as their guiding principle. When visiting a criminal court in the US, we attended jury selection where the candidates received the following instruction:

When you step into your role as a jury member, imagine you're walking through a disinfection airlock, as if you were a surgeon on the way to an operation, and in this airlock, all your emotions and all your personal prejudices are washed away.

(Observation notes, San Francisco Criminal Court)

That jury members are reminded of the irrelevance and undesirability of their emotions echoes how lay judges engaged in deliberations in Swedish courts are kept focused on their task. Should the latter make a blunt or a 'sentimental' remark, they are promptly reminded to only pay attention to facts – emotions have got nothing to do with it. Similarly, when lay judges break the stone-faced norm of the Swedish courts, they commit a more serious breach than a professional judge doing the same. While, in both the US and Sweden, lay people need to be reminded of the norm to be able to remember it or understand its fundamental nature, legal professionals have presumably habituated the emotive-cognitive judicial frame. Therefore, they have more room to occasionally transgress the frame's feeling rules than do the lay members of the court.

In the more traditional civil-law systems in Europe, the judges are active during both the court process and the investigation, and they can display a range of (comparatively strong) emotions. Although these systems remain under-researched from the perspective of law and emotions, given that they, too, operate in accordance with the same Western judicial values of objectivity and dispassion, our findings can be analytically generalized to them as well. Besides what we have already argued above about the emotional expressions being interpreted *within* the dispassionate frame, we may find that the judges in civil-law systems in Europe take care of balancing their emotional displays in a manner similar to their Swedish counterparts. That is to say, even a highly expressive civil-law judge is likely to make an effort to treat everyone equally. Accordingly, an angry judge will not be angry only at the defendant and his or her witnesses, but also at the witnesses of the state. In our study, we identified this characteristic as a feeling rule requiring the balancing of emotional display, so that both sides are exposed to it to approximately the same degree (see Chapter 6).

## Structure of the book

This chapter has presented the incentive for writing this book. We take an interest in action that usually is regarded as purely rational (unemotional), but which is in fact intertwined with background emotions as motivators, guides, and shortcuts to our memory bank of experience. We chose to study judges and prosecutors because legal professional practice allegedly has nothing to do with emotions. The aim of the project Emotions in Court (2012–2016), on which this book is based, was thus to study emotions and emotion management in Swedish courts. Based on the departing from theoretical distinction between background and foreground emotions, we wanted to find out not whether, but in which ways, emotions are active and acted upon in legal practice.

As an example of our research interest in this empirical field, we discussed the concepts of trustworthiness and intuition, concepts that – within the emotive-cognitive judicial frame – straddle the juxtaposition between emotion and reason. Mapping the international research field of emotion and law, we concluded that previous research has examined moral emotions, empathy, emotion management, and emotions of power, though almost exclusively in the common-law system. Our research takes the field forward by empirically investigating background emotions in naturally occurring socially situated interactions in a broad area of court practice. We thereby offer a detailed analysis of background emotional processes in several dimensions of judges' and prosecutors' work. In taking the Swedish judicial system as the context of our fieldwork, we furthermore extend the research field of emotions and law to the civil-law system.

We then proceeded to present the Swedish legal system as a hybrid between the adversarial and inquisitorial systems, the functions and main responsibilities of the different legal professionals, as well as the procedure of the hearing. Next, we introduced the theoretical framework of our data analysis. Main concepts defined and discussed were background/foreground emotions, emotion management, habituation, ritual, front stage/backstage, the emotive-cognitive judicial frame, emotional profiles, power, and status. Finally, we discussed the potential for theoretical and analytical generalization of our findings to courts in other countries sharing the modern Western regime of judicial dispassion, and across cases of common law and civil law. Throughout the chapter, relevant methodological information was offered in "How did we do it?" – boxes.

Chapter 2 presents an overview of the professional profiles of judges and prosecutors. These profiles are the outcome of judges' and prosecutors' different functions and work tasks in the legal system and of how they are selected for their respective careers. These partly shared partly profession-specific circumstances generate emotive-cognitive dispositions and challenges. Uniting features are professional pride, a highly valued independence, and a sense of belonging to 'a uniquely valuable group', which means that prosecutors and judges are legal professionals on the 'right side' of justice. They thus share 'group charisma' although as distinct professional groups the group charisma is not equally distributed between them. Judges are closer to the ideal of pure objectivity and further removed from messy reality, while prosecutors perform the 'dirty work' of purifying and translating reality into legal codes. Judges' professional pride revolves around autonomy and comfortable power. Prosecutors' professional pride is centred on independence, which is 'bounded' in character yet capable of manifesting itself as independence based on power. Judges enjoy higher professional status than prosecutors do, but they also depend on the 'dirty work' performed by prosecutors. Different emotive-cognitive orientations thus result from these profession-specific circumstances.

Chapter 3 takes a further look on the joint and divided hardships, to which the professionals submit in order to prove their worth in the group of judges and prosecutors, by presenting how emotion management is embedded in the organizations of the courts and the prosecution offices. We first demonstrate how neoliberal management ideology organizes time with an implicit effect on judges' and prosecutors' emotion management vis-à-vis their cases, pushing a less personalized and more detached relation to them. We then proceed to demonstrate how the management of fear is connected to organizational security concerns and discuss how fear relates to institutional self-confidence and generalized trust, tied to the legitimacy of the rule of law. The last part of the chapter deals with the organizational silencing of emotions resulting in a 'teflon culture' shared by the two professional groups. Teflon culture is fundamental to the apparent accomplishment of unemotional legal practice by generating various techniques to separate the professional from the emotional, but also to provide spaces and ways to, in fact, manage strong emotional experiences on an informal and collegial basis. The different emotional profiles are furthermore seen in that judges are manifestly lonely, but also more protected from the emotional impact of horrific cases, in their autonomous position, while prosecutors are backed up by a strong and protective collegial group solidarity and are, to a larger extent, tolerated to breach the norms of the emotive-cognitive judicial frame.

Chapter 4 shifts focus from the organization to the staged drama of the court ritual and how emotions and emotion management are tamed and silenced by the entire dramaturgy of the rule of law, including props, script, and language. Subsequently, we demonstrate how the performance of the different legal roles, nevertheless, relies on skilled empathic engagement in and management of the emotions of the lay people coming to court. The concerted performance of objective justice furthermore requires the professionals to communicate emotions between themselves, both tacitly and openly. When doing it openly, the emotional communication is performed to meet the expectations of lay people in court. In other words, emotions are required to give the impression of authentic performance; that the defence lawyers, for instance, indeed care about their clients. Tacitly, the professionals exchange emotions like worry, doubt, assurance, irritation, and contempt – giving cues to and arriving at agreements about how to proceed to secure a smooth court procedure. Background emotion and emotion management are thus essential for the legal professionals to navigate the court drama. The encounter between the ordered and purified legal version of a crime and the fuzzy and emotional reality of crime is not always easy to manoeuvre in line with the silencing of emotions. The legal professionals perform a tricky balancing act, requiring skilled emotion management and empathic capabilities, and they sometimes slip; when the two 'realities' of the crime clash too hard, legal professionals experience dramaturgical stress, giving rise to foreground emotions.

Chapter 5 examines judges' and prosecutors' background emotions and emotion management from a power and status perspective. How do the dynamics of power and status in the courtroom influence emotions and emotion management strategies? How do judges and prosecutors deal with power in their work roles? How do professional power and status shape judges' and prosecutors' interactions with other professionals and with lay people? The increased workload requires faster decisions from both judges and prosecutors, which, as combined with the serious consequences of their decisions, put great pressure on their capacity to confidently perform autonomy and independence. Thus, we examine the background emotions conducive or disruptive of the use of power, and the emotional outcomes of power and status challenges. The chapter also examines the emotion management strategies of power and status. While judges are required to habituate a feeling of comfort with being in power as part of their autonomous emotional profile, prosecutors' power is circumscribed by their bounded dependence, orienting them to mitigate power with status ('being liked'). However, the essence of prosecutors' independence is seen when they sometimes use power in spite of losing status. In all these different dimensions, the legitimacy of the rule of law is key to a confident use of power.

Chapter 6 scrutinizes the core of a legitimate rule of law and power usage: objectivity. The emotive-cognitive judicial frame holds positivist objectivity to be static, something one 'is'. Furthermore, objectivity is assumed to be unemotional, because emotion, as opposed to instrumental pure reason, carries social bonds and affiliations, and morality (good and bad, likes and dislikes). We challenge this notion of objectivity by showing, first, that objectivity is profoundly emotional because the emotive-cognitive judicial frame sets its own moral standards and orients professionals by the pull of professional pride (doing good) and the push of professional shame, or shame-trigger warnings (doing bad). Second, we demonstrate the multiple ways that objectivity is done in situated processes of actions and interactions, involving emotion management, and how this situated doing of objectivity is distinctly different for judges and prosecutors. Judges primarily focus on impartiality, while prosecutors primarily focus on objectivity, which was enacted as a self-reflexive internal dialogue. In summary, while emotions can be rendered formally insignificant by the legal system, they will nonetheless be present. A lot of skilled emotion management goes into upholding the positivist ideal of unemotional objectivity itself.

Chapter 7 presents a summary of the book's empirical results and thereafter develops and discusses the theoretical implications relating to its main concepts: the emotive-cognitive judicial frame, emotional profiles, and background emotions. We conclude that the emotive-cognitive judicial frame lacks workable concepts for disentangling and evaluating emotional information. The judicial frame thus serves a disciplining and performative function by excluding emotions from the professional arena. Background emotions sustain and reproduce this silencing of emotions in the various dimensions of legal practice. Our analysis, however, shows that emotional processes are fundamental to legal practice as well as to professional life at large.

**How did we do it?**

In the early stages of transcribing and storing our data, all potential identifiers such as names of persons, places, and cases, along with all other pertinent details, were removed or changed to protect confidentiality. As a result, our manner of referring to our data requires some explanation. When quoting from an interview transcript, the words of the participant are followed (in parentheses) by the fictitious name of the interviewee, along with his or her professional role and approximate age (rounded down to the nearest five years) to give a rough indication of the interviewee's work experience (e.g. Margareta, judge, 40+). In the quotes, "[...]" indicates that some words are cut out, and "[---]" indicates that several sentences have been cut out. Spoken emphasis is marked by italics. When presenting excerpts from our observation notes, the excerpt is followed by the type of case, the professional role of the person shadowed, and his or her fictitious name and age (e.g. Observation, fraud, Prosecutor Jacob, 50+). This helps to distinguish between our notes from hearings and our other field notes, which is important in light of the fact that our hearing notes represent data collected through non-participant observation, in which notes were recorded in vivo on a laptop. The addition of the person shadowed gives information about the perspective (judge/prosecutor) of the observation. When we present fieldnotes from general observations and shadowing backstage – in and out of the office, during lunch breaks, and so on – the excerpt is followed by the location of the researcher when the observation took place (e.g. Field notes, court or Field notes, prosecution office). The fieldnotes made during such observations were transcribed and elaborated at the end of the day with the aid of brief memory notes made during the day.

## Notes

1 Defence lawyers have not been the focus of our data collection, but interviews with defence lawyers were carried out as part of two master theses associated with our study (Holt, 2015; Rampling, 2015).
2 In Swedish, the plaintiff/injured party/victim is called *målsägande* (literally "he/she who owns the case") and the suspect/accused/defendant is called *tilltalad* (literally "he/she who is addressed"). Among the different English terms used for the corresponding parties, we have opted for the use of "victim" or "injured party", interchangeably, to denote the equivalent of *målsägande*, and "accused" or "defendant" interchangeably to denote *tilltalad*.
3 Compared to other European countries, prosecutors in Sweden possess considerable judicial power (Zila, 2006). If the prosecutor finds that there is sufficient evidence, the suspect has admitted to the criminal act, and the alleged offence carries a conditional sentence or a fine, he or she can order a summary

punishment (e.g. when the case is of a traffic offence, shoplifting, or theft). In cases where concurrent sentences are passed or the offenders are young (15–18 years), the prosecutor can also grant a waiver of prosecution or initiate mediation. In 2016, 22% of the decisions by the prosecution authorities led to a notification in the criminal records registry without a court being involved (Åklagarmyndigheten, 2017).

4 Emotional socialization begins in early infancy, and emotions are usually managed without much conscious reflection. A professional setting usually calls for more deliberate emotion management strategies, but eventually also these become settled in the body and habituated, and can thus be operationalized without conscious reflection.

# 2   Background emotions in legal professional life

> While we are sitting outside the courtroom during the break, the trial pros-
> ecutor approaches us, stating: "I'm curious, seeing you write so much". Re-
> searcher 1 replies: "We're researchers studying emotions in court". "What?"
> the prosecutor asks; "emotions in court?" Looking sceptical, she asks: "So
> you're writing about us?" Researcher 1 sidesteps the question, replying that
> "we've got a lot of writing to do from today's hearings", with Researcher 2
> adding that "we're mostly comparing our notes right now". The prosecutor
> seems to relax a bit. Researcher 1 explains: "We study neutrality". The pros-
> ecutor assents and says, "Right; there's not supposed to be any emotions in
> there."
>
> (Fieldnotes, court)

The vignette illustrates the routine silencing of emotion in the courts by demonstrating the barely observable emotional processes of the prosecutor when we bring the topic up as our area of study. The curi-osity, scepticism, consternation, and relaxation she expresses are examples of background emotion that she is entirely unaware of. To us, they reveal the feeling rules of the emotive-cognitive frame by indicating that our study area is slightly alarming to her. To calm her, we say that we study neutrality and this being in line with the feeling rules makes her relax.

The aim of this chapter is to present an overview of the professional pro-files of judges and prosecutors, based on the background emotional pro-cesses that orient career choice; adherence to joint and distinctive core values and the associated feeling rules; and the development of necessary emotion management strategies. We relate the distinct emotional processes to the different work tasks of prosecutors and judges, arguing that the dif-ferent context-bound requirements associated with these professions are what account for their different emotional profiles, which nevertheless re-main within the shared emotive-cognitive judicial frame. Part of the shared frame are emotive-cognitive values such as excellence, professional pride, autonomy/independence, and objectivity. In the conclusion of this chapter, we then link these core or sacred values to the concept of 'group charisma' (Elias and Scotson, 1994).

Even though the primary focus of this book is on the state-employed judges and prosecutors, our interactional perspective demands some attention to the third professional actor in court, the defence lawyer. Although they are also lawyers, the defence lawyers stand out as different from both prosecutors and judges; they are often also described this way by the two latter groups. The position(ing) of defence lawyers thereby reveals something about the professional identities and emotional profiles of prosecutors and judges. We therefore begin the chapter with a brief excursion on the emotional profile of defence lawyers, as described in interviews with them and as seen through the lens of prosecutors and judges. Thereafter we continue with the emotional profile of the judge, followed by the emotional profile of the prosecutor.

## The emotional profile of defence lawyers

The first and foremost duty of the defence lawyer is to represent the client. One of the defence lawyers interviewed in our study, Ester, stated: "Everywhere where there is rule of law, I think everyone has the right of defence, no matter what the charges are". Taking the example of a paedophile standing on trial, she elaborated: "I don't defend the action; I defend a system of justice in which no one is judged without adequate evidence" (Ester, lawyer, 50+). Another interviewed defence lawyer, who worked as both victim's counsel and defence lawyer, explained:

> When I act in my role as the victim's legal counsel, I do things the exact same way [as I do when I'm in the court for the defendant]. I try to relieve them of their anxiety [about the trial], asking them the kind of questions that the defence will ask. We practice the upcoming hearing here in my office, so that they get used to what will come, and afterwards they usually tell me, "It was hard in court, but not as hard as in your office", which means the preparations worked.... Of course, [when you are in court] you have a case to win and your job is to win.
>
> (Bengt, defence lawyer, 55+)

Ester's and Bengt's statements suggest that defence lawyers employ a specific emotion management technique in their work. In general, their primary engagement and pride is in the upholding of the rule of law (see further Siemsen, 2004). With this goal in mind, depending on their role (as a victim's counsel or as a defence lawyer), the same lawyer can switch from accusing to defending people in the same type of criminal offenses (e.g. domestic abuse). Pride in the rule of law helps them keep the emotional distance needed to do their job equally well on either side of the law. Whether they appear as defence lawyers or as victim counsels, they are able to keep their deep professional engagement focused on the weaknesses of the opposing party, on identifying and effectively sowing doubt on the credibility of both that party and, if they are on the defence side, the evidence.

The emotive-cognitive judicial frame primes all legal professionals to take pride in their particular judicial skills, but in different ways and to different degrees. The judge's focus is on the matter itself, the evidence, the correct application of the law, and – in the courtroom – the empathic chairing of the procedure (what we call 'emotional presence'). The prosecutor's focus, on the other hand, is on the translation of actual events into a legal code and on the collection of the kind of evidence that will hold in court (Tilly, 2008). In court, as a party to the trial, prosecutors may grow emotionally engaged (develop emotional presence) with the case and the victim. Even if they take pride in, and primarily focus on, their legal skills – and on the requirement to remain objective even when being partial – this emotional engagement provides them with additional motivational emotions to boost their performance as prosecutors (Wettergren and Bergman Blix, 2016). They may thereby become focused on revealing the 'truth', which, from their perspective, is that the victim whose interests they represent is 'right'.

Defence lawyers, for their part, may or may not sympathize with their clients. The mere fact that the prosecutor has made the decision to bring the matter to court means that there should be enough (objective) evidence for the guilty verdict against the defendant. Therefore, as far as they are concerned, they will likely be defending someone losing the case (Scheffer et al., 2010). Their focus on winning (as expressed, for instance, by defence lawyer Bengt above) thus represents an emotive-cognitive orientation to perform in an antagonistic way in court, rather than a realistic goal. However, this very orientation (desire for 'winning') may also go too far, explaining a pattern among the prosecutors in this study where they could not imagine themselves working as defence lawyers. Karl develops this common stance:

PROSECUTOR KARL: The thing with working as a defence lawyer is that … you're not always on the right side of things. But I am always that. If I am not, I withdraw. But that's not possible for defence lawyers…. They are megaphones for other people. That's their job.

RESEARCHER: They are in a tricky position.

KARL: Yes, of course, and sometimes they really sit on their client's lap. But even when they don't, they're still acting as someone else's megaphone. And, I mean, they have to believe their clients and at the same time they don't. It's a really weird situation for them.

(Karl, chief prosecutor, 55+)

Also the judges sometimes expressed this desire to be "on the right side of things". Both prosecutors and judges voiced the opinion that, of the legal professional categories they interact with, defence lawyers were the ones most likely to arouse irritation or anger. In interaction ritual theory, irritation and anger are emotional responses to the violation of one's sacred values (Collins, 2004) and thus indicate that defence lawyers are often liable to cross the line between doing their job as they should (which, all parties agree, is about defending the rule of law) and "sitting on their client's lap".

The reserved emotive-cognitive attitudes towards defence lawyers – suspicion, doubt, and irritation, while at the same time there is relief that someone else does the important job of defending the suspect – thus mark the boundaries of the judges' and prosecutors' emotion management in their job. These attitudes unite them in the self-image of being the legal professions working for a higher purpose – justice – rather than for the sake of individual motives and clients. We will now turn to the judges, and thereafter to the prosecutors, probing more in depth into the formative aspects of their respective emotional profiles that make them quite different legal professions.

## The judge

### *A formative shame or pride moment*

To become a judge in Sweden, one needs excellent grades from the law school. This is required even for the very first step in the process, which is working in a court as a court clerk for a period. Then to be able to complete the next step, entering the ranks of the judges in training, excellent recommendations are required from the judges whom one served as a court clerk. To get these recommendations and be suited for a career as a judge is a moment of pride in accomplishment, regardless of one's original career plans. As recounted by Leo,

> When I finished my time as a clerk I got really good recommendations from the district court, among other things because I worked real hard as a clerk.… But I really didn't think about becoming a judge back then. That came only when I saw my recommendations and thought "Oh really; I guess I did pretty well".
>
> (Leo, associate judge, 35+)

In Leo's statement, the recommendations appear formative for his subsequent career choice. In his interview, he said he had gone on to try some "other things for a couple of years" after the clerk period, but he later on returned to the career as a judge. Reversely, the choice not to become a judge can be influenced by negative experiences such as the (background or foreground) shame of not being among the selected few, as in the following case:

> Those working as a judge at a district court, they're, like, exalted to the skies, in my view. Compared to them, the rest of us are basically dirt [...] But then you get drawn into that, and I did apply to that appellate court position, but I didn't have the recommendations I needed, and since, as a rule, you can only get in there if you have the best recommendations, I wasn't accepted, hrmph…. But then I think that it wouldn't really have

been good for me anyway to get there and work at the appeals court. [Prosecution] is so much better. But I did apply. And I wasn't even called for an interview, or anything.

(Clare, prosecutor trainee, 25+)

In this quote, there are several indicators of shame ("the rest of us are dirt", "I wasn't accepted, hrmph", "wasn't even called for an interview"), indicating the pain of being rejected. But Clare also defies the shame, emphasizing that prosecution is "so much better". The examples of Leo and Clare illustrate that the recommendations received at the end of the clerk period come as a moment of shame or pride, shaping the persons' emotional orientation, either pulling them away from or attracting towards the judge's profession, regardless of their original career hopes.

The criteria applied in recommending some individuals over others for the judge's career are likely to be strongly biased towards social similarity. They draw upon feelings such as those of liking someone, of comfort and safety, and of recognition (Kemper, 2011); in turn, the fact of being the one 'chosen' evokes feelings of pride and self-awareness (as Leo stated above: "I did pretty well") and thus a readiness to conform to the values one has been seen to fit (cf. Elias and Scotson, 1994). The selection process is therefore likely to reproduce established professional traditions, along with a certain type of habitus (Bourdieu, 1999) among the judges' ranks. In this study, 33% of the judges self-identified as upper class or upper-middle class, while 18% of them thought of themselves as lower-middle class or working class. For the prosecutors, the corresponding figures were 15% and 34%, respectively. An almost identical proportion of judges and prosecutors self-identified as middle class (49% of the judges and 51% of the prosecutors). Though the numbers here are not strictly speaking representative,[1] they lend some support to our qualitative assessment that for someone with an atypical background, it is easier to break into the prosecutors' ranks than into the judges'. The typical judge is middle to upper class and native-born Swedish. The change from male to female predominance that has been taking place in Swedish legal education in the last two decades has recently begun to also manifest itself in courts and, even more visibly, prosecution offices.[2]

### Pride in status and comfort with power

The average age of appointment of Swedish district court judges was 44 in 2013. At that point, one has spent up to ten years in various training positions (see Chapter 1), at each stage subjected to critical evaluation by one's peers. This means a long exposure to implicit pressure for conformity to established behavioural and emotional norms. Habituating these norms, judges come to identify with the law and legal institutions. Although, in Sweden, judges do not wear robes or wigs to publicly underscore their embodiment of a bureaucratic organization at the expense of human personality, what they do wear – a dark suit and a stone face – nevertheless serves a clear symbolic marker. Indeed, the stone face is a crucial element in the judges' public performance of objectivity (Chapter 6).

Shadowing judges in the field – in the district courts – conveys a feel for their comfort with being in power. When judges deliberate, people listen, and when they indicate through small gestures that they find a topic interesting or, alternatively, irrelevant, those in the room adjust their talk and actions accordingly. The judges' high status is not something they reflect on – it is a backgrounded part of their professional role – but some judges have come to reflect on their habituated comfort in power and status in situations beyond their professional sphere. The judge in the following quote used to work as a prosecutor for several years before becoming a judge, and she described the difference between the two professions as follows:

> We talked about that the other day, that it starts to affect my private life – that, as a judge, you never engage in a dialogue. You get so used to the fact that if you say something, then that's the way it's going to be. That I'm the one who decides. I don't have any colleagues to run things through, but when the lay judges try – well, it's me who decides, and that's the way I always do it. If I decide that you need to leave [the courtroom], you leave; there's no discussion about it. If you're a prosecutor, you discuss and you argue and – well, you do it in a very different way. In my private capacity, I sit in various boards, and when I say something in them and someone questions that, I go, like, "What the heck; take it to an appeals court!" [Laughter] […] I thought about that just the other day and laughed, the way I do that "What the heck – you talking to me?!" "I'm the judge here!"
>
> (Monika, judge, 45+)

As we can see from above, Monika "discovers" her comfort in being in charge, while to some extent also distancing herself from it and analysing its roots in her autonomous role as a judge. According to the Instrument of Government, she is to decide autonomously (Regeringsformen) without basing her decision on the opinion of others, implying, among other things, a need for habituating a sense of comfort about being in charge. While, according to the positivist ideal of objectivity, this comfort with power ought to be grounded in legal expertise only, for judges 'sound judgement' is equally important as a factor legitimatizing their powerful role and their pride in their performance:

JUDGE BRITTA: The way I think is like this: someone's got to have [the decisive power], because that's how we've built our society, and if someone has to have it, I think I'm a good candidate for that, compared to many others.
RESEARCHER: Because…?

BRITTA: Because I know this [law] book and understand its purpose. I think I have the right understanding of what the courts are there for, I'm rather clever about solving problems, and I think I use my power in a right way. Now and then it makes me uneasy, for sure, but not that often.

(Britta, judge, 45+)

As autonomous guardians of justice, judges embody the law, and they do it proudly with dignity. Their objectivity work strives to remain closer to the ideal of positivist objectivity – the God's eye perspective – than that of prosecutors, while, indeed, also depending on what is usually described as 'sound judgement': the ability to embrace the values of responsibility, seriousness, and integrity. On the other hand, it is only possible for judges to uphold this ideal thanks to the translation work done by the prosecutors, implying a certain purification of reality in order to fit within the legal code (Abbott, 1981). While the performance of justice front stage (in the courtroom) is rooted in ceremony and ritual to secure lay people's emotive-cognitive compliance (Tyler, 2006), the dramaturgy of justice (Chapter 4) also works the other way around: it reflects and reproduces justice's image of itself.

### Autonomy

Justice's autonomy is, arguably, a fundamental principle stipulated in the Swedish constitution, and representing a deeply held value in judges' training and in judges' professional performance. Chief judge Arni (50+) emphasized that he tried to guide court clerks "to become autonomous legal professionals, because the ones I respect are those who have an independent opinion; and I try to make the clerks understand that". Arni thought that clerks today tend to "blend in with the wall … like chameleons", and he did not appreciate their "obsequiousness". It did not seem to occur to him that the clerks' compliance in this regard might have had to do with the insecurity they tend to feel when trying to crack the code of exactly what type of independence is and is not called for if you do not want to be considered unsuited for a career as a judge. The notion of judges' autonomy indeed denotes a specific pattern of conformity during education and training. The same autonomy also serves as the rationale for the expectation to "do other things" in between serving as an assessor and receiving one's appointment as judge. As Arni explained it:

During your career as a judge, you are, in fact, encouraged, almost forced to do other things, before you can get appointed as a judge. Those who only work for courts almost never get a permanent appointment; it's considered a merit to broaden yourself and do other things, too. So most people pick up work as government enquiry secretaries, or at ministries or the Parliamentary Ombudsmen's office or the Ministry of Justice or something.

(Arni, chief judge, 50+)

Autonomy thus becomes an acquired capability and a personal performance, and thereby also a performance of self-confidence and self-assurance. As seen in judge Monika's case above, autonomy is tied to the comfort with power in the sense that its successful performance demonstrates comfort of power and vice versa. Implying impeccable personal integrity and independence, the notion of autonomy obscures the judge's actual dependence on other legal professionals.

### General intellectual dealers

Swedish district court judges are expected to possess broad substantial knowledge of all sorts of juridical matters, covering a wide range from criminal law to family law, from white-collar crime to civil disputes. In principle, all judges handle all types of cases. At trials they act as chairs, preside over the proceedings and control the conduct of the parties involved. In preparatory negotiations (in civil cases), they act as mediators between parties, chiefly to help them settle their disputes by agreement before going to trial. In this book, while our focus is on criminal cases, it should nevertheless be mentioned that successful mediation in preparatory civil case negotiations – be it about family or contract law – was repeatedly described by the judges in this study as their most gratifying work experience, in terms of professional joy and satisfaction received. As described by judge Ola:

RESEARCHER: What's the greatest source of job satisfaction for you, working as a judge?

JUDGE OLA: Ahem; well, I enjoy the kind of legal issues I encounter, the juridical problems; [solving them] that's fun. And, in civil cases, I also really enjoy trying to help the parties reconcile, both in family law cases and in other civil cases – trying to see what's behind the parties' view of the dispute and understand the motivations for their wanting or not wanting to reach an agreement. I think those kinds of things are among the most enjoyable things for me, really.

(Ola, judge, 40+)

In contrast to criminal cases, mediation in civil law cases in Sweden allows the judge considerable space for expressing strategic emotions of frustration and dissatisfaction with the quarrelling parties, and for strategically manipulating the parties' feelings of anticipated success or failure (Wettergren and Bergman Blix, 2018). Judge Ola's statement expresses this pattern of gratification associated with civil cases, but it also expresses a more general source of delight, characteristic of the judge's profession: opportunities to go in depth into the legal analysis of a case. In this study, an intellectual inclination for, and satisfaction from, the latter was evident in particular in cases where the juridical aspects were challenging rather than straightforward. Judges enjoy digging deeper and pondering.

This intellectual aspect of the judges' work is closely related to the writing of judgments. Many judges described the writing of the judgment as a crucial part of their work, reporting it to take roughly as much time as the actual trial. The 'pedagogics' of writing a judgment is a topic of professional development among judges in terms of both the intelligibility of the text – the written judgment is read not only by lawyers, but also by the lay people involved – and necessity for it to clearly reflect the fact that both parties have been heard by the court. At the same time, prosecutors mentioned this intellectual side of the judges' work as one of the reasons why they did not want to be judges. As one of them expressed it: "I felt like I didn't want to dig into matters so much; I like it when there is speed and motion and when a lot of things are happening simultaneously" (Anneli, assistant prosecutor, 30+).

Being "general dealers", as chief judge Ruth (65+) described it, could, however, also be seen as a burden to judges in the judicial status competition in our increasingly complex society requiring more and more specialization. In complex cases, judges' general competence can, Ruth suggested, undermine their status vis-à-vis prosecutors and defence lawyers: the latter professions allow for possibilities to develop and deepen one's skills and knowledge in specialist areas. While, on the one hand, judges in Sweden have a highly varied job role, decide as they do in all sorts of cases, there, on the other hand, are fewer routes available for them to develop their career, which makes their profession relatively static in comparison to that of prosecutors and lawyers. No judges in our material, however, expressed themselves as feeling any professional lack of confidence in relation to their highly competent and specialized defence lawyer or prosecutor colleagues, although it was possible to observe gifts of deference and respect shown to them. Judge Niklas (40+), for instance, shadowed during a tax evasion trial, spoke of his admiration for a prosecutor specialized on economic crime that he sometimes dealt with, describing him as "extraordinarily skilled".

> Niklas spoke warmly about the prosecutor, openly admiring his cleverness, his ability to keep all the facts of a case well ordered in his mind, and the way he could begin attacking from one angle only to soon after, unexpectedly, hit hard in an entirely different direction, like a brilliant baseball slugger or a well-trained terrier.
>
> (Fieldnotes, court)

### Procedural justice: an increased service orientation

In this study, there was one area regarding which judges talked openly about emotions and emotion management, and that was the treatment of the lay people in court. In line with a generally increased focus on procedural justice, this articulation represents a broader societal shift, of which the recent service orientation of state bureaucracies in Sweden is part (cf. Du Gay, 2008). As a result, courts are required to develop 'good treatment policies' and for this purpose to investigate how lay people in court experience their 'visit'. During our data collection, we observed such investigations undertaken as face-to-face standardized interviews with lay people in the entrance and waiting halls, by project groups consisting of volunteering judges and administrative staff at the courts. There were also exchange-projects going on where courts investigated each other:

> As part of the collaborative good treatment project, judges from the court in [name of city] will come today to observe different trials and to inspect the environment, such as the waiting halls. They have even called the administrative office to check out the treatment on that end.
>
> (Fieldnotes, court)

The focus on good treatment requires personal representation to some extent, as it recommends all judges to present themselves and the rest of the court by name and, postulating empathy, forcing all judges to situationally adapt to the lay people in court. Indeed, making lay people in court feel less stressed out and more comfortable is becoming a notable goal for some judges, who gain professional satisfaction from achieving that goal, as elaborated by judge Sanna who starts by referring to civil case mediation:

> CHIEF JUDGE SANNA: It's a true joy when you can make a difference in the courtroom, through the way you treat people, by making them feel seen and listened to, by finding a solution – that's all very nice. And the same is true also about criminal cases, when you deliver a verdict to someone who actually is pleased [laughs] or satisfied or thanks you. It's gives you a very nice feel when you can reach someone.
> RESEARCHER: How do you notice that: you get feedback?
> SANNA: Well you [light laughter] – you feel it in the courtroom, yes, when people are satisfied, yes.
>
> (Sanna, chief judge, 50+)

Typically, judges in training have been taught to be even more mindful of the importance of treating people coming to court well. However, the fact that the judge's profession is primarily about exercise of power complicates the notion of good treatment as a service rendered to the citizens. This can be seen when – as sometimes happens – the focus on being welcoming and service-minded obscures the power positions in the court, as in the following case:

> The defence lawyer asks if his client may leave. Judge: "Yes, of course!" The defendant gets up, and begins to walk towards the door. The judge,

staring at his back, with a cheerful voice: "Thank you for coming here today!" The defendant, not turning around to look at the judge, answers quickly over his shoulder in a bitter, ironic tone: "Yeah, but I had no choice, did I."

(Observation notes, drunk driving, associate judge, Asger, 30+)

The cheerfulness of the nice and welcoming approach illustrated in this excerpt appears thoughtless and clumsy and is rejected as hypocrisy by the defendant. It stands in sharp contrast to the seriousness emphasized by chief judge Ruth in Chapter 1 (p. 3). Seriousness, indeed, was for her the right respectful approach to the lay people subjected to her power in court. In the following quote, judge Ruth points out the contradiction between this "serious" power and the above-noted diminution of judges' status to that of "any civil servant":

It's in some ways taboo to speak about our status, that judges ought to act from a position that invites public respect and is not like that of any ordinary civil servant [...] I mean, it's a profession in which you, throughout your life, have to keep in mind that you're a person with an awful lot of power. [---] It's a power-amassing profession, one that should for that reason perhaps be more special in society than any ordinary civil service profession, which is nevertheless the direction in which we're heading now I think.

(Ruth, chief judge, 65+)

The examples of Asger and Ruth highlight different understandings of how to achieve procedural justice in courts. On the one hand, there is the "good treatment approach", which risks conflicting with the factuality of the judges' exercise of power, while, on the other hand, there is a traditional approach, emphasizing respect for and the seriousness of the exercise of power.

To summarize this section on the general elements of the judge's emotional profile, we found pride in the exclusivity of being welcome to join the judges' ranks: pride in one's status as a professional judge; a sense of assurance and comfort about possessing and exercising significant power; a strong and highly valued sense of autonomy; and an interest and pleasure in the intellectual challenges presented by complicated juridical matters. As 'general dealers', the judges derived pleasure from emotionally deviating from their otherwise habituated stone-faced demeanour when engaging in civil case mediation. Another source of professional satisfaction is related to the recent focus on good treatment of lay people in court. This focus made judges pay attention to how their demeanour affects lay people in court, highlighting the importance of deliberate emotion management strategies. It also problematised their position of power, while, to some extent, obscuring their status as "not just ordinary civil servants". Turning now to the prosecutors, we begin with the shame/pride moment of receiving one's recommendations from clerk service.

## The prosecutor

### *An issue of personality?*

RESEARCHER: You never thought of becoming a judge?

PROSECUTOR HENRIK: I did, for a while, but still, in my experience, the prosecutor's profession is more independent, you know, because [in that role] I set the framework for the trial: this is what the court is to decide about. And I like investigations, collaborations with the police, being there from start to finish, and, like, moving things around and piecing them together to deliver a good product. And I like the mixture of work tasks; it's not like being a judge who just sits and listens to the parties and then rules. As a prosecutor you can be active in so many different ways.

(Henrik, prosecutor, 45+)

The formative shame/pride moment of receiving one's evaluations at the end of one's clerk period also means that some clerks' hopes to become judges will go unfulfilled. Prosecutor Henrik, as quoted above, however, illustrates a pattern among prosecutors in this study to characterize their profession as in many ways more attractive than the judge's, seeing it as more varied and multifaceted than the latter. Indeed, the work tasks of a prosecutor differ much from the work tasks of a judge.

Prosecutors lead investigations and give directives to the police, decide whether to close down cases or to prosecute, and speak with the police, defence lawyers, lay people, and a number of relevant authorities such as the prison and probation service and the social services. Shadowing prosecutors gives a close sense of the rhythm and pace of their work, entailing frequent phone calls, overflowing email inboxes, meetings with the police, discussions with colleagues, communicating directives to the police, and drafting of strategies for presenting cases in court. Prosecutors can work on up to 40 cases at the same time. There may be people to talk to or decisions to be communicated in one investigation but when that one runs into a momentary pause or deadlock, the prosecutor puts it aside and immediately continues with another investigation, or issues indictments in investigations that have been completed, or closes an investigation that cannot go any further, or prepares for the case/s that she or he is taking to court the following day. There is restless activity in the prosecution office, a constant movement of people going in and coming out of the individual offices. It is also true, as suggested above by Henrik, that the prosecutors' work may be more influential and powerful *in essence* as compared to the judges' work, since the prosecutor is the one who elaborates and encodes the material to be presented for the court. Since prosecutors may specialize later on in their career, becoming experts in specific types of crime, they also become highly knowledgeable in particular sections of the law. The experienced specialized prosecutors can thus wield considerable power and status in court, particularly through the way they define, develop, and, in general, handle their cases. Thereby, they truly "set the framework for the trial".

Given these differences between judges' and prosecutors' work, it is no surprise that prosecutors stress personality as the main reason for having inclination for either one or the other of the two professions. Karen (prosecutor, 30+) in the following quote suggests that the personality traits precede the recommendations:

> Karen is convinced that it's one's personality that steers one in the choice between a prosecutor's and a judge's career. According to her, you can see already during the clerk period which people will end up going in which direction. Those who are more reserved, very, very meticulous, and show ambition are the ones who will get good recommendations and go on to work for appeals courts, since it is permanently appointed judges who evaluate them and they tend to choose people who are like themselves. The extrovert and talkative ones become prosecutors. Karen says there is a more open atmosphere in the prosecution offices, but there's a bit of a macho culture there, too. There it's not meticulousness that's valued, but instead toughness, the ability to "throw yourself in it".
>
> (Fieldnotes, prosecution office)

Karen in this excerpt suggests that, when assessing clerks' performance, judges view more positively those individuals who demonstrate personality traits similar to their own. She also indicates, however, that court clerks who are aware of their own personality characteristics have an idea about the options they are likely to have available to them at the end of their clerk period. They may then begin to orient their interest towards a prosecutor's career, concluding that that of a judge is "not their thing", as chief prosecutor Inga expressed it, continuing:

> I don't really like the … I'm not good in writing long judgments. So being a prosecutor fits me fine: it's a reasonable effort for me to write and issue indictments, kind of, and I'm the sort of person who likes the speed….
>
> (Inga, chief prosecutor, 50+)

It is worth noting here that the selection process for a position of prosecutor relies less on peer evaluation and more on standardized criteria (various tests), which may then result in there being a more diverse group of people working as prosecutors. Today, there are more women than men in the profession, and there were also some prosecutors of foreign origin in our material. As we saw earlier in this chapter (p. 38), more of the prosecutors categorize themselves as having a working-class background. The average age of appointment of Swedish prosecutors (after approximately three years of training) is around 30, or considerably younger than that of the judges.

## *Mediators, translators, and purifiers*

The above-quoted chief prosecutor Inga, in her interview, went on to explain that she chose prosecution because she "wanted to stay closer to the reality somehow". This was a quite typical statement from the prosecutors. Unlike judges who ought to remain detached and in principle not engage in the kind of theoretical reduction of complexity implied in judicial encoding, prosecutors do the translation work of purifying fuzzy reality, encoding it in judicial terms (cf. Abbott, 1981; Tilly, 2008). This translation work puts them in contact with ambivalence and insecurity, calling for explicit and conscious management of their own emotions and the emotions of others (Wettergren and Bergman Blix, 2016). Put simply, prosecutors purify the complex reality of the case into the form of legal categories that enable the courts to decide on it. As prosecutor Lara explains below, her and her colleagues' position in between "reality" and the judicial world makes them into mediators between the court and the police, doing translation in both directions:

PROSECUTOR LARA: I feel that we prosecutors operate somewhere in between. The police prefers to solve things practically and the courts are even more theoretical than we are, and juridical, so you've got to accommodate these different values somehow.

RESEARCHER: It becomes your task then to do just that?

LARA: Yes, and to understand. For instance, if the police get called in, they may have to separate the parties first instead of collecting evidence, although it's supposed to be their first priority upon arrival. And then you sit there in court and the judges are, like, "Right, so why did you move these things around, why didn't you just secure the evidence!?" and then you have to explain…

RESEARCHER: …that this is the way reality looks?

LARA: Yes, somehow, and then the police already thinks that prosecutors are otherworldly, but the court is even one more step further removed from reality. But we understand better that you need to do this the proper juridical way. And then you have to explain to the other side [the police]. So people may get irritated and there can be misunderstandings, because you don't know one another's roles and the conditions shaping everyone's work [---]

RESEARCHER: Could you say that prosecutors act as kind of translators between reality and the legal code?

LARA: Yes, in a way it amounts to that.... I suppose that's why you get these juridical expressions.... You use one language in there [in the court-room] because you transform that, I mean, what happens in reality, into juridical language.

(Lara, prosecutor, 30+)

Whether the prosecutors work in investigation teams, draft the indictment, or argue the case in court, they are constantly mediating between the two worlds: the "dirty work" of the police and the "pure" world of the judges (cf. Ashforth and Kreiner, 1999). As already noted, part of the prosecutors' purifying work consists of deciding about the framework, which also involves the presentation of the evidence: what to state and in which order, which piece of evidence to present first, and whom to examine first, all of which has importance for the court's interpretation of the case. In cases like fraud that involve complicated technical evidence, the prosecutors think about and calibrate the presentation continuously. In the below quote, one prosecutor describes how he would proceed in developing his case during the first day of a longer fraud trial:

I will have a PowerPoint presentation: first I'll show how to connect the phone to Defendant 1 – calls to his wife, some car photos, and a film. I want them to become convinced about that first. After that we can go through the charges one after the other. So, first for the whole thing – who is Defendant 1? What relationships does he have? Where does he live? Where does his telephone "sleep" at nights? And I do all that to make them [the judge and lay judges] convinced that this is actually Defendant 1's phone. Because if they don't buy that, it doesn't matter what I come up with next; they first have to become convinced that it is his phone. All that I do before noon, and then in the afternoon we'll go through the charges, one after the other.

(Linus, prosecutor, 40+)

Although prosecutors in Sweden have to investigate circumstances both incriminating and exonerating for the defendant, the development of the investigation tends to orient the prosecutor towards either increased or decreased commitment to the case (Bandes, 2006). In other words, when the evidence becomes stronger and stronger against a particular suspect, the prosecutor's rising assurance that the suspect can be proven guilty reinforces background emotions of commitment like interest, excitement, and dedication. Assured commitment forecloses further investigation of (for the suspect) exonerating circumstances and the prosecutor's focus turns to the presentation of the case in court, with the hope to win the case. Below, prosecutor Wenche complicates the requirement that prosecutors remain objective both during the investigation and as parties in court:

There are those kinds of cases where you have to make out the connections, you have to put a lot of time in establishing the details – like that they wear the same clothes in different surveillance camera shots – you must emphasize that evidence and point out the connections and so forth; but it's still all based on facts. You just have to work on the right way to present them.

(Wenche, prosecutor, 35+)

When prosecutors proceed to "emphasize that evidence", "point out the connections", and "work on the right way to present" the material, their purifying work includes interpretation. It implies that one can, and also must, do more with "facts" than merely translate them into legal codes to be presented to the court. Indeed, the presentation of evidence may require time-consuming preparations even before the decision about prosecuting the case and taking it to the court is made.

### Committed to justice

I like what you do [as a prosecutor]; you try to work for justice, in a way. I think that's the difference between prosecutors' work and the task of the defence lawyer, which is to protect the client, and the judge, which is to evaluate the evidence. They don't work for justice in the same way, to reveal what's right; judges just evaluate the evidence presented by the parties. Whereas, in my opinion, we're the only ones who can fight for justice, for what's right, whether the defendant has done it or hasn't done it. We have to objectively uncover everything. And I think that's beautiful, a beautiful thought.

(Agnes, prosecutor trainee, 30+)

Agnes's description here reveals a recurrent fundamental motivation that drives prosecutor's work: a desire to reveal the truth and further justice. It is rarely articulated as explicitly as Agnes does here, owing to a deep ambivalence built into this motivation. Prosecutors are expected to be committed to the pursuit of justice, while at the same time also steadfastly adhering to the objectivity requirement (Bandes, 2006).

Following the emotive-cognitive judicial frame, justice is not concerned with the truth but with 'facts', evidence. The positivist ideal of objectivity in the legal system rests on this focus on facts. In the embedded mundane work of prosecutors, however, commitment, justice, objectivity, and facts/evidence are complicated. In the previous section, we saw that for prosecutors, growing commitment to a case walks hand in hand with growing evidence against the suspect. Growing commitment thus involves increasing conviction that the suspect is guilty, as will be proven, and justice becomes confounded with truth (which is the case in Agne's excerpt given above). Preparing the case for the court, the purifying and translating work of prosecutors entail reduction of complexity and interpretation. Roughly described, one could say that prosecutors produce legally encoded facts and evidence for the court. For this reason, the requirement to be committed and objective at the same time is fraught with problems. It necessitates prosecutors continuously to reflect upon if and how commitment carries them away from objectivity. Chief prosecutor Ingvar illustrates this reflexivity below:

> You are prosecutor for a reason, of course, and in court you pursue the case, but that doesn't mean you're always right, or that things always turn out the way you anticipate. Even prosecutors can be wrong, or things can appear in a different light [...] A prosecutor needs to have this sensitivity, so a good prosecutor is objective and sensitive and influenced by impressions; you can't successfully pursue your case without listening [...] You should be engaged and do your homework well, but that's different from taking things personally.
>
> (Ingvar, chief prosecutor, 45+)

As described by Ingvar, objectivity for the prosecutor means remaining sensitive to potential changes in the evidence and taking into account others' perspectives throughout the process, which demands a capability for constantly shifting commitment. It also presupposes a foundational sense of pride in remaining objective. This pride in objectivity was accentuated when prosecutors compared the different roles of prosecutors and defence lawyers. When doing so, they often emphasized the importance of the defence lawyers' role per se:

> The defence lawyers have the most important role in the justice system, and they are often the ones who take the most shit from society and in the news ... they have an undeserved bad reputation.
>
> (Dagur, prosecutor, 35+)

On the other hand, they could also describe their own choice of profession as an objective antipode to that of a defence lawyer:

> I think I do what's important for society, if you think about the other side, the defence lawyer, it's an important task too, but it's more like "Well, I make lots of money" that's their main thing. As prosecutor I tend to think that I'm an important cog in democratic society.
>
> (Josefin, prosecutor, 35+)

Josefin expresses the suspicion and doubt directed against defence lawyers, discussed in the beginning of this chapter (pp. 36–37), by saying that "making money" is their main motive. Comparing her own job as prosecutor to the defence lawyers thus makes prosecutors stand out as objective cogs in the machinery of democratic justice; prosecutors become inherently objective.

Complicated cases that highlight the taxing paradox between objectivity and commitment include those that involve violence and abuse in close relationships, sexual abuse, and child abuse. In this kind of cases, factual evidence tends to be weak due to the victims' failure to report them properly and there are frequently no or few witnesses, owing to which prosecutors many times have to rely primarily on the trustworthiness of the victim and the witnesses. At the same time, victims of violence and abuse in close relationships, for instance, tend to have low trustworthiness in court, either because they are children and, as such, are seen as unreliable as witnesses (Landström et al., 2013), or because battered women are prone to regret and withdraw the charges (Enander, 2010). There is an organizational (managerial) fear that prosecutors feel too strongly about these cases: they become too committed (to justice/truth) and are believed to lose sight of the objectivity requirement (focus on facts/evidence) guiding their work. It is also well known that these prosecutors are more prone to burnout because of high levels of stress, frustration, and disappointment. Spending much time and energy in investigations only to conclude in the end that there is not enough evidence to pursue the case is very common among these prosecutors (Törnqvist, 2017). As a prosecutor of child abuse cases, Ursula (30+) explained, child abuse prosecutors – contrary to other prosecutors – spend a lot of time assisting the police interrogations with the children in the investigation phase. Due to this, and to the fact that most of the investigations are closed down, child abuse prosecutors "go to court less frequently than the others" (Ursula, prosecutor, 30+), making the work with these cases less varied and rewarding.

Closing down an investigation of abuse in a close relationship actualizes the gap between justice as being "what's right" and "the truth", on the one hand, and justice in the legal sense (that which can be proven), on the other hand, giving rise to ambiguous emotions regarding the meaningfulness of being a prosecutor (Törnqvist, 2017). One way to solve this potential emotional dissonance is to embrace the division between truth and justice. Thereby, prosecutors can maintain their belief that a person is guilty in a moral sense, while taking some comfort in the feeling that they follow the objectivity ideal and act professionally when deciding to close down the investigation. Moreover, as Chapter 3 in this book shows more in depth, the structure and organization of prosecutors' work tasks contribute to the ability to both be committed and quickly let go, moving on to the next investigation. Prosecutor trainee Clare describes discovering this:

> Someone said the most important thing to know here is how to be able to let go of things. And I suppose when you're doing 20 different things simultaneously … you must be able to work with them in parallel and you can't be afraid of letting go of some of them…. So, if you can't let go of things that way, you can't do this job.
>
> (Clare, prosecutor trainee, 20+)

A large part of the emotional burden of prosecutors then arises from having to deal with the potential disbelief and outrage of the lay people involved. They need to explain to the latter that the decision not to pursue the case further is only because of judicial circumstances, not any moral judgement concerning the perpetrator, the victim, or the crime itself. The incompatibility in practice of the combination of commitment and positivist objectivity embedded in the prosecutor's in-between position as a "translator", the paradoxical upholding of opposite stances emotionally and cognitively, was nicely captured by Karl (chief prosecutor, 50+): "You should be empathic. You should have a certain amount of callousness. You can't be too empathic. Or you should be empathic but still ... callous".

### Independence and collegiality

As noted earlier, the protection of the judges' highly valued autonomy is built into the nature of their training and actual employment as judges. Among the prosecutors, it was, instead, 'independence' that was emphasized. Throughout the book, we will highlight the 'boundedness' of this valued independence, referring to prosecutors' complex web of relations to other professions, on which they de facto depend to do their job (e.g. the police). Prosecutors need to make the relations to these groups work with as little friction and frustration as possible; usually by means of skilled emotion management – to become "well-liked" prosecutors – rather than using whatever formal power they may have over these groups. When prosecutors' commitment to their professional goals conflict with the nurturing of these relationships, the actual strength of their independence is demonstrated by disregarding its boundedness. This can be achieved by means of power exercise (as when a reluctant victim is forced to carry on with the charges) or by means of pretending not to see the needs or expressed wishes of others. Prosecutors' independence is thus tricky to master, because it requires, on the one hand, keen attunement to others and, on the other hand, capacity to be completely insensitive to others. In this section, we will focus on the way that independence, for prosecutors, emerge as a core professional value in tandem with their position as notoriously exposed to criticism and pressure from all possible directions. As Karl explained it:

> This is – it must be one of the toughest legal professions, as I see it, given our independent position. We drive investigations, we decide about prosecution, we go to court, and we are entirely independent, eh, we are surveilled, we have results to achieve for the boss, we've got to be quick and so on; the mass media, the victims, the courts are onto us, and the lawyers. I mean it is difficult to imagine a tougher job, actually.
>
> (Karl, chief prosecutor, 50+)

This excerpt contains two seemingly contradictory statements (on the one hand, prosecutors are 'independent', and, on the other hand, they are 'surveilled') separated only by a sign of hesitation ('eh'), illustrating the way that prosecutorial independence is paradoxically shaped in response to control and critique. Autonomy for judges means to remain immaculate in one's judging and thus protected from contamination by messy reality, while independence for prosecutors means developing a protective shield while remaining embedded in the messiness of reality. Independence then assumes, first, an ability to deal with guilt feelings that stem from demanding things from people without promising anything in return. That is to say that prosecutors demand from the police to provide material and witness reports, and from victims and witnesses that they perform their part, while all these efforts may also lead nowhere in the end. Second, in relation to their peers (defence lawyers), independence, for prosecutors, means having to deal with feelings of resentment and humiliation as part of the antagonistic court interaction. In relation to judges, prosecutors' independence means having to deal with humiliation and frustration arising from the judges' structurally superior position and power (see also Chapter 5). "Dealing with it" in all these arenas and interactions amounts to an effort to balance one's commitment and detachment, to keep being committed to the pursuit of justice, while all the time prepared to "letting go" and to be able to withstand critique and ridicule.

Given the high workload and fast pace of work characterizing the prosecutors' profession, emerging connotations of the core value of independence are also flexibility, improvised problem solving, and having a good ball sense. Indeed, various metaphors from ball games were frequently used by the prosecutors: dealing with suddenly emerging issues, for instance, was called "taking it on the volley", while the situation where one pursued several cases at once was described as "having many balls in the air", and staying focused "keeping your eyes on the ball". Ball games and prosecution may indeed not be very far apart, as illustrated by Peter in the below quote, talking about how his experience as a soccer referee got him the job as a prosecutor:

> I was an almost elite-level football referee when I became a prosecutor; I think it contributed to my getting the job. I got this first interview [at the prosecution office], it was a short one, and it felt like just blah blah blah and then the last question. I had mentioned my football thing, and so this last question was: "Tell me why you'd be a good prosecutor". And I felt like that was what the entire interview was for. And I just said: "Well, I'm used to making quick decisions, I'm used to making uncomfortable decisions, and I'm used to getting so much shit for those decisions." And then I looked up and it was, like, "OK".… But then I felt "Ah, that nailed it!" [laughter].
>
> (Peter, prosecutor, 40+)

The comparison of the prosecutor to the soccer referee is telling of how prosecutors perceive of themselves as exposed to critique. In most situations, being independent also means acting on your own, alone. In contrast to the judges' comfortable and symbolically inaccessible position when presiding in court, there is a palpable sense of loneliness and vulnerability surrounding the prosecutors in their position in court, underscored by the staging of the courtroom; prosecutors sit, often alone, on the left long side facing the defence lawyer and the accused, with the judge and lay judges and the clerk in an elevated bench on the short side of the courtroom.

Meanwhile, this loneliness of prosecutors in their professional front stage is alleviated by a very strong sense of loyalty, collegial solidarity, and team spirit backstage. We experienced this team spirit hands-on when shadowing prosecutors. The following excerpt from a lunch break illustrates the team spirit being pointed out as alleviating the hardships of prosecution:

> "But", says Prosecutor 1, "at the same time it's the most enjoyable job in the world", with Prosecutor 2 agreeing and saying that there is a very tolerant and collegial atmosphere at the office, with everyone helping and supporting one another. "We're a team", Prosecutor 2 agrees and clarifies that he means the entire prosecution office. Prosecutor 1 adds that since the work pace is so fast, people in the office have to constantly ask one another for help, because it takes too much time if you check everything on your own.
>
> (Fieldnotes, prosecution office)

The organizational context of, and support-providing collegiality between, prosecutors make them less prone to consider errors and mistakes made by their colleagues as an embarrassment to the entire judicial system. In this sense, prosecutors were less judgemental about their colleagues' mistakes than judges. While they often extensively criticized judges and defence lawyers, they rarely spoke badly of other prosecutors. Indeed, what truly triggered a moral outrage among prosecutors was an attack on their profession as such, for example, by claiming that the prosecution office does not work as it should or fails to maintain its objectivity. Such accusations were sometimes made by defence lawyers in court and would be a sure way to upset the prosecutors. Thus, while the emotive-cognitive judicial frame produced for judges a strong sense of pride in, and protectiveness of, the legal system as a whole, for prosecutors it produced a strong sense of pride in, and protectiveness of, the prosecution office.

To summarize this section on the general elements of prosecutors' emotional profile, we found an emerging awareness of and pride about the actual power of one's profession, a profession that in the judicial world nevertheless still has a lower status than that of judges. When ordering and encoding reality for the judicial process, prosecutors purify the messiness of it (Wettergren and Bergman Blix, 2016). Performing this translation, they get to decide and shape the framework for the court's decision-making, and, by means of well-crafted presentations in court, they mark the matter with their interpretations. This ability can be further enhanced by specializing in specific areas of criminal law. Prosecutors in retrospect (but sometimes also early on, during their clerk period already) defined their personality as more suitable for the prosecutor's than the judge's career, because they could both endure and enjoy the pressure and the fast pace of the job. In their intermediary position, however, prosecutors found themselves subjected to the paradoxical requirement of commitment along with the positivist objectivity called for by the emotive-cognitive judicial frame. Independence was highly valued by prosecutors as a means to juggle contradictory demands, withstand workload pressure and cope with vulnerability: as mediators between 'reality' and the judicial world the prosecutors were exposed to criticism and assaults from frustrated police officers, lay people, defence lawyers, and judges. Consequently, there was a high degree of collegiality and solidarity between them, along with a higher threshold of tolerance of collegial mistakes.

## Conclusion

This chapter has analysed key dimensions of the tacit everyday background emotional processes and emotion management strategies of legal professionals. This was done by looking at the specific features and conditions that distinguish the judges' and prosecutors' profession, respectively, beginning with the shame/pride moment at the end of the court clerk period. Based on acceptance to do clerk service – which requires excellent grades from law school – and the emotive-cognitive boundary drawn towards defence lawyers, excellence and professional pride in the independent pursuit of objective justice were shown to be some of the key elements of the emotive-cognitive judicial frame shared by the two professions. Yet, these elements were elaborated differently in practice, given the different organizational contexts and work tasks distinctive of the two professions.

Judges typically enjoy the highest status among all legal professions, with inclusion into the judges' rank functioning a sign of recognition fuelling judges' professional pride. Several of the prosecutors in this study had at some point realized having the wrong 'personality type' to pursue a career as a judge, but developed a strong sense of pride in their purifying, translating, and mediating function – a function on which the judges, paradoxically, depend for their performance of autonomy. In the context of the judge's profession, independent pursuit of justice is given by autonomy, and the meaning of autonomy is connected to the positivist objectivity ideal, the ability to stand free to assume a God's eye perspective. The habituation and performance of autonomy by the judges thereby becomes central for the legitimacy of the legal system as a whole and judges come to proudly embody that system.

In contrast, prosecutors were exposed to critique and pressure from all directions, due to their mediating position. Compared to judges they are immersed in fuzzy reality, with the task to purify reality by way of legal encoding. To prosecutors, independence is accentuated to enable them to withstand the work load, the fast pace, the loneliness, and the constant attacks on their professional self. Towards that end, they also relied on their strong sense of solidarity with other prosecutors and the relatively high degree of tolerance among themselves for collegial mistakes (cf. Asforth and Kreiner, 1999). In contrast to judges, independence for prosecutors also meant navigating a double consciousness, encompassing an imperative for both positivist objectivity and committed truth-seeking. They took great pride in this flexible capacity to move between the two opposite stances. The division of labour between the prosecutor and the judge is vital for the emotive-cognitive judicial frame's systematic silencing of emotions, and thus, for sustaining the core ideal of positivist objectivity.

The way the emotive-cognitive frame and its feeling rules orient legal professionals' work can be elaborated using Elias's concept of 'group charisma' (1994). The term refers to the sense of comfort, pride, and security one receives from membership in a powerful, high-status group and the way this comfort is transformed into values of purity and superiority.

> Pride in the incarnation of one's group charisma in one's own person, the satisfaction of belonging to and representing a powerful and [...] uniquely valuable [...] group is functionally bound up with its members' willingness to submit to the obligations imposed upon them by membership in that group.
>
> (Elias and Scotson, 1994: xxiii)

Group charisma thus provides a motivational pull to shape professional subjectivity in line with the emotive-cognitive (judicial) frame. It furthermore implies that the hardships and suffering involved in becoming a member of the group are accepted as necessary. In other words, the pride orienting professional performance in line with the emotive-cognitive frame and the shame of failure are linked to group charisma. While the shame/pride moment and the way the ranks of judges are reproduced accentuates the superiority of judging inducing judges with, in a sense, more group charisma than prosecutors, the distinguishing emotive-cognitive features shared by prosecutors and judges also indicate shared group charisma in relation to defence lawyers and legal counsels. Underscoring this connectedness, as we have seen, regardless of their higher status judges' privileged removal from fuzzy reality relies on a "double bind" (Elias and Scotson, 1994), or interdependence between judges and prosecutors. Although the sense of purity and superiority is stronger among judges, they effectively depend on the prosecutors who purify, encode, order, and present the matter for them to decide upon.

## Notes

1 The sample in this study was not representative. Judges and prosecutors volunteered for it, with the only criteria that we attempted to control being age/length of work experience and sex. This meant that our participants were mostly individuals who for some reason were interested in reflecting about the role of emotions in their work. To the extent that an experience of social mobility might make individuals more conscious and aware of – and reflexive about – their acquisition and performance of pertinent norms of behaviour, it is therefore possible that persons from a working-class background were over-represented among our participants.

2 According to data obtained from district courts, there were approximately 750 judges working at the Swedish district courts in 2016, while the proportion of male judges decreased from 78% in 1992 to 48% in 2016. In 2016, there were approximately 950 prosecutors working in the country. Of them, the proportion of men was 40%, having been 58% in 2000.

# 3 Organizational emotion management

[Burn-out] is to large extent a matter of individual dispositions. [---] We, the managers, speak a lot about "good enough". Sure, there are lots of urgent deadlines, and obviously as managers we check that things don't take too long time, so in that sense we don't ease the pressure, but we also say "this is not what you should be doing right now, now you should do this other thing because that's more important" and we also say "go home", but it's not as easy for everyone to let go.

(Nadja, chief prosecutor, 50+)

There is a macho culture in the prosecution office entailing that you should wade through [the horrors] unaffected.

(Göran, prosecutor, 35+)

The staff manager says that it's difficult to get judges to speak about themselves or their emotions and feelings in the staff development meetings. The elitist mentality of legal education inculcates a notion that you should be tough and not break down under pressure, something that marks the judges throughout their career. So you don't notice if a judge is not feeling well, as they keep walking around carrying their load until they crash.

(Fieldnotes, court)

We saw in the previous chapter that the group charisma of judging and prosecuting requires 'submission to hardships' proving the individual's worth as part of a 'uniquely valuable' group. The quotes and excerpt above refer to some aspects of these hardships at different levels of the organization, at the prosecution office and the court. Chief prosecutor Nadja asserts that withstanding the hardships is an individual quality, continuing that the management at the prosecution office have almost to force the employees to let go and go home. Prosecutor Göran states that the macho culture of prosecution entails that one should "wade through the horrors" unaffected. And a resigned staff manager at one of the courts complain that having staff development meetings with judges renders nothing; judges will not talk about themselves and they certainly will not reveal any problems until they crash under the weight of them.

In this chapter, we discuss how organizational structures embed emotions and emotion management techniques. This embedding is done by directly addressing emotion at the structural level, as when fear is addressed by organizational security measures, or indirectly, as when increased workload and time pressure contribute to increased emotional distance and detachment. As we will see, the idea of the practice of law as unemotional has implications for how courts and prosecution offices manage actual emotional outcomes.

We will start with the obvious emotional process associated with organizations: time as an organizing principle operationalized through high workloads, generating loss of time for the judges and lack of time for the prosecutors. We then continue to examine the one emotion that is explicitly dealt with through organization, fear, via organizational security work. This is to say that formal management of fear is mostly prevalent in relation to security, generally dealt with but not felt. This brings us to the notion of 'teflon culture', in which structurally embedded presumptions entail that emotions are not supposed to 'stick' to either judges or prosecutors. Debriefing exists but is seldom used: being a professional implies an ability to manage emotions, making the need for debriefing unprofessional. The end of the chapter demonstrates how teflon culture leads to informal collegial emotion management strategies, raising the question of individual coping strategies when faced with particular emotionally challenging cases.

## Time as organizing principle

When asked about the unpleasant aspects of their work, the most common answer by both judges and prosecutors was high workload and stress (cf. Roach Anleu and Mack, 2017). The answer reflects an ongoing development of neo-liberal government policies and New Public Management (NPM) approach that, through their reliance on technological development for increased organizational control, output, and efficiency, lead to more administrative and self-monitoring work tasks for staffs in public service (Svensson, 2018). Digitalization has led to more standardized procedures and ways of recording, archiving, and keeping track of different investigations and court cases. It has also enabled the introduction of various instruments for measuring work efficiency and turnover time for each investigation or case, with higher expectancy on shorter turnover-times and a steadily shrinking managerial tolerance for 'waste of time' and budget transgressions.

Digital 'aids' have also become part of the stressful dimension of work. One example of this will be seen in Chapter 4 (p. 108), in which judge Margareta opens the trial, at last, but the video link to the accused fails to work. The prosecutor's understanding refers back to his own experience; lack of synchronization between the digital platforms – which are also highly securitized and encrypted – used by the courts, the prosecution offices, and the police is a daily source of frustration for prosecutors. This technological addition to stress should be kept in mind as we turn to the social and professional dimensions of time as an organizing principle.

### Judges: lamenting the loss of time

Along with the NPM reforms, there have been quite a few associated attempts to reorganize the Swedish court system since the turn of the millennium. Smaller district courts – those employing 5–10 judges – have been merged into larger ones, closing down some local courts. In consequence, judges today handle more cases and, apparently, do that more efficiently. The impression of judge Folke (60+) was that instead of the approximately 40 cases a year he had when he was a young judge, he now handled 40 cases every month. Did judges have way too much time before, then? Probably not, since time emerges as an important work tool in the judge's profession, emphasizing the intellectual quality of the job: time to ponder on the juridical aspects of cases, time to study related laws, and time to write judgments in a well-poised manner. Increased workload thus implies loss of valuable time to think and to elaborate on details in the cases. As described by retired chief judge Ruth:

> Everything moves so fast in the courts today, *too* fast, so the judge's capacity to really get into [the case].... Keeping budget balances is more important than writing good judgments. I think it's a pity, because lawyers used to say that it's so good when they get a written judgment with properly argued reasons, because they can use those arguments when talking to their client and deciding whether to appeal or not, helping the client to understand why he was sentenced.
>
> (Ruth, chief judge, 65+)

In this quote, Ruth looks back at her professional experience, comparing the process of "getting into the case" in the past to how the focus today is on keeping budget balances. Ironically, while speeding up turnover times, this focus on efficiency has created a need for client-oriented policies such as the "good treatment" policy discussed earlier in this book. There are also ongoing projects for standardizing the style of judicial paperwork like written judgments, to make these more intelligible to the public. Such concerns, according to judge Ruth, used to be an integrated aspect of judges' work when there was more time. In her interview, Ruth also spoke about time required for taking a pure and honest interest in each and every individual coming to the court, giving a "closer personal relationship" to each case, as opposed to the trained empathy suggested by the present "good treatment" policy.

While larger trials are of necessity allowed to take the time they need, smaller trials running overtime may cause domino effects. The smaller trials are often scheduled for an hour or two and they frequently begin one right after the other without a pause between them. Normally, the same judge and the same prosecutor conduct four to eight short trials a day. Given the tight schedule, there is little room for improvisation, for which reason these trials may cause emotive dissonance (Hochschild, 1983) between pride in the principle of "good treatment" and pride in the principle of staying on time (Roach Anleu and Mack, 2017). Even if the good treatment policy is introduced in a period when the mechanic efficiency of the courts threatens to jeopardize the public legitimacy of the rule of law, good treatment is not really meant to require more time. The task to achieve the tricky balance of a respectful, empathic treatment while remaining impartial and staying on time, thus relies on the judges' individual emotion management capabilities (compare p. 43–44).

It is important to note that high workloads force legal professionals to quickly let go of cases. Thereby legal professionals become implicitly oriented towards emotional distance vis-à-vis their cases. As explained by judge Folke:

> Especially now that everything is done so fast you don't have time to [feel], because as soon as you're done with the mutilated body, someone has committed a tax offence and you have to rule on that and then that other thing is pushed aside. You see, if you have five trials in a day, when you're done with the last one you can't remember the first without checking your notes.
>
> (Folke, judge, 60+)

As suggested in this quote, while memory and emotion are closely entwined, a constant shift of focus prompts forgetting, and thus detachment. In other words, the high workload can be considered an implicit organization-induced emotion management tool to uphold some values inherent to the emotive-cognitive judicial frame, such as detachment and objectivity.

### Prosecutors: constant lack of time

The prosecutors in this study did not lament any loss of time, but rather the lack of time. Prosecutors do not work 'with' but rather 'against' time. This becomes particularly evident when the suspect is in detention, which, according to the law, is time limited. Prosecutors' work tasks are diverse and dependent on the police and the police's effective collaboration. Prosecutors handle up to 40 cases at the same time making time an adversary haunting the prosecutor's work, not a tool to enhance its intellectual quality. The difference between judges' and prosecutors' relationship to time is illustrated by Monika, who had formerly worked as a prosecutor:

> If you compare prosecutors to judges, work is not fast-paced for judges. You can always take a break to contemplate things. You can't do that as a prosecutor when they call you in the middle of the night and need a decision. So we have an entirely different leeway as judges, compared

to prosecutors. [---] I actually felt that the court was like a protected workshop when I first got here [laughs]. I somehow miss that life. Four telephone calls going on at the same time, investigations here and directives there, and – I sometimes miss that.

(Monika, judge, 45+)

The quote highlights the fact that time pressure in prosecution is not experienced merely as something negative. It can also be exciting, something that one can even "miss" as a former prosecutor. As we have seen, prosecutors often position themselves as more of action lovers than judges.

The intermediary position, the exposure to critique, and the extreme speed and workload of prosecutors' work situation contribute to a strong team spirit and make prosecutors less prone than judges to be ashamed of individual colleagues' mistakes. Too many decisions have to be taken, on the spot and without a minute to contemplate, entailing that no individual prosecutor can feel safe beyond reproach. But the ability to take all these quick decisions, knowing that some of them may indeed be mistakes or simply wrong, requires emotion management to keep anxiety and remorse at bay. The effort to learn to trust the people that one depends on to be able to work effectively as a prosecutor is captured by prosecutor Saga, who was formerly a judge:

[As a prosecutor] you need to deal with many things going on around you, all the time, and you must have the courage to make quick decisions based on rather sparse information. You can't ponder on things forever and ever. And that's one difference from being a judge. [---] You must learn to trust people around you. I mean, primarily your colleagues and the police whom you work with. I still sit and read investigation protocols and double check everything, which means I am overloaded with work. But you can't work like that. I haven't got rid of this need to stay in control yet.

(Saga, prosecutor, 35+)

The organization of the prosecutors' work encourages not only interdependence and mutual trust, but also, as the above quote indicates, letting go of discrete cases and investigations. The way their work is organized, entailing high speed and high workload, thus becomes an implicit tool helping prosecutors to balance commitment and detachment in their work.

Contrasting the judges, prosecutors regularly do night-call duty, which means that they stay at work all night, answering phone calls from the police and making immediate decisions about directives and means of coercion, such as arrest warrants. Prosecutors and prosecution offices in one geographical region take turns in being on night-call duty, so the area covered at night-time is much larger than during the daytime. An ordinary prosecutor may have one to two night-call duties per month. On busy nights (e.g. on weekends or holidays), the phone lines tend to get congested, with many officers on hold needing an urgent decision in order to proceed with their work. At night, the prosecutor on call gets both lonely and tired, with the collegial buffer groups unavailable. Prosecutor Lara below tries to capture the anxiety that may arise during those hours:

> I don't know if it's a generally used notion, but here at this office we talk about night-shift anxiety: it's the feeling you get after you're done with your night shift that – I mean, it's a joke, but still – "what the heck did I just decide about? All these cases and these people that I spoke to..." [---] It's not just that it may turn out that you've done something wrong.... I mean, you learn early on that the one thing you must *not* get wrong is the coercive measures, when we use that power over people, of course. But otherwise, I think, you get a lot of understanding when you're on night duty; your colleagues know what it's like to be sitting there.
>
> (Lara, prosecutor, 30+)

The anxiety at the amount of decisions needing to be made and the speed at which they are taken during night shifts are balanced with Lara's sense of assurance and comfort in knowing that there are colleagues who understand what it is like. When shadowed during a night shift, Lara lingered about at the office in the morning, speaking to colleagues about the night and orally communicating her decisions to them. This was kindly received by the colleagues, who, however, also commented that if they were Lara, they would rush out of office at eight o'clock sharp to go home and get some sleep. On this, Lara commented that she had a habit of staying on for a little longer so as to be able to reflect on her night and get some positive feedback for her decisions; for her, this was a way to manage her "night-shift anxiety".

Whether implicit or not, time pressure as an organizational tool to manage commitment and detachment was ambivalent for both judges and prosecutors because it gave rise to insecurity. For judges, this insecurity was about demeanour and reflection, and respect for the people coming to court no matter the pettiness of the crime. For prosecutors, insecurity was primarily associated with the speedy decisions, and the risk of getting them wrong. The dimension of "getting into the case" mentioned by the judges, of getting a feel for the case at hand, was also important to prosecutors, but this happened as a more or less unavoidable part of the investigations. They struggled, rather, to keep emotional distance to the reality of suffering, which is present in their work as purifiers (see, e.g., Chapter 2).

In the next section, we will look at the organizational approaches to security and the way that organizational security measures relate to fear. Such measures evoke, dampen, and direct fear at the workplace and thus also function as implicit organizational emotion management shaping the different emotional profiles of judges and prosecutors.

## Fear and organizational security work

Fear is an emotion that alerts the subject to danger. When danger is a possibility in the future, fear serves to fuel and orient action to avert the danger (Barbalet, 1998). In this sense, fear propels a cognitive assessment of one's potential vulnerabilities and can be a background as well as a foreground emotion (Kleres and Wettergren, 2017). Yet, taking measures to avoid dangers may also create or worsen fear, by increasing the focus on risk. In this way, fear is both silenced and evoked by the organization, through organizational attention to security.

In 2012, when we first began frequenting the courts, we were impressed by the fact that we could simply walk in and take a seat at any ongoing trial, for as long as it suited us. This openness spoke of an almost naïve emotional regime of downwards trust. As related in Chapter 1, Sweden has high generalized trust in state institutions (Rothstein and Stolle, 2008), and this generalized trust presupposes mutuality, meaning that institutional transparency and openness signal the trust of power in its citizens. This is important to keep in mind when we discuss the courts' apparent reluctance to think in terms of security.

### *Court fears*

As we later found out, there had been ongoing discussions and concerns about security following incidents in Swedish courts in the 2000s. In 2012,

*Figure 3.1* Court house of Lund, Sweden. Photo: Stina Bergman Blix.

starting with a government initiative that secured money to improve the courts' security, larger courts began to introduce rigorous security checks at public entrances: security guards, and bag and body scanners. It is worth mentioning that while district courts tested and, in some cases, have subsequently implemented security checks at the public entrances, appellate courts have been lagging behind, remaining without any visible security measures. This is also the case with smaller district courts, as evidenced by our data:

> There is one security guard but he is out sick again. There is thus no security control. The windows of the courtroom at the ground level that reach down close to the ground have ordinary two-glass panes. In the morning, a court clerk opens one of them wide open to let in some fresh air and then she leaves the room.
>
> (Fieldnotes, court)

The stark contrast here to the security concerns we observed at larger courts led us to highlight the situation in an interview with one of the judges, Jessica (40+), who worked in the court described. Jessica admitted that the security situation was bad, but then went on to laugh the issue off, saying that if someone would jump into the courtroom through an open window, she would just "jump out on the other side". With the security concerns at the larger courts in mind, the researcher pointed out that "anyone could fire a gun right through the window", at which Jessica responded:

> [Mockingly] I never thought of that; now I'll be afraid the rest of my time here. [Serious tone:] No, I never, ever thought of that.... I guess these are things you think about before you get used to them. But of course our security here is bad; it is, that's true.
>
> (Jessica, associate judge, 40+)

Jessica's reflections tell of a rather habituated sense of security that might have permeated the courts before 2012, in line with judges' habituated self-assured autonomy and distance from the messy reality, as if reality could never really touch them. To claim not feeling threatened was rather common among the interviewed judges. On the other hand, when security was improved, they generally acclaimed it, in particular as they learnt of the amount of knifes actually found in the security checks. As jokingly remarked by Jessica, above, when risks are pointed out, fear emerges. Security measures and fear as mutually reinforcing each other may explain some of the lack of emotional backup for considering security, leading to some courts lagging behind in this regard (Roeser, 2012).

We suggest that this sense of security is premised on a mutual trust regime, which, in turn, is premised on the idea of a "just society" (Clark, 1997) and, implicitly, on the idea of perfect justice. Judge Jessica's reactions to the questions about security above may seem naïve, but the fact is that the emotive-cognitive judicial frame is not easily amenable to the consideration of security issues, in terms of "feeling the fear of risk". The self-image of representing the cornerstone of democracy contains within itself the institutionally self-assured notion that people naturally respect justice. The emotionally anchored belief that judges are autonomous servants of objective law, equal to all, is incompatible with any fear of resentment or retaliation. In other words, fear would signal doubt in the legal system. Instead, institutional display of confidence is warranted, and for judges that display is part of their performance of autonomy.

The organization of courts is geared towards keeping judges away from contact with the parties and the public at large (by, e.g., having separate entrances for them), even if this, too, may differ between small and big courts. In a staff meeting in one of the big courts, judges complained that they had too little contact with the parties, to which the administrative chief responded by telling that the administration wanted to let as few calls as possible to get through to the judges: "To allow callers to get through to a judge would count as a failure" (Fieldnotes, court). At the small courts, administrative staff is smaller and work tasks tend to be less specialized. This led its chief judge to complain that people called too often, reflecting a decreasing respect of the courts as compared to the past: "25 years ago it would have been unthinkable to call a chief judge to complain, but now people ... get in touch far more often". Interestingly, at the small courts it was more common for judges to move about in the public areas of the courthouse, contributing to a general sense of closeness to the public that was lacking in the bigger courts. Together with fewer security measures, this may tell of reluctance to feel fear, as closeness may be a valued aspect of legitimacy in non-urban areas.

Fear is, furthermore, a strongly private connoted feeling (see below), which means that it is an emotion that may be very deeply backgrounded in the judges' professional emotional profile. While there were many stories in our material about situations in the courtroom that had warranted some kind of security measures – like calling in security guards or even pressing the alarm button – judges tended to describe these situations more in terms of their "responsibility for everyone in the courtroom" than in terms of fear for their own safety. In the excerpt below, judge Margareta discusses such a situation with two other judges during a lunch break:

Judge Margareta describes a trial she once had in which the parties were so angry at each other that, to be able to drown out their voices and break the argument, she had to shout louder than they. She wasn't angry, but she shouted angrily to interrupt them. She repeats this and it appears to have been a very uncomfortable situation to her. She says that in that kind of cases she feels the enormous responsibility that comes with being a judge: "I was responsible for the clerk, for the lay judges, for everyone's safety!" She had pushed the alarm button but that doesn't help much since it takes time before the security arrives so she had to do something to stop them shouting. [...] All three judges agree that it is a good thing with the security control now in place at the courthouse.

(Fieldnotes, court)

In this excerpt, the interpretation that Margareta's story is a story about an apprehension of fear is validated by the mentioning of safety, alarm buttons, and other security measures in the courtroom. Margareta, however, emphasizes that her apprehension of fear concerned her responsibility for others. We call this displacement of fear to others, or to a fear for others, 'othering'. Othering works to legitimize talk about fearful situations without directly admitting one's own fear; it is a sort of 'ventriloquism', similar to the way that researchers in academia have been found to talk about their professional achievements in a collegial environment that strongly discourages such talk (Bloch, 2016). Nevertheless, as a story about fear, Margareta's story contradicts the display of the self-assured security of the judge's position. The same lunch break also involved a fear story by another judge:

Judge Johanna enters the lunchroom, her face pale. She says she just came from a situation that made her all shaky. It was a civil case hearing in which one of the parties was a war refugee with scars all over his face. Johanna asked several times about his plea to the charges and then he began telling his whole story, whereupon she interrupted him and said: "You may tell your story later, but now I just want to hear your plea." And at that moment she felt that she "lost him". He became upset, and she felt that he might attack her. She became afraid, but it was only afterwards that she understood how afraid she had been. When leaving the courtroom, she was shaking.

(Fieldnotes, court)

In this excerpt, Johanna joins the group, coming from a hearing where she herself had experienced fear whose bodily effects are still present – she is shaky and pale. As the discussion continued, however, she shifted from expressing fear of the actual threat to a fear of not living up to high standards. Johanna's tangible fear opened up for situational intimacy between the three judges sitting in the lunchroom, and Johanna eventually turned her focus on her role in the incident, saying that "she knows exactly what she did wrong, but it is hard to talk with colleagues about it as [judges] don't want to admit mistakes". Her mistake was to push the defendant to tell his plea to the charges. At this, judge Margareta remarked that she herself tries to be careful not to push the defendant, and instead let go of the issue, and then ask again later.

As we can see, Johanna's fear story is remodelled into a story about inadequacy revealing the underlying assumption that a competent professional demeanour could have prevented the situation. The remodelling that we see exemplified here was aimed to maintain the autonomy and distance of judges: a judge should be able to navigate around becoming emotionally involved in interactions with people in court. This ability is reflected in Margareta's telling about her strategy to let the person be and then return later to the subject.

While there is a similar reluctance to cede any ground to fear among prosecutors, their actual physical situation looks quite different. Judges are more or less physically separated from the public, while prosecutors normally enter the courtroom through the same door as the defendant, the victim, the witnesses, and the general public. In all courts, however, prosecutors have a separate space for them to withdraw into during breaks, but, as a rule, to get there they need to walk through the public area. As they are more exposed, it is perhaps not surprising that prosecutors are much more aware of risks when moving about in court.

### Prosecution fears

There are various ways for prosecutors to approach the lay people in court, but a common strategy encouraged by the prosecution authority is to greet and shake hands with not only the victim but also the defendant if the latter is present in the waiting hall before the trial begins. This is generally considered a good way to signal to the defendant that the prosecution is not 'personal'. Yet, it remains a fact that the prosecutors' free movement among the parties in the court can also be a risk. There were several stories of glances, shouts, and insults received from lay people. In the following quote, Dagur recalls being once provoked by "street kids":

PROSECUTOR DAGUR: I've had such ... small incidents.... I was never threatened or anything, but I do remember a youth criminal case once where there were these cocky kids from the suburb of [suburb name].
RESEARCHER: In the audience?
DAGUR: Yes, and I was hard on their friends [the defendants]. I was pretty hard, and [laughs:] since I had twisted my ankle the previous day, I was also limping around pretty badly. [...] So I'm limping, right, and these guys of course see that. And they sit there ... you know, laughing a bit and messing around and looking at me in a funny way. And then, on our way out they – because I don't want to yield and let them go first, I go, like, "I'm walking here and I'm not going to back down and give way to them" – you know. So they group up around me on our way out, and I feel how someone [stamps down hard on my foot].
RESEARCHER: Ouch!
DAGUR: And right on that injured foot of mine [laughs]! And they laugh and I can't see who it is, but I don't make a sound, I just keep walking. [...] I felt quite small there, a bit vulnerable.

(Dagur, prosecutor, 35+)

In this quote, we see Dagur, while assuring that he never felt directly threatened, having no difficulty recounting a story about how his authority was challenged and he himself literally hurt by "kids". He admits having felt "small and vulnerable" in the situation, but nevertheless, looking back at the event, he rather represents it as a funny story. We also see the institutional confidence mentioned earlier in the discussion of judges, that is, the refusal to cede any ground to fears or become influenced by threats, as a representative of the rule of law ("I don't want to yield"). While judges can do this in their relatively protected position behind the bar, prosecutors must maintain their facade even when literally caught in a situation of potential danger. A similar account was given by prosecutor Klara (35+), who had been threatened by an accused person:

> Prosecutor Klara says that in a trial she was involved in, a police witness was threatened by the accused, so he asked for police escort when leaving the court. As the accused was angry with her, too, she just did not go to her usual place to pick up lunch. "Imagine that: the police officer was so affected that he asked for protection!" She seems to find that strange. She says the threats were rather vague, both the one directed at her and the one aimed at the police witness, but the accused is known to carry weapons and to have a short fuse. But "you can adapt, right – like now when I knew he would be going my way, so I chose to pick up lunch in a different place. Before, I used to insist on going wherever I wanted, but now that I have children I don't do that anymore". She says that the accused anyhow doesn't know that she changed plans because of him.
>
> (Fieldnotes, prosecution office)

In this excerpt, we see how Klara appears to be puzzled by the fear shown by the police officer. She rejects the feeling on her own part through othering; her "adaptation" is warranted because of her children. She also defends her adaption by saying that the accused does not know that she avoided him because of his threats. Along the same lines, also prosecutor Dagur above shifted away from reasoning about his personal vulnerability in the situation described, to the question of respect for the legal system, or "society", as a whole. He thus stepped up to defend his institution and let out emotions of indignation and worry on behalf of society at large – a form of othering turning personal concerns into professional worries:

> It's a bit worrying this disrespect. [...] You need to have *some* respect for society, in a way. [...] They crossed the line! I'm an adult and they're just kids. I would have never, ever dared to do that myself at that age. And it shows that they lack boundaries, which is dangerous. If you can do this sort of thing, you're capable of lots of other things as well. And these group dynamics: they sit there and incite one another. That's damn unpleasant. Not to me personally, but more as a social phenomenon.
>
> (Dagur, prosecutor, 35+)

This shift from personal (private) to professional fear indicates how the emotion work that goes into balancing the line between personal fear and the professional self-assured appearance is more foregrounded for prosecutors than for judges. Professional security signals belief in the general legitimacy of the legal system, while fear would cast doubt on the authority of that system. As representatives of the state in court, prosecutors frequently find themselves targets of defendants' resentment, and thus they need to actively negotiate the emotions associated with their position and its vulnerability. The question about fear is therefore not as remote to them as it may be to judges.

The generally increased attention to the risks involved in prosecutors' work comes in the aftermath of incidents occurring in Sweden over the past decade, incidents in which prosecutors have been severely threatened. While only a few of these incidents have been given media coverage, they are common enough to be represented in our material. In the quote below, chief prosecutor Agata gives a long account of fear. It starts out as a general reflection:

> I have felt fear sometimes when I have been threatened; then I've been scared. [...] But I've felt that it was difficult, like – in the actual moment it was hard to connect to fear, but then afterwards, when thinking about it, what I felt was indeed fear, fear of – I mean fear in the sense that you can't sleep at night, you notice every sound, of a newspaper dropping into the mailbox, and you wake up. [...] Fear of what? For your own safety, but above all for your kids' safety.
>
> (Agata, chief prosecutor, 45+)

Here Agata speaks of backgrounded fear: she realizes that it is fear she feels when thinking back on past incidents, trying to figure out the reason for her waking up to, for instance, the sound of the morning paper being delivered. The assessment of fear comes afterwards "when thinking about it". Subsequently continuing her account, Agata clarifies that "it has happened maybe four or five times that I was actually scared", and gives a vivid example of foreground fear. In the quote below, she also describes the security measures surrounding high-risk cases: there is always at least two prosecutors in such cases, and, in Agata's example, they were assigned bodyguards and had to sleep in a hotel:

> The police evaluate the threat and the potential for violence, but of course sometimes you feel that you look over your shoulder a lot. And at one particular time I, in fact, felt that kind of fear. We were two prosecutors in that trial, and there was this security information that the two of us would be shot, so we had moved away from home and lived in a hotel, with bodyguards driving us back and forth. [...] That's how we then went to and from the court, because we were in the middle of this trial, and then this person came in.... It was in a high-security courtroom, and so there was security control as well, but this person.... I was

the second prosecutor so I was just watching. Then suddenly this person in the audience raises something in the air, but I can't see what it is, I can only see that it's an object of some kind.... I got even physically scared, the way you get when you get into these dangerous traffic situations. [---] Well, you knew that there was security control but.... I was so damn scared.... That was really difficult and my son was very small then. Makes you really think about your career choice.

(Agata, chief prosecutor, 45+)

This quote represents an account where fear is foregrounded and becomes disruptive of one's professional performance. Agata mitigates her personal experience of acute fear – panic – by generalizing her argument in places ("sometimes you feel" that you look over your shoulder, "you really think about your career choice"), but she also explores her "feeling the fear" by visualizing how it knocked her off balance, and, in particular, how irrational her fear was, since there really could have been no way to get a gun through security.

We see that the acute feeling of fear surfaces against the context of the security information that Agata and her colleague would be shot, and of the action taken to prevent it (bodyguards, sleeping in a hotel). Awareness of the security surrounding the trial did not help when Agata thought the shooting was about to take place. Fear, in the form of precaution and heightened cognitive awareness, enables assessment of risk and can thus lead to action taken to deal with the sources of fear (Barbalet, 1998), but the increased alertness also foregrounds fear and allows it to interfere with one's work; it was fear that made Agata "see something" not the other way around. In the everyday work of prosecutors, fear needs therefore to be kept backgrounded if one is to perform professionally. One could, moreover, say that this backgrounding takes place in spite of, rather than thanks to, all the security measures taken to ensure prosecutors' safety.

As seen in Agata's case above, organizational security is prepared if a true threat emerges. However, it is also common to shift prosecutors, and even prosecuting offices, if minor threats occur. Prosecutors are, furthermore, continuously informed by the security departments about general risk levels and about how to adjust their daily lives and take precautions even when there is no concrete threat against them and even when the investigations and trials they work on are not high risk. They are advised to avoid habitual roads to and from work, to keep a very low profile on the Internet – preferably not having things like a Facebook or a Twitter account – to never post pictures or information about their children online, and to always hide their addresses and telephone numbers (removing them from online telephone books).

A recurrent pattern among the prosecutors in our study in relation to these general security measures was that they followed some pieces of advice given to them while shrugging off others. Prosecutor Jakob, for instance, who worked with severe crimes, had a secret phone number and "had no interest in Facebook anyway". Yet, as he described:

You should keep a lock on your mailbox ... and you should check the tires before you get into the car.... No, come on! [laughs] I refuse! And you're not supposed to bike the same way to work [laughs] everyday. Now, I don't bike to and from work the exact same hour every day, right, but I think if someone wants to harm me, they'll get to me anyway, right? It's not like you can do something about it.

(Jakob, prosecutor, 50+)

Jakob in this quote speaks of how the advice of the security department forces him to negotiate his emotional response (fear) to the organization's heightened risk awareness. He does not yield to fear and yet he does (deciding not to bike to or from work at the same hour every day), and in the end, he decides to simply accept the risk, rather than to live in fear.

Emotive-cognitively, prosecutors positioned themselves moderately in relation to the precautionary measures they were advised to take, because this positioning itself was about fear management: fearful action may evoke fear. This fear management kept their professional dignity and belief in a just world reasonably stable, yet they did not embrace the studied naivety that judges sometimes show. As mediators, translators, and purifiers, prosecutors have good reasons to feel exposed to risk. In the courts, prosecutors' risk awareness clashes with that of the judges, as seen particularly in (small) courts where security arrangements remain all but non-existing. Prosecutor Wenche (35+) compared the small and the big courts she used to work at, wishing that the small court would develop its sense of security, but concluding that "it's not going to happen until someone gets stabbed or something, so it feels. [...] They are rather naive about security".

The way new district court houses are built mirrors an increased concern for security also in the courts, however. Typically, they are built so that the justices never have to enter the public area, with more secluded rooms for prosecutors, and high-security entrances for defendants in custody. New courts, furthermore, may have at least one high-security courtroom that keeps the audience seated behind a bulletproof glass. Interestingly, while this arrangement may improve the feeling of safety of all those in the courtroom, it makes the spectators feel potentially excluded and exposed to the very threat the court wishes to exclude. Contrasting the openness when we initialized our court project, the public now finds themselves subjected to security checks by uniformed guards when entering the courts. By positioning citizens as 'suspects' until it is proven that they carry nothing dangerous, downwards trust is becoming conditional.

Security alertness is thus a double-edged sword: it both orientates focus towards potential threats and thereby foregrounds fear and emotion management to contain fear. Yet, it is seen as necessary in a world where it no longer seems wise to take the existence of 'respect' for justice and mutual trust between the legal system and the citizens for granted. Denial of fear is a way to assert legitimate authority and it is implicit in the self-image of objective law. When the organization moves in to increase security, it inevitably weakens this institutional self-confidence.

## Teflon culture: emotion management as self-discipline

Working hard, working long hours, and not complaining or being self-complacent are part of a self-disciplining culture that we have labelled 'teflon culture'. Under the influence of this culture, legal professionals are expected to deal with hardships in their work and, in particular, with hardships associated with horrific cases, as if the emotional aspects of these hardships would just bounce off one's professional (teflon) shield. Participants in our study commonly brought up the fact that working in courts, one becomes exposed to great human misery and gruesome pictures; "it's something you need to be able to deal with". They suggested that some individuals were born with the ability to manage it, while others were not: either you were a non-stick person or you were not fit for this line of work. The teflon culture, according to the participants, permeated both the courts and the prosecution offices, but played out somewhat differently in the two contexts. We will start by looking at the judges.

### Teflon culture in court

As noted in earlier chapters, judges must measure up to high demands on being overachievers: "Everyone should perform 110% all the time and be in top shape all the time, but that's not the way it is, because we're human" (Eva, associate judge, 30+). While it is not possible to always be in top shape, the continuous evaluations during training and the importance of displaying confidence and autonomy turn the 'human' features of feeling tired, sad, vulnerable, and so on into weakness, and thus into something associated with not being 'professional'. A professional, it is posited, should be able to keep emotional distance to others' emotions and to those of one's own. When asking chief judges about whether the clerks were somehow prepared for gruesome trials or whether they could avoid participating in certain types of trials like those involving a rape or a murder, it was clearly something that had not crossed the judges' minds before:

> Well, the issue has never been raised to me, but in a way [sighs] it comes with the territory: if you're not able to handle all kinds of trials, why choose this profession, right? If someone said, "I've got some experiences of [rape] myself, and I don't want these kinds of cases as they bring so many memories and emotions", then I would of course respect that, but, generally, judges cannot choose only to do civil cases or business law, so....
>
> (Arni, chief judge, 55+)

Even if Arni says that he would accept personal experiences of one's own as an excuse, it is clear from his reasoning that he would not recommend such a person for the judge's profession. Although it seems perfectly reasonable that all judges should be able to work with all kinds of cases, the implication is that "taking all kinds of trials" should not be emotionally difficult.

As with any workplace in Sweden, the courts provide their employees formal access to free occupational healthcare services including free sessions with a therapist. According to our interviewees, this possibility, however, was never made use of; even the idea of doing so was so remote that some interviewees did not even mention the possibility or did not know how to make use of this right. Occupational healthcare relies on individual initiative, and taking such an initiative would make colleagues suspect one of suffering burnout, the symptom of one's ultimate failure to endure one's workload and withstand pressure in general. Participation in formal debriefings arranged upon the initiative of one's organizational leadership – something that had not been done in any of the courts we studied – would, apparently, also give rise to such suspicions. In one of the few cases where debriefing had been arranged for by a judge following a particularly taxing court case, the judge found that the lay judges had gossiped about her. Resenting the gossip, the judge described the long hours of listening to different victims' descriptions of the same torture-like incidents over and over again:

JUDGE MONIKA: There was this lay judge going around saying that I had asked for debriefing. But, I mean, I did that due to this trial we had that lasted for two weeks with eight victims telling basically the exact same story over and over again. You got like brainwashed by them. So I asked the staff administrator [about debriefing]....

RESEARCHER: Right. That's the person you should turn to?

MONIKA: Well, I turned to anyhow; I have no idea, I guess she can talk to [the chief judge] later. But, I mean, the debriefing was on behalf of the lay judges and the court clerk. I mean, as a judge [sarcastic tone] you're not supposed to have any feelings.

RESEARCHER: But you're human just like them.

MONIKA: Yes, but that's the culture.

RESEARCHER: Yes ... but would you be able to speak to someone?

MONIKA: I don't know.

RESEARCHER: You arranged debriefing only for them?

MONIKA: Yes.

RESEARCHER: OK. And you yourself never spoke to anyone?

MONIKA: No.

RESEARCHER: If you'd want to, is there any sort of debriefing....

MONIKA: No.

RESEARCHER: Because, I mean, as you said, you've had murders and child pornography and ... do you talk about it?

MONIKA: Yes, you talk a lot, with your colleagues, you do. And I've said many times during coffee breaks that this particular case took a heavy toll on me. It was, I did say that, probably the nastiest case I've had.

(Monika, judge, 45+)

The quote is telling in the way it both rejects and reproduces the teflon culture. It begins with expressing a sense of discomfort about lay judges' speaking of her, explaining that she raised the issue of debriefing not for her own sake, but for the lay judges and the court clerk at the trial in question. Monika's description here represents a variation of the technique of othering, of speaking up on someone else's behalf. She then admits not knowing whom to turn to, because she has never asked for debriefing before. Then follows a sarcastic rejection of her own presumed need to talk, "as a judge you're not supposed to have any feelings". She does not know if she even could talk with someone even if she wanted to, and the short answer she gives reveals her unfamiliarity with talking about these issues. At the end of the quote, she, however, tells that she did talk to her colleagues, indeed stating that the particular case in question was the nastiest she had ever had. Her actual 'talk' with her colleagues is nevertheless presented as mere chatter during a coffee break, an example of the collegial emotion management that can be labelled 'ventriloquism' (see Bloch, 2016). We will return to this subject later. In summary, while Monika partly distances herself from the ideal of the emotionless judge, she still subscribes to it as a professional requirement.

### Teflon culture at the prosecution office

Also prosecutors subscribed to the ideal of emotional distance, but, as described earlier, their required commitment rather puts the emphasis on the ability to let go. The predicament of continuously needing to put up with critique and anger from several directions, together with the relative closeness to the lay people involved in the cases, requires an ability not to let expressions of strong emotions get under one's skin. Nevertheless, encountering angry victims when closing down (or even prosecuting) cases also raises the prosecutors' own moral standards. If they, for instance, ask people to make a witness statement even if they are afraid, the prosecutors themselves need to live up to the same principles. The prosecutor in the following quote had been threatened, but when her boss asked her about the upcoming trial, she declined all assistance offered to her. When her boss then came up with the idea that she could participate in the trial via telephone, her first reaction was shame:

I felt so ashamed for feeling such a relief. I mean, I argue [with victims and witnesses] all the time, saying "you have to turn up, because it's really important". In the end, you do the "what kind of society do you want to live in" appeal; "should we let the bad guys" and so forth. You know, these high flying ideals. And I felt ashamed for feeling so damn relieved about my not needing to then go myself.

(Hildur, prosecutor, 45+)

As we can see from Hildur's account above, her ability not to let her fear stick, even when she failed this time, was linked to living up to the moral expectation of preserving the legal system in practice. If judges' adherence to the teflon culture originates in the intellectual ideal of being overachievers, prosecutors' more practice-oriented ideal has to do with living up to the high moral standards of the system that they spend their days defending. Their closeness to the messy reality of crime and criminal narratives, combined with the objectivity demand on them, can make prosecutors uncertain of their moral right to feel affected by the tragedies they face in court.

Prosecutor Lisa (25+) who had a case of repeated domestic abuse of a woman, involving also children caught in the middle, confessed feeling guilty for emotionally taking sides, empathically "tuning in" with the victim: "After sitting with this case for three days, it breaks my heart a little. I guess I'm not supposed to feel that, but I do anyway" (Fieldnotes, prosecution office). The prosecutor felt this way even as she represented the accusing party in court.

The need to continuously heed evidence in both directions makes empathic involvement with the victim a tricky business: if, during the trial, evidence emerges that is in the defence's favour, the prosecutor needs to take it into account and thus be prepared to question the victim as to the account she or he has provided, in effect questioning also the prosecutor's own feelings of compassion with the victim. Feeling with any layperson can jeopardize an objective and professional practice (see also Bandes, 2006). Confessions of feeling with a victim or a case thus often turned up only when we talked to prosecutors alone, without any of their colleagues present.

Given their intermediary position, it might be that prosecutors are more strongly than judges subjected to the requirements of the teflon culture. But this fact also makes them more reflexive regarding how they manage their emotions when involved in a difficult case. They are also more open to the possibility of formal debriefing. In their work, prosecutors meet other professionals, such as social workers, for whom debriefing has become a standard procedure. Prosecutor Henrik below pinpoints the in-between position of prosecutors and the difference regarding their view on emotion management as compared to social workers:

In my view, it's really strange that debriefing is not part of our culture in any way. Two different cultures meet here [...] and ours is a different world where you are expected to handle your own emotions. When you work with social workers, it's absolutely natural to have debriefings, to not have that would be like "What! This workplace is sick, something must be wrong with the management" – right?

(Henrik, prosecutor, 45+)

The judges in our data never compared their work to that of other professions, while the prosecutors who brought up the importance of emotional reflection did. The same way as the judges, the prosecutors usually used othering to exemplify the difficulties in managing emotional hardships:

> At the office where I worked before it was normal that people at least sometimes sat in their offices crying. [...] In particular people who worked with emotionally demanding cases, like people with children investigating child abuse cases as if these cases came on an assembly line. There is a macho culture in the prosecution office entailing that you should wade through [the horrors] unaffected. I've never been in that situation myself ... and I've never been in a situation where I was sitting in my room, crying, I don't think I am that type of a person.
>
> (Göran, prosecutor, 35+)

As we see in the excerpt, the mixture of a sometimes unbearably stressful workload and emotionally demanding cases is said to cause breakdowns among prosecutors. Göran's description nevertheless represents a variation of the technique of othering that we also saw in judge Monika's case above. Prosecutors who themselves are parents who investigate child abuse as if they came on an 'assembly line' are susceptible to emotional breakdowns, implying that cases can be demanding due to the prosecutors' own private circumstances, not due to the cases' being emotionally demanding in themselves. In the last part of the quote, we see rejection of this 'macho culture', yet the teflon culture is also reproduced the same way as in the case of judge Monika earlier; it is personal qualities that make the difference between those who break down and those who do not (Göran is "not that type of a person").

Nevertheless, prosecution offices have come further in their organizational preparation for emotional ventilation. In principle, all prosecution offices have someone in the staff who is trained in debriefing. These trained persons, however, do not conduct debriefing at their own office but are only called to other offices to do so. This way of organizing debriefing is to avoid collegial conflicts, but it also implies that the trained debriefers do not necessarily acknowledge the need for debriefing at their own office. While the teflon culture can be articulated and debated in various ways in the prosecution offices, the culture's structural orientation towards individualized emotion management is reproduced by silencing. As prosecutor August said:

> The prosecution authority has got debriefers, but they're not used and they're entirely invisible; no one ever asked me, "Do you need to talk about this?" [...] And I was wondering if it's me who doesn't dare to show that I'm affected, but I contest that; I've raised the issue that I feel it's difficult now. I've got nothing in response though. So I wish it could saturate the prosecutors' training more so it wouldn't scare young prosecutors away if they feel bad, instead showing what to do with it when

you do feel bad and how to prevent such situations from developing in the first place. But there's no such change, as far as I can see.

(August, prosecutor, 35+)

As long as speaking up is left to the individuals themselves, the risk of revealing one-self as potentially unfit for the job remains. If and when the silence is broken, it may be disguised by othering. In August's statement above, we see how he admits being "affected" himself, but then calls attention to the needs of "young prosecutors", thereby trying to shift the focus from himself to another level of analysis. Yet it appeared from our interviews that it is in the nature of the prosecutors' work – and not due to personal incapacity – to wear down those doing it. It is thus a reasonable conclusion that it is the organization's responsibility to prevent such wearing down from happening. In our interviews with managerial-level prosecutors, some indeed articulated the importance of organized fora for ventilation and reflection. However, even the managers then found themselves confronting the teflon culture, as described by Nadja:

We have arranged debriefing for those working on big, taxing cases. Twice I've told prosecutors that "Now, let's book an appointment for you", with both of them responding, "No, I don't need it". But I insisted, saying that "You can tell me that afterwards, and you'll only have to go once". I think that it's hard to determine your need for something like that yourself, because you're in the middle of it. [...] I don't think that you realise when you've reached a level that's beyond what you're expected to manage. After those kinds of cases, you can feel completely empty.

(Nadja, chief prosecutor, 50+)

Nadja has had a lot of experience of tough cases herself and knows what it is like to "feel completely empty". In this quote, she describes how she alleviated the responsibility on the individual prosecutor to take the initiative to talk, but meets resistance ("I don't need it"). The management can implement strategies for promoting reflection, but the teflon culture is deeply built into the emotive-cognitive judicial frame's construction of professionalism.

As we have seen, the teflon culture in many ways prevents reflection about emotions and emotion management strategies. How do judges and prosecutors, then, reflect about and manage emotional strain? Starting with the judges, we will see how emotion management as an individual responsibility goes hand in hand with the judges' quest for autonomy.

## Individualized and collegial emotion management

When asked about how they managed emotional strain, a common response by the judges in this study was to refer to their own responsibility. As described in the section on fear, if a potentially dangerous situation occurs in the courtroom, judges need to make sure that others are not hurt. This form of othering can be efficient in the moment, but also accentuates judges' standing alone. Managing own emotions becomes an individual responsibility: "Judges are individuals and each one has to handle these situations in line with one's own personality" (Kerstin, judge, 60+). Kerstin emphasizes that as individuals, judges need to manage their emotions in a way they themselves best see fit. Individualizing emotion management can also be understood as inherent to the specific requirements of being a judge:

> Independence is fundamental. There are these projects run by the National Courts Administration. We're supposed to participate in supplementary training, talking about soft skills, and that's of course very good, but there's one problem. We're supposed to meet and talk about difficult cases and then one can suspect that there are colleagues who'll say, "Is that how you handled it? I'd have done it this way instead". And that can undermine something and – I don't know, it's not easy. It's fundamental that the rule of law be observed and that the individuals' rights are protected – all that has to come first. And then, of course, one should try to make all judges feel all right, but it's difficult to get a joint approach to that, to prepare templates for each specific situation.
>
> (Mikael, judge, 35+)

Mikael here stresses the importance of autonomy for the rule of law, and although he noticeably struggles to articulate a hitherto unarticulated stance, he puts legal autonomy in opposition to collective emotion management, or the identification of joint emotion management strategies. Later on during his interview, Mikael developed these reflections further, proposing that since talking to other judges might influence one's decision-making, it would be better to talk individually with a professional therapist, as a way of separating out the emotional aspects from the legal aspects. Independence, here articulated as autonomy, is depicted as fragile and easily swayed in a collective setting when the focus shifts from (hard) legal reasoning to 'soft skills', including emotion management. It seems as if the expression and sharing of emotions, not the feeling of them itself, is what presents a threat to the rule of law. Not talking about emotions would then safeguard against emotionally influenced decisions and reproduce trust in the legal system. By this logic, individualization of emotion management can be understood as a fundamental professional sacrifice. Nevertheless, judges also did talk about emotions with trusted colleagues in the backstage areas of the court:

> How many times have we gone from a hearing straight to some colleague, stamping our feet on the floor and saying, "What a god-awful hearing I just had, he was so stupid!" I think those kinds of emotions are pretty common, as is going backstage to talk about them.
>
> (Asta, judge, 60+)

In this quote, judge Asta talks about instant emotion ventilation, about "stamping our feet", to relieve tension after a difficult hearing. In our study, female judges referred to collegial emotion ventilation more often than their male colleagues, but when asked about gruesome cases and unsuccessful emotion management, judges more generally described having "dealt with it alone". In one case involving child pornography, the judge was completely unprepared for his own strong emotional reaction:

> I couldn't handle it; I had to take a break. It was the most repulsive shit I have ever – just horrific. And that poor court-clerk young woman. I bought her a [laughs], a six-pack of beer and told her, "Go drink this fast."
>
> (Erik, judge, 50+)

Erik excused himself for sending the young clerk home with alcohol by saying "There was nothing else I could do". It is interesting to note here that apart from Monika earlier (page 74), Erik was the only judge in our study to mention any clerks and their need for emotional assistance in cases the judges themselves found too gruesome to handle. Taking a break or repressing emotions in some other way could be momentarily successful for the purpose, but 'flashes' of 'images' could occur, as could lingering physical discomfort:

> It was this child pornography case I had, it's been a while now, but I suffered from these pictures that kept popping up in my head for six months afterwards. I felt really bad. And some awful rape cases: I had one when I was still relatively young, no more than an associate judge.
>
> (Kajsa, judge, 45+)

Similarly to Kajsa's recollections here, the gruesome cases judges recounted were often from a long time ago, but had stayed fresh in their memory for months and even years. Dealing with gruesome cases also entailed talking in private with partners. Although our study was limited to the work sphere, there were several indications of also partners having to "deal with it": "I've had a lot of violent crimes and sometimes there are gruesome pictures.... I've just handled it myself, so to speak, talked about it at home" (Ola, judge, 40+). Or, as the spouse of one of the judges in the study spontaneously remarked when hearing about our study, "You should talk to partners, relatives, they have a lot to tell!" (Fieldnotes, court). This spouse's remark suggests that there was more emotion management taking place at home than what the judges were willing to reveal. There were also spouses refusing to be implicated in this emotion management, as was the case with Kajsa's (cited above) husband. Kajsa said: "I don't really have anyone to talk to, as my husband said that he can't take it, so it's more like I'm talking more to my colleagues. Some of them you can talk to". The ambivalence regarding the colleagues in Kajsa's statement ("I don't really have anyone" vs stating that she can talk to "some" colleagues) indicates the general pattern that judges may have one or a few colleagues they confide in. It also signals the precariousness of needing to "talk"; it is not safe to be open about this need.

While the teflon culture assumption that judges "have no feelings" is clearly misguided, judges get support in remaining emotionally distant by the prosecutors' purifying and translating work. Handling and being faced with all the details of a crime, prosecutors make some important decisions when taking the cases to court, notably regarding how much of the evidence actually needs to be presented at trial. For instance, some prosecutors like to present photos of murder victims when they were still alive. The pictures create a point of identification, which is hard to do when having to depend on images of dead – and perhaps severely mutilated – bodies, and prosecutors believe that this is fair to the victim and that it strengthens their case. Most judges find such pictures out of place and unnecessary, however, precisely because the pictures evoke emotions and emotions are considered misplaced in court. Similar reasoning may be found in cases involving child pornography, in which there are judges who think that showing video recordings or pictures taken by perpetrators is abusive in several ways:

> Watching these films is in itself an abuse of these children but also of us who sit there, so I try to avoid that [...] And if that can't be done, I try to minimise the suffering for us by watching picture by picture instead, with no sound.
>
> (Viktoria, judge, 50+)

From this quote, we can see that there are subtle ways to manage the teflon culture. Viktoria actively works to preserve her emotional distance to pictures and video recordings showing grave abuse by only looking at them frame by frame and turning off the sound. Prosecutors are not always happy with this solution. Prosecutor Karl (55+) described a child pornography case where he had accepted the request of the district court judge to skip some of the video recordings at the trial. The result was...

> ...a verdict in which the accused was found guilty of "child pornography, not severe". "The images were not that severe". So I appeal and bring the pictures to the appeals court, and after a while the chair says: "Do we really need to watch this?" I say: "I refer to the verdict from the district court."
>
> (Karl, chief prosecutor, 55+)

In the appeals court, Karl won a verdict for severe child pornography. Hearing the verbal description of an event is not the same as seeing it, and prosecutors know this. The judge, at one end of the legal encoding chain, is exposed to no more than a selection of pictures or films, while the investigating police officers at the other end need to see them all. The prosecutor in the middle needs to manage more of these pictures than the judge. Repressing emotions of grief, fear, and disgust is the most common way to individually deal with these pictures. Some come out as "good copers" with an ability to switch in or out of their emotional performance (Fineman, 1995: 130).

> I remember a case I had many years ago, one in which a girl had been raped by her father many times, I mean, really many times, and she got pregnant. [...] Then I sat at the kitchen table at home, snivelling a bit, but that would never happen now – never. [...] You get hardened, and I think that's important if you are to survive in this job. You can't go home and weep once a week; then you have to change jobs.
>
> (Ingvar, chief prosecutor, 45+)

Becoming "hardened" was often described as an ideal, but it could also be problematized in that prosecutors were seen to need the ability to empathize in order to perform well. They should not grow 'cold' (Wettergren and Bergman Blix, 2016). Consequently, the prosecutors who described themselves as hardened and as being able to cope could elsewhere, in another discussion or in another part of an interview, recount stories that still described them as affected by some cases. Below, prosecutor Jakob talks about a debriefing session following a case of severe and repeated sexual abuse of a child:

> We had a meeting that night and talked about it. [...] [upset tone, low voice] I thought it was absolutely horrible and, well, then I let it all out, as it was, I mean, it was a real boy, and child pornography is also actually about *real children*. Everything is real. But to have to *see* this, that it actually has happened, that's so horrible; it's, well, yeah, it's sickening. There are, like, a million feelings swirling around inside you, you know.
>
> (Jakob, prosecutor, 50+)

Jakob had a low and steady voice throughout his description of the case and the debriefing session, yet he conveyed deeply felt disgust and grief. Working with rape and sexual abuse cases was also told by some prosecutors to affect their own sexuality; producing a "skewed idea of your own sexuality, I mean it becomes – it's hard, like – because these images pop up all the time..." (Agata, chief prosecutor, 45+).

As we have seen, prosecutors in our material commonly expressed interest in regular debriefing, while managers described difficulties in making people attend them ("there was no interest"). Another option is informal collegial emotion management. Prosecutors often stated that they could discuss and ventilate all kinds of experienced hardships in one's vulnerable professional position as a prosecutor but, even among prosecutors, ventilating about emotional repercussions of horrific cases in the company of one's colleagues breached the norms of teflon culture. Talking about emotions was to be done indirectly:

I guess we – well, we don't talk about it, but we do, because we talk with one another a lot, so that, I mean, if something happens we do talk, do kind of debriefing or whatever you want to call it. And if I think before [a trial] "How am I going deal with this?" I know that the defendant will be really angry at the victim, and then I will brainstorm about how I ought to handle this. So, we talk with one another, but what we talk about is not really articulated, we don't make it clear that we're talking about emotions, about how we're going to handle our emotions. We don't say that; what we say is "How will I deal with this situation?" and "What would you do if this or that happened?" That's how we do it.

(Josefin, prosecutor, 35+)

Emotion management here is achieved using codified talk, talking about emotions without talking about them – through what we call "ventriloquism" (cf. Bloch, 2016). Ventriloquism was used as a way to avoid breaching the feeling rules while still dealing with difficult emotions together. However, it seemed to amount to collegial support in that it shifted the focus away from the emotionally burdening contents of a case onto the judicial and formal aspects of it.

Alternatively, strong emotions could be redirected towards professional relationships: lawyers are frequent objects of frustration, disappointment, and anger, and, for prosecutors, judges can be objects of strong emotions, too. In the following quote, prosecutor Elsa speaks about the latter and draws a rather sharp distinction between collegial informal emotion management and formal debriefing sessions (of which she has experience):

We talk a lot anyway – you notice when you sit there during the coffee breaks that there's constant debriefing processes going on – but in a simpler form. And some do it better than others. [...] Because you always have opinions about the judge or the defence lawyer or the accused or the case as such – I mean, there are billions of opinions each time that some feel a great need to talk about, and it's good that there is this possibility at your workplace. We're quite tolerant, so I must say you're also allowed to talk. But [debriefing] is probably the only occasion when I actually get in touch with my feelings a bit more deeply and in a way that allows me to show my feelings. [...] The fact that you can react to things because you're carrying so many other things that all of a sudden something makes you burst, although it might not be a big thing, in itself [---] Something can suddenly make some other thing surface that happened to you quite a long time ago.

(Elsa, prosecutor, 50+)

No matter how important coffee and lunch breaks might be as occasions for people to let go of some of their experienced pressure, ventriloquism first and foremost achieves emotive-cognitive reorientation and thus does not relieve the weight of accumulated grief, horror, and disgust. Interestingly, the quote also indicates the accumulated weight of emotions that have not been properly ventilated, suggesting that these may surface much later.

Another version of ventriloquism in our study was achieved through joking cultures (Bergman Blix and Wettergren, 2018). While joking occurred frequently at all the courts and prosecution offices in our material, it is telling that prosecution offices exhibited a rather distinct, dark sense of humour. Humour relieves tensions and dark humour may act as a way to let out dark emotions without actually talking about them.

## Conclusion

Organizational contexts shape the emotional profile of both the judge's and the prosecutor's profession. We have seen that the judges' work is fundamentally organized around time as a tool: they take pride in contemplation and reflection. Prosecutors' work, on the other hand, is organized around time as a challenge: they take pride in their capacity to make quick decisions and to let go. The organization of time supports an orientation towards teamwork in the prosecutors' emotional profile, while there is an orientation towards autonomy in the judges' emotional profile. Whether time is a tool or a challenge, workload appears to steadily increase for both judges and prosecutors. For both professions, increased workload and pace of work function implicitly as organizationally induced emotion management, pushing towards detachment. This, in turn, calls for organizational policies of good treatment, to counteract an emerging mechanic approach (due to the focus on staying on time and getting done with the process) to the lay people in the courtroom, especially on the part of the judges.

Organizational attention to security, becoming more and more prominent in the past few decades, works to heighten the attention to risk and thereby produce fear, but it also increases the demands for a secure environment (especially for the prosecutors). These demands in many ways go against the presumably transparent, open, and trust-based legitimacy of the legal system. Increased security controls undermine institutional self-confidence and public trust. There are rather sharp differences in how far this development has gone, insofar as the two legal professions investigated in this book are concerned: prosecutors have a higher risk awareness and higher demands for security than judges. Both professions, however, are reluctant to admit any actual danger and feelings of fear, which is in line with the performance of institutional self-confidence and belief in the legitimacy of the legal system.

Teflon culture – the feeling rule that emotions should not stick to a professional – is thus related to both the performance of power and legitimacy and the emotive-cognitive frame's systematic silencing of emotions. As we demonstrated in this chapter, the absence of any professional mechanisms for rendering emotion management explicit and legitimate gives rise to techniques such as othering and ventriloquism and identifies the individual as the locus of emotion management, highlighting innate personality traits as decisive for success or failure in this regard. One's (lack of) capacity to deal with emotional hardships, work pressure, and stress reveals one's (un)fitness for the job. As a consequence, even if and when there are debriefing and therapeutic talks provided at one's workplace, there is a general reluctance to use these resources.

# 4　The dramaturgy of court emotions

It's a ritualized process in which I play a formal role that I can always fall back on. It can happen that you cross the line, get too aggressive when cross-examining someone, but that usually results in some kind of reprimand – there is a control mechanism – and then you back down. The role I play in the process is controlled to the extent that if I sometimes lose control, the ritual holds me within the boundaries.

(Göran, prosecutor, 35+)

Göran describes how the court ritual and the improvised coopera-tion with the judge serve as emotion management strategies; the judge's reprimand serves as a 'rule reminder' (Hochschild, 1983), keeping his professional role performance in line with the feeling rules of procedurally correct boundaries. In the previous chapter, we investigated the emotion management embedded in organizational structures. In this chapter, our focus will be on the backgrounded (interactive) emotion man-agement of role performance and the trial as a dramaturgical ritual. We thereby build our argument that the performance of justice as unemo-tional relies on empathic and skilled emotion management, and emotional exchange. This is related not only to the emotional expressions of others but also to one's own. Background emotion and emotion management are essential for the legal professionals to navigate the court drama and their re-spective roles in it. The first part discusses the court process as drama. First, we set the scene, which is the courtroom, describing how it is meticulously structured to orient and tame emotions. The code of legal procedure serves as a script, further taming emotions through its detailed rules of conduct and conversational turn-taking. Judicial terminology and language itself transform emotional narratives into a legal code that silences emotion.

In addition to the dramaturgical setting, script, and language, legal actors need to perform their roles in concert and in a convincing manner. The sec-ond part of this chapter narrows down on the interactional and collaborative emotion management in trial situations, looking at it through the prosecu-tor's and the judge's perspectives. Through these, we can then elaborate a set of dramaturgical elements used by legal actors in order to sustain their role performance: 'situated adaptation', 'tacit signals', 'front-stage strategic empathy', 'dramaturgical stress', and 'emotional toning'.

## Setting the scene for the non-emotional ritual

In the court, as on the theatre stage, everything is there for a reason, from the placement of furniture and equipment to the costumes and accessories. This reason is often two-sided: both symbolic and practical. Unlike the theatre, the court has no director and set-designer to decide which symbolic meaning the setting and the roles should project in a particular hearing. Instead, the legal actors are socialized into norms and value systems about the procedure and their roles in it. These norms and value systems are part of the emotive-cognitive judicial frame.

When asking the legal actors about the setting and the dress code in court, most informants talked about practical aspects. The elevated bench where the judge, lay judges, and clerk are seated when the parties enter, and also remain seated until the latter have left the room, is "practical" because, from it, the judge can keep a careful watch on everybody present. Nevertheless, our informants were also aware of the symbolic meaning of this arrangement. As associate judge Kristin described it:

> This thing with us sitting higher up … it's practical, because the audience sits in front and then the court can see everyone, and in a way it's the case that the judge rules, I mean we're also de facto elevated, we put ourselves above the people we judge.
>
> (Kristin, associate judge, 30+)

The elevated bench thus symbolically accentuates the power of the judge. The message here, furthermore, goes both ways: the judge feels empowered and sitting below one also feels "pressed down", as associate judge Leo (30+) noted when changing places once: "Sitting down there, I really felt myself sinking down; I felt more pressed down than how it appears to be, looking down from up there" (see Figure 4.1).

The correct attire in court is a dark suite, which is also considered both practical and respectful of the audience. Judges and prosecutors keep suits or blazers in their offices, slipping into them before going to court. Thereby, they also slip into their official role: "Dressing up for trial, I kind of enter my trial mode, readying me for the hearing" (Eva, associate judge, 30+). Putting on a jacket or a full suit signals a role transition, entailing strict adherence to the feeling and behavioural norms governing the public performance of a legal professional:

> I enter a role. I put on my suit and thereby I become my role. […] For me, clothes are important, because they show that … now I'm an authority figure, and then the state expects me to act in a certain way.
>
> (Dagur, prosecutor, 35+)

*Figure 4.1* Interior of court room and an ongoing trial. On the left side: the victim
counsel, the victim, and the prosecutor. At the central bar: (from the
left) a lay judge, a lay judge, the professional judge, the court clerk, and
a lay judge. On the right side: the defence lawyer and the defendant. The
picture is arranged. The persons in the picture are not related to any real
trial, nor are they participants in the research study behind this book.
Depending on when the courtroom is designed, the bench can be more
or less elevated. Photo: Åsa Wettergren.

For prosecutors, the dress code is more relaxed than for judges, except in
the appellate courts. In the district courts, combining a blazer with a pair of
jeans can be perfectly fine for them. Yet, the dress code also varies, depending on the nature of the trial. In prolonged trials, a particularly strict dress
code marks the seriousness and ceremoniousness of the opening and closing
days, while in between the two the code may become more relaxed. The
clothes worn by the professional actors outside the courtroom often give
clues as to what is at stake inside. A murder trial, for instance, unfolds as a
full-blown drama with all the costumes and rituals in place, while the four
more minor cases quickly dealt with, one after the other, in the courtroom
next door constitute more of a habitual improvisation.

## Script and legal terminology

The script of a typical Swedish criminal proceeding consists of the code
of judicial procedure (hereafter CJP) and the penal code. Judges in training usually use a cheat sheet to keep track of the order of events in a trial:

charges and claims, defendant's stance, development of facts, examinations, personal matters, and closing statements. Prosecutor trainees often write down their developments of facts and closing statements beforehand, also in simple trials. Procedural correctness is the backbone of an objective legal process, and the script is the guarantor of a legally correct hearing, invested with professional pride by the professional actors. The CJP directs the sequence of events and the kinds of articulations allowed, and, along with judicial language, it becomes a crucial manifestation of the emotive-cognitive judicial frame, taming and silencing emotions.

In Chapter 2, we proposed that the translating function of the prosecutors is a key aspect of their emotional profile: prosecutors purify fuzzy reality into judicially encoded packages. This argument builds on Tilly (2008), who discusses how the frames of social interaction influence the way people give reasons. In most everyday accounts, people explain themselves by telling stories, while specialized or expert reasoning come in the form of codes or technical accounts (Tilly, 2008). Tilly uses the example of legal experts and describes how, for example, an examination during a court hearing requires translation by the prosecutor or the defence lawyer, in order to turn the stories told by witnesses, defendants, and victims into codes for the court's evaluation (2008: 23). That kind of legal encoding disciplines emotions, both because encoding generally entails omitting the emotional content of an account, and because encoding represents the authoritative account in court: people generally accept that codes override ordinary language. In the following quote, a young woman witness takes the oath before giving evidence. According to CJP, the judge is to remind the witnesses of their "duty to tell the truth" (1942: Ch. 36, Art. 14) and of the fact that lying under oath can carry a prison sentence. In their everyday work, quite many judges indeed put it in such simple terms. In the case involved in here, however, the judge instead resorts to a legal phrase:

> The judge asks that the witness repeats after her: "I, [Name] promise and affirm on my honour and conscience that I shall speak the whole truth and will not conceal, add, or change anything". The witness repeats. The judge looks at her and says: "This oath is a declaration of truth, the violation of which may be penalized as perjury, but you presumably knew that already". The witness looks stunned and remains silent. The prosecutor begins the examination of the witness.
>
> (Observation, fraud, prosecutor Linus, 40+)

The purpose with the use of codes and procedural correctness is to ensure fair and objective proceedings. However, when legal phrases are used in communication with lay people in court, the latter's reactions tend to be similar to that of the witness above – consternation and intimidation deriving from not fully understanding what the phrase means. Some of our participants therefore talked about the importance of using vernacular language to make themselves understood by lay people. In their view, many of the common expressions in court do not actually promote correct procedure but rather tell of habituated bureaucratization. Assistant prosecutor Abraham (30+) exclaimed: "I'm so tired of all that 16th-century Swedish. [...] Just give me plain, regular Swedish!"

Nevertheless, inter- or intra-professionally 'legalese' is useful since it conveys specific professional meanings and thereby minimizes the potential for misunderstandings among legal professional actors. Experienced legal professionals furthermore manoeuver the codes in order to send tacit signals to each other, signals that are not intended to be transparent to lay people (see below). Legalese may also be used in situations of inter-professional status and power challenges and inexperienced legal professionals may use it to conceal their nervousness or shame, displaying surface self-assurance.

Legal encoding of stories told in court furthermore achieves removal of the emotional underpinnings of these stories, with an implicit emotion management effect. This is achieved both through the choice of terminology and the particular way that the reasoning inherent to legal encoding splits stories up into legally relevant sequences. Below a woman stands accused of beating her 14-year-old son. At the time of the incident, she lived with her three children in a small apartment and the son in question had been in a bad mood for several days before the incident. The hearing lasted for approximately 30 minutes, with the mother crying silently for most of the time, and when speaking, expressing regret and shame for what had happened. First, the prosecutor presented the facts of the case, reading them directly from the prosecution file:

> The prosecutor reads with a monotonous voice: "[The victim] had been ill-tempered towards his siblings all week. One evening the siblings come into the living room, complaining about their older brother. Their brother then enters the room, and the mother tries to prevent him from entering. The boy takes a shovel and hits his mother on her elbow with it. She wrestles the shovel from him and either hits with it or throws it at her son. He suffers a wound in his head requiring six stiches."
> (Observation, assault, court)

After this, the accused mother was examined about her version of the events. She had already pleaded guilty and agreed to the prosecutor's description. Her narrative was thus basically the same as that of the prosecutor's, while also differing from it in the way it described the flow of events and their emotional framing:

> The accused has tears running down her cheeks and she speaks in a broken voice: "He called me a cunt, a whore, and a bitch all week long, and every time he passed by me, he shoved me so I got bruised all over my body. That evening, his little siblings came running in, hiding behind my back, screaming, with their brother following after them with a

shovel in his hand. When he hit me, I yanked the shovel from his hands and tried to push him away, and I threw the shovel at him. It all took like no more than a second."

(Observation, assault, court)

Note the difference between the two descriptions of the same event. The prosecutor's version, read out in a monotonous voice, on the one hand, includes all the facts of the case, presented as a sequence of disparate events, while all emotional cues are toned down or eliminated altogether. The accused mother, on the other hand, describes a flow of events with no precise beginning or end, and even though she does not use any emotion words, the narrative and its articulation are emotionally highly evocative, conveying the emotional rationale behind the action.

While questioning the defendant, the judge continued the legal encoding initiated by the prosecutor, but now in vivo, enquiring about exactly how the shovel could hit the son in the head: "Did you hold the shovel above your head or in front of your chest?" From the legal-encoding perspective, the question sought to clarify whether the strike was intentional (shovel was above the mother's head) or more of a defence reflex (a shove from the chest level). The focus in the question, however, also had the effect of calming the mother: she stopped crying and tried to remember with the help of body gestures. The emotive-cognitive judicial frame thus keeps both professionals' and lay peoples' focus away from emotionally engaging aspects of the narrative.

## Front-stage performance and emotional communication

Apart from setting the scene and the language, the court ritual also needs to be performed. Goffman's definition of 'performance' provides a useful starting point:

> A performance ... is that arrangement which transforms an individual into a stage performer, the latter, in turn, being an object that can be looked at in the round and at length without offence, and looked to for engaging behavior, by persons in an 'audience'.
>
> (1974: 124)

In ordinary face-to-face interactions, it is impolite to stare, and people show respect to one another by continuously switching between looking and averting one's gaze. In court, however, the legal actors can be looked at incessantly. This arrangement underscores the centrality of performance to fulfil the demands for positivist objectivity postulated by the judicial frame.

In particular, the bench, with its elevated position in the centre of the courtroom, remains exposed to looks. The judge, lay judges, and the clerk all need to perform impartiality, that is, they should not express any feelings or subjective views about the case. This requirement is usually met by putting on a 'stone face'. This expression, or, rather, lack thereof, is the standard facial role performance of the court, although permanently employed judges can deviate from it based on their personal styles. They may, for instance, mimic puzzlement, surprise, attentive listening, or thoughtfulness, or they may smile, for instance when welcoming witnesses.

Although both defence lawyers and prosecutors can mobilize a whole range of facial expressions as part of their adversarial repertoire, the defence lawyers usually tend to be the more expressive of the two. Prosecutors usually keep a face that remains expressive but controlled, we may call it a 'poker face'. While it is similar to the stone face in that it can hide actual feelings, it differs from the latter in that it displays emotions as part of a broader strategic emotion management. The poker face may, for instance, become tender when turning to the victim (display of sympathy), but stern when turning towards the accused (display of moral outrage). When the defence lawyer talks, the prosecutor can demonstrate disinterest, disbelief, or irritation by combining a stern poker face with bodily gestures.

The two distinct faces are employed as part of strategic emotion management front stage, belonging primarily to the performance of justice for a real or imagined lay audience. Indeed, the 'audience' may consist only of the lay judges and the defendant. At the same time, however, also emotional communication that legal professionals hope their audience not to understand takes place. In the following quote, judge Eleanor describes a very common way for presiding judges to communicate to other legal actors present in the room their encouragement and interest as opposed to boredom and irritation:

> I take notes to be able to keep actively listening for longer periods at a time, but I also look up every now and then at the person speaking to show that I understand and that I actually find what they say relevant enough for noting down.... And then, if prosecutors or lawyers stray from the subject matter, I put down the pen, lean back, and turn my head away, to signal that "this doesn't interest me at all". [...] I don't do that with the defendant or a witness, however ... they might misunderstand those types of signals. But lawyers and prosecutors, they get the message right away.
>
> (Eleanor, associate judge, 30+)

As we see in this quote, in the context of the 'non-emotional' hearing, the judge's use of the pen becomes a crucial indicator as to the standing of the legal professionals. Depending on the situation, putting the pen down can communicate anything from feeling blasé to feeling angry (Bergman Blix and Wettergren, 2016). Purposeful use of looks and gazes is a communication technique resorted to by all legal professionals. Prosecutor Karen (30+) explained how "every trial is a game of looks" as the opposed parties try to win support from the lay judges. The "game of looks" thus blends with the poker face, staged for the lay people in court. Karen went on to describe how the looks can also be a way for professional actors to cooperate in the interest of a smooth procedure:

> There are also things that can only be tacitly expressed in court. For example, I had this witness who might have been mentally disabled; we weren't told of that beforehand. Or if someone – something that you don't want to say directly, like if you need an interpreter even if they don't want one. You know, things like "Can we pull this through?"; things like that. "How're we going to solve this? Should we continue the examination…?" Then you exchange looks.
>
> (Karen, prosecutor, 30+)

Looks here communicated concern or worry about potential obstacles to the procedure that could not be discussed openly due to respect for the lay people present.

But looks can also be part of the poker-face strategy to communicate things that lay people should pick up, such as the antagonism between prosecutor and defence lawyer. Defence lawyer Bengt explained how he used his poker face and bodily gestures to influence the proceedings during the prosecutor's examination of his client: "I lift my eyebrows, I lean back, or I lean forward, looking sternly at the judge, or I even interrupt the prosecutor: 'I must say that that was an odd question'" (Bengt, defence lawyer, 55+). Bengt here wants his client to see that he is engaged and alert on the client's behalf (cf. Flower, 2016).

Looks and discrete gestures, such as the positioning of one's pen, communicated emotions between the professionals not suited for an audience. The stone face and the poker face, bodily gestures and postures, on the other hand, were vehicles for communicating emotion that could be shared with the lay people in the audience without tarnishing the image of justice as something purely rational. The reason that there has to be a modicum of visual emotional communication, we argue, is that it is essential to convey a convincing role performance (Goffman, 1959). Complete lack of emotional expression would undermine the legitimacy of rational justice in the eyes of the public.

### Front-stage collaboration to control emotion

In order for the court ritual to run smoothly and achieve its goal of presenting justice as unemotional, the professional actors need to collaborate. Particularly when lay people involved in a case bring vibrant emotions into the courtroom, the professionals collaborate to either disregard these emotions or display joint empathy in response to them, depending on the circumstances (see Scarduzio and Tracy, 2015).

In one trial involving a 15-year-old male youth offender reported by his own father for driving the family's car (minimum driving age in Sweden is 18), the prosecutor, the defence lawyer, and the judge all acted in concert to embed the hearing ritual in a framing mindful of the vulnerability of the accused. The female judge displayed a soft and kind demeanour from the very start, addressing the defendant as a child, while the prosecutor displayed a more strict and judgemental style and the defence lawyer, a man in his 70s, put on a calm and fatherly appearance. The judge assumed the role of a guide, carefully steering the visibly remorseful and ashamed accused boy through the procedure, calming him down and making sure that he was able to follow what was going on:

> The judge, looking at the defendant, explains with a calm and kind voice how a trial works and asks if the boy understands. The boy responds: "Yes, we've talked about it in school".
>
> (Observation, unlawful driving, Inga, chief prosecutor, 50+)

After the prosecutor had developed the facts, the judge turned to the defendant again: "Now it's your turn to tell us what happened". The boy described how he and some friends wanted to go and join a party, so he got "this stupid idea" to borrow his father's car. The father was asleep at home, but woke up when the boy returned from the party and called the police. Following his description of the events, the prosecutor began the examination:

> Prosecutor [in a stern, lecturing tone]: "How did the drive go?" Defendant: "I guess it went well". Prosecutor: "You're an experienced moped driver?" Defendant: "Yes, and I've driven cars on, what's it called..." The defence lawyer fills in: "A simulator". The prosecutor asks the accused if he has given any thought to what *might* have happened and if he understands the seriousness of what he has done. The boy answers in the affirmative and the judge concludes the examination with a dry "Thank you".
>
> (Observation, unlawful driving, Inga, chief prosecutor, 50+)

While the prosecutor in this case used a lecturing tone, her questions were not particularly harsh. In a follow-up interview, she explained that she was "caught off guard", learning only during the examination of the boy that it was his father who had reported him: "I thought, what an idiot father! [Laughs]... I didn't want this to fall too hard on the boy".

Towards the end of the trial, when the judge detailed the defendant's personal matters, it also turned out that, by reporting the event, the father wanted to teach his son a useful lesson. The mother had expressed concern about her son's cannabis habit, and had contacted a treatment clinic about what she saw as his addiction problem. The defence lawyer asked the boy about the treatment programme and thereafter asked the judge's permission to allow the father, who was sitting in the audience, to say something. The father embarked on an emotionally highly charged narrative about feeling guilty for reporting his own son while simultaneously hoping that he did the right thing, teaching his son a lesson. When he was done, the prosecutor took over with her closing statement:

> The prosecutor leans back and with an authoritative tone asks the defendant if he understands that he should not drink at his age, nor take any drugs. In her closing statement, she proposes that the sanction suggested by the probation authority will suffice. The defence lawyer agrees with the prosecutor and adds that it is good if the defendant now understands the seriousness of the matter, as an outcome of this trial. The judge concludes by saying that the judgment will be issued shortly. Everyone leaves.
>
> (Observation, unlawful driving, Inga, chief prosecutor, 50+)

In this excerpt, the defence lawyer's suggestion that the trial is a good thing for the boy can be seen as an effort to reduce the father's previously expressed anxiety. It also tells the boy that his father had good intentions, and that the boy should not resent him. The defence lawyer's emotion management here reaches beyond the judicial domain and into the domain of care. In our material, defence lawyers emphasized that both of the two domains were important aspects of their professional interaction with their clients. The prosecutor proposed a lenient sentence that was agreed to by the defence lawyer, and later issued by the court. Afterwards the prosecutor explained that she wanted to remain stern without intimidating the boy. On their way out of the courtroom, she then talked to him to prevent him from "feeling that we're on opposite sides".

This case illustrates how the legal professionals collaborate in a tacit agreement to perform their respective roles impeccably but smoothly, a rather common practice in youth cases where the hope is to prevent the youngsters from engaging in further crime by applying a preventive rather than punitive approach. The judge can adopt a 'kind' though still objective demeanour when the prosecutor takes on the judgemental role, and the defence lawyer acts supportively and caring for his client, while agreeing with the prosecutor on the "seriousness of the matter". Upholding procedural correctness through ritual, script, and role-adherence, such cooperation mitigate the harshness of the performance of justice while at the same time carefully controlling the emotionality of the lay people involved. Such smoothly concerted performance of justice builds on the subtle emotional communication described in the previous section.

So far, we have focused on front-stage performance. In what follows next, we will show how backstage preparations, front-stage presentations, and backstage venting are interlinked and reveal background emotional processes and emotion management from the perspectives of prosecutors and judges, respectively. We will highlight specific dramaturgical features used by the different legal actors to sustain their performance of procedural correctness: 'situated adaptation', 'tacit signals', 'front-stage strategic empathy', 'dramaturgical stress', and 'emotional toning'. We begin by looking at a brief 'grey trial', shadowing the experienced prosecutor Jakob. A grey trial is a minor offense trial, usually a matter of quick and routine handling by all the legal professionals. At the same time, because they may, as in the trial with the 15-year old discussed in this section, involve first-time and one-time offenders, as well as experienced recidivists, they can become unexpectedly emotional.

## The prosecutor's perspective: enacting backstage/front stage

The waiting room in the courthouse constitutes the backstage to the courtroom but for the prosecutor it is a space of layered front stages. Prosecutor Jakob has had a full day of grey trials. He is dressed for the occasion in a pair of jeans and a grey striped jacket. Entering the court's waiting room for his fifth trial of the day, aggravated theft, he identifies the injured party, an old man looking a little misplaced on one of the sofas, and approaches him:

> They shake hands, after which the old man sits down again and asks Jakob if he is the person representing him. Jakob keeps standing and says with a disinterested voice that he is partly representing the old man's insurance company that has claimed compensation for the money they have paid him, the victim. The old man, who turns out to be in his late 80s, apologizes that his hearing is bad. Jakob replies with a louder voice: "Yes, I'm here to help you". The old man wants to show him papers concerning his compensation, arguing that he has not been correctly compensated. Jakob protests at first but eventually sits down with the old man when realizing that there actually has been some problem with the insurance company.
>
> (Observation, theft, prosecutor Jakob, 50+)

When Jakob first introduces himself to the victim he establishes a certain distance, even stating that he is partly representing the man's insurance company, not the injured party. This is in line with the prosecutor's objectivity demand: prosecutors represent the state, not the victim, contrary to a common misunderstanding by victims that prosecutors themselves are keen to correct. During his follow-up interview, Jakob explained: "I usually approach the injured party to say hello, but I don't want to, so to speak, convey the impression that I'm close to anyone, anyone who's going to tell their story [in court]". In other words, also the waiting room, the backstage arena of the courtroom, may demand front-stage presentations from legal actors: it is a semi-front stage. Jacob takes great care to display an objective demeanour, not associating himself too overtly with the victim. However, the victim also appears to be in need of assistance from him, which makes Jakob change his approach:

Jakob and the victim sit side by side, with Jakob showing a slightly protective attitude by sitting close and articulating his words clearly, so that the old man can hear him. Eventually, they agree on a new damage claim, for both the victim and the insurance company.

(Observation, theft, prosecutor Jakob, 50+)

When Jakob understands the victim to be right in his argument and it becomes obvious to him that the victim has already fought a lot in vain with his insurance company, he becomes more engaged. Besides representing the state, prosecutors in Sweden also have a far-reaching obligation to assist the victim during the preliminary investigation. As Jakob explained: "Since the police did not ask these questions, I've got to do that. [...] So as prosecutors we have to step in and, well, we help victims, and naturally we grow very close". Accordingly, in order to perform objectivity, Jakob at some points needs to demonstrate distance, while at others he needs to become empathically involved. As we can see from the above, the shift from disinterested distance to engaged proximity and back can be swift and requires from the prosecutor a certain level of emotional astuteness.

Jakob's involvement with the victim results in a changed damage claim. After their agreement on the matter, Jakob glances around for the defence lawyer. They have had hearings together earlier that same day, and they like to chat a little in between trials. The defence lawyer, who stands a bit further away, talking with his own client, notices Jakob and comes over. Jakob greets him and tells about the issue with the insurance company, giving him a heads up about the adjustment to the damage claims. Thereafter the two both complain a little about the trial's being late: "It's disrespectful to let people wait like this".

For prosecutors and defence lawyers to chit-chat with each other during grey trials is common, offering a way for them to exchange neutral information about the case and often also, if they know each other from before, talk about this and that. The older, more experienced legal actors see these professional interactions outside the courtroom as the 'fun' part of grey trials, with the hearings themselves tending to be routine. The younger professionals described their collegial interactions more in terms of an emotion management strategy: "If you have a relationship – not one between best friends, but a work relationship – then we can take that with us when we go into the courtroom. It doesn't get personal; we don't get the trench warfare" (August, prosecutor, 35+). This experience was shared by defence lawyers:

We meet in court a lot, us defence lawyers and prosecutors, so it would be dull if we wouldn't chitchat a little every now and then. I find it quite nice. But then again, it depends on who your client is. [...] If you represent someone who's traumatized, then you have to focus on taking care of that person. Or someone who is very angry with the prosecutor: then you need to create a bit of distance, you need to be sensitive to that. But I think that many of our clients understand that we do have this collegiality.

(Selma, defence lawyer, 40+)

Collegial interaction in the waiting hall creates fleeting shifts between the position of demarcated distance that marks one's front-stage performance and moments of pleasurable chit-chat constituting an interactive back-stage for inter-professional ventilation and relaxation. Situated emotional communication – through looks and bodily gestures – is the means by which the appropriate course of action is agreed upon.

### Situated adaptation to ordinary surprises

Although grey trials are often seen as "easy" assignments, they may still be full of surprises (cf. Roach Anleu and Mack, 2017: 33–35): the accused, the victim, or some of the witnesses fail to show up, new evidence surfaces in the examinations, or technical devices fail. Emotive-cognitive astuteness about unexpected events, the dramaturgical feature of 'situated adaptation', is essential here. In the trial with Jakob, the hearing did not even start before an unexpected event occurred: the judge announced himself to be an acquaintance of the victim, which could be a cause for disqualification.

When everyone has entered the courtroom, the presiding judge begins by telling the court that he and the victim are members in the same Rotary Club, quickly proceeding to explain that he has "talked to the chief judge, and I do not think it disqualifies me". The defence lawyer appears to disagree, however. Telling the judge about the new damage claim that came up in the waiting room, he states this circumstance to cause potential "complications". Through this, he signals the defence's wish to request disqualification of the judge, although avoiding any direct articulation of his intention. The judge decides that the prosecutor should first present his new, revised claim, after which the court will take a break to deliberate. In his follow-up interview, Jakob commented:

> The judge must have realised this rather late, I guess…. Had he noticed it before, they'd have put another judge on the case and this would never had happened…. I mean, it's an administrative matter. It's not that common, but it has happened to me, too. A couple of times I've noticed that I actually know the person sitting in front of me in the courtroom…. But it's good if you – you should be transparent about it.
>
> (Jakob, prosecutor, 50+)

The quote suggests that incidents like this happen, and, while in themselves not that noteworthy, they become troublesome primarily if they take place in front-stage settings because they seem to disrupt the performance of objective justice. It is interesting to note that Jakob only refers to the potential problem of presenting an impartial demeanour, not in any way questioning the objective state of mind of the judge. This points to the habituated professional belief that the mere idea that legal professionals would be influenced by their emotions contradicts the very definition of "the professional".

The professional judge chairs the court sessions and enjoys the highest status in the court hierarchy. Ritual deference (cf. Clark, 1987; Scheff, 1990) towards them by the other legal professionals present is key to a smooth procedure (see Chapter 5), contributing to the performance of objective justice. The professional judge's opinion is hardly ever questioned, and in the case with Jakob, the issue was even more delicate than that: the question was about whether to express doubts about the judge's self-proclaimed capacity to remain objective. The defence lawyer swiftly adapted to the situation, however, resorting to addressing a matter (the new damage claim) that did not directly put the judge's decision under question.

In the waiting room, while the court discusses the objection presented, Jakob manifestly moves away from the defence lawyer and his client, walking to the water fountain at the opposite end of the hall to quench his thirst. Knowing that the lawyer will now need to talk with his client about the possibility to request the disqualification of the judge, Jakob keeps a distance; the waiting hall has now turned into a front-stage arena. After a while, the defence lawyer approaches Jakob again and tells him that his client is not at all happy that the judge knows the victim. Jakob agrees that someone else should chair the hearing. The defence lawyer elaborates on his client's reasons:

> "Especially, as my client tells me, because he was at the crime scene in different business. I've tried to reason with him, but if he wants to stick to his story there's nothing I can do about it." The defence lawyer shrugs his shoulders, showing that he knows his client's denial to be ultimately pointless.
>
> (Observation, theft, prosecutor Jakob, 50+)

When the defence lawyer has left, Jakob explains to the researcher that the judge is clearly not disqualified, but it is still "important to consider delicacy disqualification". Thus, even though he does not really believe that the judge should be disqualified, he offers the defence lawyer his support. This can be seen as an emotional gift of sympathy, a claim, according to Clark (1987), to friendship and intimacy. In return, the defence lawyer gives Jakob a heads up about the version his client is going to give of the events: he is going to stick to a completely unbelievable story. While information is a valuable gift already in itself, it also serves as the reciprocation of the sympathy gift given to the defence lawyer by Jakob, thereby reproducing and confirming a trusting collegial relationship between the two. At the same time, this emotive-cognitive interaction between the trusting colleagues marks the transition into a backstage arena again.

What we also see, however, is the way the defence lawyer distances himself from his client: "if he wants to stick to his story there's nothing I can do about it". Lawyers need to balance their duty to prepare a defence in their client's best interest with their duty to present and stand by their clients' version of the events (Flower, 2016), and the two duties may sometimes conflict from the professional point of view. In the trial with Jakob, by talking to the prosecutor beforehand, the lawyer releases some anticipated shame and saves his professional face; in court, he will (be forced to) present remarkably weak arguments due to his obligations to his client (cf. Harris, 2002).

Shortly afterwards, the judge shows up in the waiting hall to speak with the victim. At most courts, it is only seldom that a judge enters a public section in the building, rendering another surprise in the course of this trial. The sudden presence of the judge transforms the waiting hall into a front-stage arena again, causing the focus to be put on procedural correctness. The judge first speaks a few words to the victim and thereafter approaches the prosecutor. He informs Jakob that the victim has decided to pursue damages separately from the criminal case, leaving them to a later civil case. As the judge explains, this solves the problem with the victim's new claim, "and so we can continue with the trial". Finally, the judge turns to the defence lawyer to speak also with him, returning thereafter to the courtroom. Jakob and the defence lawyer do not talk to each other again after the judge's arrival at the waiting room: it remains a front-stage setting for them. Soon afterwards, the trial commences again, with Jakob commenting to the researcher: "Now we get to see if someone made a request for disqualification or not".

Up until here, we have seen how 'situated adaptation' requires emotional astuteness to see when strategic non-interaction (display of disinterestedness) becomes preferable over strategic interaction (sympathy exchange), and vice versa, in the ongoing professional interaction. The marking of distance and discretion turns the waiting hall into a front-stage arena, while closeness and emotive-cognitive exchange make it a collegial backstage setting. This way, the prosecutor and the defence lawyer can maintain a good relationship without its affecting the adversariality of their roles in court. We have also seen how situated adaptation is necessary in the front-stage arena to maintain a deferential demeanour towards the judge, a theme that we will elaborate in the next section.

### Adjusting to the judge: situated adaptation, emotional toning

Back in the courtroom, it is the chief judge who is now presiding. Yet no one comments on the fact that the previous judge has been replaced. The presiding judge himself does not explain his presence, and the prosecutor now includes the damages in the claims he presents, without any indication of the backstage decision that they were to be pursued in a separate civil trial instead. Jakob reads out the charges very fast, like a radio talk-show host. After the trial, he explained that he knew the chief judge to prioritize speed. Therefore, he read the charges "like a sports commentator". Jakob's decision here represents another instance of the dramaturgical feature 'situated adaptation', through which, in this case, both the prosecutor and the defence lawyer swiftly adjusted to the presence of the new presiding judge.

Such an adjustment forms an inherent part of the prosecutors' and defence lawyers' job. It includes both the preparatory aspects of their work – trying to anticipate how patient and lenient the judge assigned to the case might be – and the performance part of it in the courtroom, where the actual situated adaptation, tuning in with the mood or style of the present judge, takes place. Unfamiliar judges may therefore cause insecurity, even among experienced legal professionals. As explained by one defence lawyer:

> If I see a new judge, I *never* know what to make of him, I need to tune in to that person. Is there something sharp, edgy, irritable? And if there is something edgy, I back off. Because I know that if I start fighting in court, there is only one loser, and that's my client. If he's annoying, or I'm annoying, it will cost him: he'll get a few extra months or something. It's not like "the lawyer is annoying, so I'll send his client to jail", but it's always human beings who judge, so you have to think about that. They represent a wide range of options, and a wide range of values.
>
> (Allan, defence lawyer, 65+)

Allan's statement highlights that empathy, emotional tuning in, is important not only between legal professionals and lay people but also between the legal professionals and in particular towards colleagues with higher rank (see also Keltner et al., 2003).

Back to Jakob's trial, the prosecution claims that when the victim came home, his front door was open and there had been a burglary, and that the police had found the defendant's fingerprints on a jar where the jewellery used to be kept in the house. Jakob shows some police photographs of the house in the condition in which it was found after the burglary. The defence denies all the allegations. The defence lawyer explains that the defendant admits to being at the crime scene, but denies having stolen anything, which means someone else must have been there after his client left. The trial continues with the cross-examination of the victim, who, due to his advanced age, talks slowly and uses a hearing aid:

> The court clerk asks the old man to talk closer to the microphone. The judge smiles and asks him gently if he can hear what they say. The victim describes his wedding rings that now were nowhere to be found, looking up at the court he says: "I don't know if they still have them?" The judge looks confused, replies: "Pardon me?" The old main explains: "If my rings are still around." The judge meets his eyes, gives a thoughtful nod, and turns to the prosecutor.
>
> (Observation, theft, prosecutor Jakob, 50+)

Lay and professional expectations in a trial clash in this excerpt. The victim hopes that he might get his rings back during the same day. His question reveals affection and innocence in a manner that breaches the conventions of the court ritual, but the judge nods anyway, as if it would sometimes happen that people get their stolen things back during the court hearings. Turning to the prosecutor, the judge instead looks startled, with raised eyebrows, uttering:

> "But [the rings] were not included in the claim." The prosecutor objects that they were indeed, with the judge then responding in an irritated and slightly louder voice: "How can I possibly *guess* what the claim includes!" Turning away, he then moves on to the examination of the defendant: "Can you describe this visit of yours in the house?" Accused: "What do you want me to say?" The judge pauses shortly, raises his eyebrows in surprise, and responds: "Well, what did you do there?"
>
> (Observation, theft, prosecutor Jakob, 50+)

Lawyers' and prosecutors' emotional adherence and behavioural adaptation to the judge have a limit contingent on their sense of professional integrity. Prosecutors in our material described their resistance to, and irritation about, judges who interfered with their work, such as when interrupting their ongoing examinations or, as in Jakob's case, suggesting that they had not provided to the court something required or necessitated. In keeping with the feeling rules of the emotive-cognitive judicial frame, and because of the need to show ritual deference towards the judge, any such irritation on the part of the prosecutor must nonetheless be managed and its expression toned down. Thus, when the judge above expressed irritation at Jakob's not having sufficiently itemized his client's claim, Jakob insisted the opposite to be true, yet retained his calm demeanour. Afterwards, however, he described having felt "crossed":

> [Laughing] That made me a bit cross, actually. I managed to swallow [my anger], but I still think the judge was just all wrong.... If someone steals seven hundred different things from you, you don't specify these in detail; you write that they stole things worth so-and-so much. [...] And I was about to adjust the amount [due to the changed claim], so saying that was just totally unnecessary! It caused my heart to beat faster for a while! [Laughs].
>
> (Jakob, prosecutor, 50+)

Even as Jakob grew angry, his emotional reaction was stronger than what he let on; in other words, what he performed was an action of toning down his emotional expression. Something similar, moreover, might have been going on with the judge: as we saw, he delivered two short comments to Jakob, of which he raised his voice in one, but then immediately let the matter go, indicating that he managed his emotion of irritation. "Emotional toning" will be elaborated with regard to its use both by judges and by prosecutors in the last section of this chapter.

To return to the courtroom in Jakob's trial, the accused now gets to tell his story. According to him, he was selling his motorcycle, and a potential buyer showed up, wanting to have a test ride, but then just drove off with his bike. The accused thought he knew the thief and that the person lived in the victim's house, so he went there to confront him. Once there, he broke into the house and rummaged around it, without, however, taking anything. When the accused is finished, Jakob refrains from examining him. As he later explained, there was really no reason, in his view, to "dig into a story that's so obviously implausible". Through his bold decision not to ask any questions, Jakob showed self-assurance brought by experience, although the example also conveys a particular prosecutorial style. Adapting to the judge's time-efficient and authoritative manner favouring succinct examinations, the prosecutor refrained from unnecessary questions. In this particular case, Jacob's decision was made all the more easier by the fact that the defendant's version of the events was so manifestly false that no questions were actually needed.

All the same, Jakob's adaptation strategy forces the defence lawyer to ask his client more questions than he normally would. The defence lawyer now asks his client about his fingerprints that were found on a jar in the victim's house. The defendant explains that he broke into the house looking for keys to the house's garage, thinking the thief had hidden the stolen motorcycle there. The photos from the victim's house, presented by the prosecutor at the outset of the trial, clearly show an elderly person's home, and, indeed, the victim is nearly 90. The defendant's story thus appears absurd in several respects, as also the judge more or less explicitly makes clear in his additional questions:

> "If you wanted to get into the garage, why did you not just break into it, and not the house?" The accused says that the door to the garage was made of steel, to which the judge responds, slightly amused: "I see; it was difficult to break through?" The examination is over. The judge turns to the prosecutor: "I might have missed something: what were the new damages again?"
>
> (Observation, theft, prosecutor Jakob, 50+)

Contrasting with the first time the judge raised the question of the damages, this time he is calm. The examination of, and focus on, the defendant during the intervening time period has given both the judge and the prosecutor time to manage their irritation and anger. The judge now begins to read from the accused's personal file and the prosecution and defence both prepare to give their closing statements.

### Tacit signals

The prosecutor delivers his statement in a fast but steady voice. Now he also adjusts the dates for when the crime allegedly took place. This move causes trouble for the defence lawyer, who has built his closing statement around the original dates, as appears from the following excerpt from the defence lawyer's summary:

> My client has stated that he was at the crime scene for a different reason. The prosecutor bets all his money on one horse when he says that the crime took place on Sunday the 1st of June [pausing shortly]. Well, in his closing statement the prosecutor just now changed the dates, saying now that it could have been any time between Sunday and Tuesday.
>
> (Observation, theft, prosecutor Jakob, 50+)

The only card the defence lawyer had left to play was the fact that the prosecutor's original time for the break-in was too narrow to cover the possible time frame of the crime. Since the prosecutor acknowledged it, adjusting the date in his closing summary, the defence had nothing else to go for. The defence lawyer's acknowledgement of the prosecutor's amendment while still keeping to his original argumentation gives a 'tacit signal' to the court and the prosecutor that the lawyer knows it is a lost case.

Tacit signals of this kind are another dramaturgical feature, similar to the subtle emotional communication discussed earlier. What these signals communicate is, to use Goffman's terminology, role distance: following a role-appropriate presentation while showing disbelief in that same presentation (Goffman, 1961). Legal professionals do not express distance from their role as such, but from conflicting aspects of that role. In principle, defence lawyers ought to remain loyal to their clients, but their clients' wish to handle the case might not agree with the lawyer's professional advice. When clients refuse to cooperate, their lawyers commonly chose to prioritize loyalty. Thereby, they satisfy the client's expectation of what a defence lawyer should do: justice is seen as having been done even when it does not hold from a legal perspective. As we will see in Chapter 6, tacit signals are, however, also used by prosecutors hoping to achieve objectivity without risking collegial loyalty.

Shadowing prosecutor Jakob, we have observed how prosecutors, to mark their objectivity, carefully control their relation to the victims. We have seen trusting collegial relationships between defence lawyers and prosecutors to be handled carefully in fleeting collaborative constructions of backstage/ front stage through the balancing between physical distance and displayed disinterest, on the one hand, and physical closeness and expressed mutual sympathy exchange, on the other hand (Clark, 1987). Doing this did not appear to affect the parties' antagonistic performance front stage, although it did strengthen the defence lawyer's confidence when acting against the hierarchically superior judge. This intervention was stubborn in character, yet performed deferentially by using the pretext of a new damage claim, allowing the defence lawyer to avoid publically challenging the judge's evaluation of his own capacity. We have seen, thus, how judicial rank and hierarchy shape subordinate legal professionals' interactive strategies, not merely to save themselves from shame but also to save the face of justice.

The case of prosecutor Jakob has also shown us how irritation is expressed and mastered front stage through the dramaturgical feature of 'toning down', and how experienced prosecutors can withstand judges' intimidation efforts. It has, furthermore, directed our attention to the dramaturgical feature of 'situated adaptation', in which both the defence lawyer and the prosecutor flexibly adapted to both the first and the second judge. Jakob did so with a self-assured impression management technique demonstrating all the qualities recommended for prosecutors earlier on, in our Chapter 2 (p. 50), by chief judge Ingvar. Finally, our case with prosecutor Jakob introduced the phenomenon of 'tacit signals', drawn upon in this case by the defence lawyer in order to communicate professional distance from his performed loyalty to his client. In the following section, we switch from the prosecutor's perspective to that of a judge, analysing what we found shadowing the fairly experienced judge Margareta before a hearing about appealing a restraining order.

## The judge's perspective: backstage preparation and front-stage presentation

Judge Margareta stands in her office in front of a computer with a court clerk right next to her, both dressed up for the court, wearing dark suits. Margareta is a permanently appointed judge in her 40s. The hearing she is to preside over this morning is on appealing a restraining order. Margareta herself explains what is going on:

> "We've just realised this hearing won't be happening. I just called the prosecutor, who told me that the defendant is in detention [so he cannot attend the hearing], and that we're the ones who put him there". She makes a face showing how embarrassing this is, as if she doesn't know what's happening in her own court.
> (Observation, restraining order, judge Margareta, 40+)

The accused, moreover, is in detention for violating the existing restraining order, the one he here wanted to appeal. What this means is that, on the one hand, he cannot be physically present at court today, and, on the other hand, as Margareta explains, it would now be better to combine the two separate hearings; the criminal case about the violation of the existing restraining order and the appeal of that same order could both be dealt with at the same time on a later occasion. Margareta's embarrassment derives from her lacking information and the poor coordination at her court. Conjoining the two hearings would restore the order and save both resources and the court's face. Professional judges' sense of pride for representing the court as such and justice in general tends to make them sensitive to fractures in the facade of perfectly rational justice (see, e.g., Chapter 6, p. 160).

Complicating judge Margareta's proposed solution, however, is the fact that the prosecutor prefers to get the appeal decision today. This is because its outcome will have an effect on how the prosecution will handle the criminal offence case. Before deciding, Margareta wants to talk with the defence lawyer appointed to the criminal case.[1] But time is running out. Margareta looks at her watch and decides to leave her office and go down to the courtroom; "We need to call them now". By 'them' she means the participants in the hearing: the prosecutor and the victim. The latter has called the court to tell of her being afraid of the defendant, but has been talked into coming to the court anyway, for the appeal hearing.

On the way down, Margareta tries to reach the defence lawyer by phone. When in the courtroom, the latter finally answers. Margareta explains the situation to him, informing him that the prosecutor wants to have the restraining order hearing now and that she wants the defence lawyer's opinion on his client's behalf. The defence lawyer's reactions cannot be heard, but the judge responds "Mmm; no, OK, I understand" in a polite voice, then hanging up. As we then learn, the defence lawyer did not even want to discuss the appeal case: he had been appointed for the criminal case and nothing else.

Although, the defence lawyer was correct from the strictly legal perspective, the possible merging of the two cases made Margareta want his opinion to safeguard his client's perspective on the issue. Refusing this, the defence lawyer in Margareta's view did not live up to her expectations on legal professionalism. In her follow-up interview, Margareta expressed resentment towards the defence lawyer, explaining that some lawyers "refuse to say anything if they cannot charge for it". Yet, Margareta had revealed no irritation at all when talking to the lawyer on the phone; since the relationship between them during that conversation remained front stage in nature, she toned down her expression.

As we saw in prosecutor Jakob's trial, it is not uncommon for prosecutors and lawyers to complain about hearings' beginning late. However, as we see, looking at it from Margareta's perspective, judges may be busy handling a multitude of tasks before any hearings have even begun. Several things can go wrong, and it happens often that judges decide to cancel hearings in the last minute owing to various complications that cannot be quickly resolved.

### Focus and strategic emotion management

It is now ten minutes past the planned starting time of the hearing. Margareta pours herself a glass of water and turns to the lay judges and the court clerk, saying: "Let's see; I just need to pull myself together a bit". Contrasting with lawyers' and prosecutors' fluent shifts between performing in backstage and front-stage roles, judges put on a stone face immediately when the parties are called in. After all the commotion backstage, Margareta thus wants to take a few seconds to recentre her focus. In the follow-up interview, she talked about these shifts between being "formal and stiff" in her front-stage appearance and being spontaneous and expressive backstage. She described it as a deliberate change between a private and an authoritative persona, effectuated as an embodied experience: "When I walk down the stairs, I kind of just – well, I re-focus a little. I just need ten, fifteen seconds.... Leaving my office and walking to the courtroom, I just forget [my private self]".

After a few seconds of silence in the courtroom, Margareta explains to the lay judges why the normal court procedure has today been altered. Ordinarily, before a hearing, the professional judge, the lay judges, and the court clerk would meet in the courtroom, with the judge briefly summarizing the case and directing the emotive-cognitive focus of the lay judges to the key issues. To help them concentrate on their task at hand, judges often tell jokes or use cheerful imperatives like "Are all on board!" and "Let's roll!"

Professional judges commonly consider lay judges as special targets of their strategic emotion management efforts for a variety of reasons. Margareta described it as follows:

> You're terrified that a lay judge will do something inappropriate. I mean, that they say something that might disqualify them. What makes me most afraid, though, is that they'll say something that can hurt one of the parties. That's what I fear the most. [...] I can prepare them by saying something like "the defendant might appear to be a bit under the influence of drugs, and he can be a bit angry, but we'll pull this through". So they won't roll their eyes when I allow the defendant to go beyond the boundaries a little.
>
> (Margareta, judge, 40+)

The management of lay judges' emotional expressions during the trial is considered necessary because lay judges are frequently elderly and often fail to keep a stone face and sometimes even fall asleep during trials, as corroborated by our own observations in court. Such misconduct influences the professional judges' self-image as those embodying justice and thus evokes shame on the court's behalf.

### Front-stage strategic empathy

Empathy is achieved by imagining the situation of others, emotionally tuning in with another person. While thus always including emotions, empathy is not an emotion in itself but "the capacity to read and understand someone else's emotions" (Wettergren and Bergman Blix, 2016: 22). The dramaturgical feature that we call 'front-stage strategic empathy' implies taking in enough of the other person's perspective to be able to anticipate and prevent that person's emotions from interfering with the rational procedure of the trial.

Before Margareta tells the clerk to call in the parties, she asks him: "Can you make sure that the video screen is on either me or the prosecutor? The victim doesn't want the accused to see her". Since the accused is in detention, he will be participating via a video link and Margareta knows of the victim's being afraid of him. The clerk nods, unlocks the doors, and calls in the parties. The victim and prosecutor enter and the clerk tries to turn on the video link.

> When everyone has entered, Margareta smiles briefly and thanks the prosecutor and victim for not sitting side by side [so they do not show in the same video frame]. She says: "The video image of the accused will be rather big" [directing her words at the victim, Margareta says this in passing without looking at her]. The video connection fails to work, however. The clerk picks up his phone and calls someone. Margareta shuffles her papers. The prosecutor starts whispering about something with the victim. Eventually a tech support person enters, and he and the clerk try to solve the problem. Margareta looks at the prosecutor and says: "Sorry". The prosecutor replies: "No problem. We all depend on technology; I know what it's like to sit in the office, trying to get the thing to start" [laughs briefly]. Margareta smiles back: "We'll take a short break while we try to get this to work." At that very moment, the video comes on.
>
> (Observation, restraining order, judge Margareta, 40+)

The thanks directed at the victim and the prosecutor for not sitting next to each other, and the warning given to the former that the projection "will be rather big", are both examples of empathic perspective-taking by Margareta. In order for the trial to go smoothly, the judge needs to employ empathy, and, having shadowed Margareta, we knew that she had openly reflected about the victim's position and talked empathically about her on more than one occasion in the court's backstage area.

Expressing empathy in an instrumental by-the-way manner is a common way for judges to manage lay people in court. The heavy pressure on the judges to perform objectively often forces expressions of empathy to be put forward rather inconspicuously. This is to avoid appearing partial, Margareta cannot both take precautions to protect the victim vis-à-vis the defendant and talk to the victim in a gentle and understanding manner – that would have been too conspicuous. The same is true about lay people engaging the judge in an interaction concerning their personal problems or emotional outbursts (e.g. crying) during a hearing. Offering a short break or a glass of water, but with one's stone face on, is a standard response from the judges on such occasions.

On the other hand, in practical matters not directly related to the conflict between the parties, empathy can be displayed in more varied ways. In the case with prosecutor Jakob above, for instance, the victim wore a hearing aid, resulting in the judge gently asking if he could follow the procedure, with the question accompanied by a friendly smile. More varied displays of empathy are also possible when judges, towards the end of the trial, ask defendants about their personal life situations in general.

Apart from pressure to moderate their empathic expressions, legal professionals also face a risk of becoming numb to the tensions lay people can feel.

Over time, all legal professionals come to witness emotionally harrowing cases and encounter people caught in dreadful situations, and it can become difficult for them sometimes to empathize with victims of more minor offences. Below is an example of a case in which the prosecutor and the judge cooperate to assist the victim, although the prosecutor believes the victim to be exaggerating her emotional expressions:

> Outside the courtroom, the prosecutor talks to the victim whose voice keeps breaking, telling her that "Crying is allowed; if it starts to feel bad in there, just look at me", pointing at her own eyes. During the hearing the victim begins to cry. Lay judge 1 hands the prosecutor a roll of kitchen paper; the latter stands up and tears off a piece that she gives to the victim. The judge asks dryly, "Do you need a break?" but no one responds. After the trial the prosecutor explains that she did not really feel so sorry for the victim: no reason to take a break as she was not a victim of abuse or rape.
>
> (Observation, unlawful threat, prosecutor Faida, 40+)

As seen from this example, empathic perspective-taking can be performed on the surface, routinely and strategically, to further a smooth procedure (cf. Hochschild, 1983).

### Dramaturgical stress

Meanwhile, in the hearing with Margareta, the technology is finally working. Margareta asks the accused his name and personal identity number:

> The accused replies: "Can you speak English?" Margareta falls silent. Lots of thoughts seem to pass through her head. She looks at the prosecutor, then back at the accused, and says: "No I can't; regardless of whether I can speak English or not, I still can't do it here. Do you need an interpreter?" She leafs through her papers. After a while, she smiles. She and the prosecutor exchange gazes. Margareta: "Now I am going to speak to the detention: We will take a break and try to find an interpreter". They disengage the video link. During the break, while walking out, the judge says: "Earlier, we [the researcher and the judge] talked about shame and embarrassment, and this represents one such situation. I feel embarrassed on behalf of the court's failure.... We should do it right".
>
> (Observation, restraining order, judge Margareta, 40+)

The judge's sense of shame on behalf of the court comes to expression clearly in this quote. It serves as an example of immediate backstage ventilation of a strong emotion, first experienced but toned down front stage. The efforts to find an interpreter, however, failed, and Margareta went back to the courtroom to ultimately – after spending the whole morning combatting one unexpected obstacle after another – postpone the hearing.

According to the Swedish CJP, all hearings are to be conducted in Swedish, while non-Swedish-speaking persons participating in the trial are entitled to an interpreter (1942: Ch. 5, Art. 6). That this need for an interpreter had been overlooked was, along with the failure to keep record of the fact that the accused was in detention for violating the restraining order he was to appeal, one more mistake for the court that morning. At the same time, Margareta knew the victim to be afraid of the accused and of coming to court. The unexpected demand for an interpreter, front stage, thus forced her to manage the failure of the court front stage with the accused, while being well aware of the consequences for the victim.

As we have seen, organizational challenges and mishaps are part and parcel of the work with pulling off hearings, with the court's backstage area serving as one arena, where the issues are being continuously solved. The situation arising front stage added extra pressure on Margareta. According to Goffman, embarrassment is a "generic property" of interactions (1956); the inability to fully predict how a face-to-face encounter will evolve implies a risk of failure in living up to interactional expectations. Along these lines, we argue that the double pressure of following procedural correctness while being aware of the "realness" of the situation can produce 'dramaturgical stress'. According to Peter Freund, dramaturgical stress arises from threats to the self or a group's boundaries, in effect endangering their ontological security (1998: 268).

Dramaturgical stress in this setting can be defined as the emotional effect on legal professionals that arises when the strictly set up court ritual and the legal encoding do not entirely achieve the reduction of real complexity and emotional silencing needed to uphold the image of objective, emotionless justice. Returning to Tilly's analysis of the contradictory logics of stories and codes "[c]odes emerge from the incremental efforts of organizations to impose order" (Tilly, 2008: 125), but people usually turn to the law not only for order, but for the truth as a moral evaluation of real situations (Rosenbaum, 2005). When the quest for the acknowledgement of this "realness" of the situation destabilizes procedural correctness, a glitch occurs that signals a disconnect between the performance of justice according to the emotive-cognitive frame and the performance of justice according to lay people's expectations. The emotional orientation of legal professionals is to perform the emotive-cognitive frame *as if* it were compatible with the common sense of justice, thereby satisfying both. The glitch disrupts this emotional orientation. Importantly, the ensuing embarrassment, as depicted by Margareta, does not primarily fall back on the individual, but on the court, or the legal system as a whole. When Margareta made sure that the victim came to court despite her fears, she put the court's "honour" – and, in a longer perspective, the public's trust in the legal system – at stake. Regardless of whether it was her or someone else's responsibility to ensure these things worked, she needed to face the situation in court and resolve the problem in the here and now, and the failure caused professional shame, not only for the judiciary, but for Margareta herself as embodying the institution of the judiciary.

When prosecutors, as representatives of the state, go to court they embody the legitimacy of the legal system too. The quote below offers an example of how truth claims are part of the "realness" that causes dramaturgical stress. It is from a murder trial in which the accused had already admitted to killing a young woman. The victim's relatives (notably her father) sat close to the prosecutor during the entire hearing, which put visible pressure on the latter to extract "the truth" about the event and secure the toughest punishment, while still ensuring an impeccably correct legal process:

> For me, it was very important to be able to get through the trial without breakdowns [from the victim's family]. That was my goal: no emotional breakdowns. It could have been cries and screaming, or [the victim's father] being escorted out and thus missing the trial for his murdered daughter. He really wanted to be there for it, to learn what had happened and what the [defendant's] motives were for executing his young daughter. I had the victim's father and his relatives sitting behind me and I felt it; it was horrible, they *hated, really hated* [the defendant], they wanted to see him executed.[2] And I *really* had to think about my behaviour, how I'd formulate questions and so on, because they noted every single detail. Every mistake I'd make and every poorly formulated question could have enormous consequences, leading to emotional outbursts and so ... it was an *extremely* demanding hearing.
>
> (Henrik, prosecutor, 50+)

Feelings of dramaturgical stress are usually described in situations when professionals, through empathic perspective-taking, reflectively acknowledge the "realness" of the situation: that it is not just another trial, it is a hearing that actually and quite concretely affects people's life. In Henrik's example above, the question was about a horrific crime, but the same phenomenon also occurs in less emotionally charged cases, as we saw in Margareta's hearing.

Shadowing prosecutor Jakob and judge Margareta, we have identified and examined the dramaturgical features of situated adaptation, tacit signals, front-stage strategic empathy, and dramaturgical stress. We also considered examples of 'emotional toning' (toning down). In the final section of this chapter, we will elaborate a little more on emotional toning as an emotion management technique crucial to performing the feeling rules of the emotive-cognitive judicial frame.

### Emotional toning

Encountering the feeling rules of the emotive-cognitive judicial frame, legal actors in court learn to both 'tone down' and 'tone up' emotional expressions of felt experience depending on their role appropriateness. The resulting adjustment leads to a habituated incongruence between the experience and the expression of emotion that seems to go mostly unreflected by the legal actors themselves.

For judges, toning down the emotional expression in relation to one's experience is very common. As ought to be clear by now, judges express their feelings subtly, if at all, when they perform front stage. Judge Margareta above, for instance, toned down her expression of the emotions (of dramaturgical stress) she experienced when realizing, at the very outset of the proceedings, that she would have to cancel the trial after all. We remember that she was first silent, keeping her stone face, then exchanged looks with the prosecutor, engaging in emotional communication with another legal professional who, too, was bound by the feeling rules of the emotive-cognitive frame. As we saw in the section on emotional communication, legal actors are highly perceptive of one another's looks and other small signs of emotional expressions. Finally, Margareta smiled. Smiling, even when acting under considerable dramaturgical stress, was a poker-face strategy. As we saw above, the poker face is usually resorted to by prosecutors, to help them conceal their felt emotions by expressing different kinds of emotions. For judge Margareta, adopting the poker-face strategy indicated that she had trouble keeping her stone face. Barely out of the courtroom, she gave full expression to her sense of shame and anger that she had toned down for her front-stage performance.

Toning up emotional expressions may at first glance look like an emotion management strategy misplaced in the court context. Yet, strategic empathy to ensure a smooth procedure tends to demand precisely that. In the case with prosecutor Faida (p. 109), we saw how this sometimes happens. Prosecutor Faida empathized with the victim, understanding her perspective, and yet her actual level of emotional engagement remained lower than the one she expressed to the victim both outside and inside the courtroom.

The adversarial nature of the court process, moreover, calls for some emotional expression of antagonism between the defence and the prosecution, even if such expressions tend to remain subtle. As we saw in the case of prosecutor Jakob, in spite of any such antagonism, defence lawyers and prosecutors may have a trusting collegial relationship. Backstage the lawyer confessed not believing in his client's story, but front stage, he nevertheless sternly contested the evidence presented by Jakob. Their antagonistic relationship in the courtroom was, in other words, toned up to satisfy lay people's expectations of how the relationship ought to be expressed. However, lawyers who "exaggerate" in their display of antagonistic emotive-cognitive confrontationality in the courtroom are generally disliked by both judges and prosecutors, since they disturb the emotional silence that the courtroom setting, the script, the legal encoding, and the dramaturgical features are all designed to uphold. They also unsettle collegial interactions and collaboration, by forcing other legal professionals to repair the damage to the image of objective emotionless justice.

## Conclusions

In this chapter, we have approached the court as a theatre, following professionals backstage, front stage, and semi-front stage to see how the performance of unemotional justice is actually done among the different actors in the court. We have highlighted the courtroom (stage), the CJP (script), and the legal code (language) that frame, direct, and articulate (non-)emotion. The legal actors need to perform the ritual or drama, each according to their own specific role. To do this, they need to emotionally tune in and communicate both openly and tacitly to ensure that they are able to move the process forward in a procedurally correct manner, collaborate around challenges and obstacles, and produce the emotional authenticity needed for the lay audience's trust in the performance of justice.

'Emotional communication' occurs on two levels: one that the actors use to alert or reassure one another (e.g. through looks), and another that is intended for the audience to pick up (e.g. through the deployment of stone face, poker face, and bodily gestures). It is on this latter level that the adversarial antagonism between the parties is played out, as conceptualized through the dramaturgical feature we call 'emotional toning', indicating the process of toning up antagonistic feelings. In contrast, the impact of surprises and unexpected events unsettling the legal actors in court tends to be toned down. The actual magnitude of the experienced emotions may not be seen at all until their airing is allowed backstage. Other identified features of the drama were situated adaptation, showing in particular the agile and quick adjustment to tacit signals and emotional communication, and tacit signals that bifurcate verbal communication into double meanings; as an example, we saw how professional distance to the performance one feels bound to uphold in court could be communicated (the defence lawyer in the case of prosecutor Jakob). Tacit signals are often about safeguarding professional pride. Front-stage strategic empathy, on the other hand, was discussed as a particular feature of the court drama to better anticipate and even avert potential obstacles to procedural correctness. This was observed to be particularly necessary for the judge although all legal actors engage in it to further their particular goals in the trial. Finally, dramaturgical stress was identified as a phenomenon occurring when, for various reasons, the emotive-cognitive judicial frame cracks under the pressure of lay people's needs for, and expectations on, justice. Justice, according to the frame, is not about the "truth" or what has actually happened; it is about the facts and evidence and their judicial value. It is, however, also about the performance of pure rationality. Most importantly, however, as should be clear by now, that performance is not unemotional at all; on the contrary, it relies on emotion and continuous collaborative emotion management.

## Notes

1 In the case of the appeal of the restraining order, the accused is not appointed a defence lawyer. Decisions about restraining orders are made by the prosecution office but can be appealed to the district court.
2 Sweden does not have death penalty. The maximum prison sentence is life, which can be converted to a time-limited sentence.

# 5  Power and status in court

We have a huge amount of power and it has to be exercised humbly, we *must* use power because that's what people want, why they come here, to get a decision. And it's really important to dare to take decisions, because some judges don't [...] Some judges think it's unpleasant [to take decisions, use power], they'd rather someone else did it, they procrastinate and nothing happens, and that's bad.

(Christer, chief judge, 50+)

The above quote from chief judge Christer illustrates some emotive-cognitive aspects of judicial power such as courage ("to dare") and confident responsibility ("we *must*") to use power, while remaining humble. Christer also talks about the discomfort ("it's unpleasant") of power that some – notably other judges – experience, to the effect that "nothing happens". Background emotions of courage, confidence, and humbleness are thus seen as conducive to using power, while unease and anxiety are disruptive. As we saw in Chapter 3, the increased workload pushes for more and faster decisions for both judges and prosecutors and this, as combined with the power effect of these decisions, put individual capacities to confidently perform autonomy and independence to the test. In Chapter 4, we also saw how continuous mundane decisions in the course of a court drama may be fraught with unease and remorse (for instance, dramaturgical stress). While judges are required to habituate a comfort of power as part of their autonomous emotional profile, exercising power itself is always bound up with a possible sense of guilt, remorse, and – in a society where egalitarian norms are highly valued – even shame. The legitimacy of power becomes key to a comfortable habituation of it. Prosecutors also have much power, but their ability to exercise it is in several ways circumscribed by their dependence on other professional categories, orienting them to use strategic emotion management to mitigate power with status ("being liked"). However, the essence of prosecutors' independence is seen when they sometimes use power in spite of losing status (Abbott, 1981).

In this chapter, we examine judges' and prosecutors' emotions and emotion management from a power and status perspective. How do the dynamics of power and status in the courtroom influence emotions and emotion management strategies? How do judges and prosecutors manage power in their work roles? How do professional power and status shape judges' and prosecutors' interactions with other professionals and with laymen? We begin with the issues of judges' autonomous power and then continue with the prosecutors' bounded independence and mitigation of power. In the end of the chapter, we examine the emotional processes of inter-professional power and status challenges.

## The autonomous judge: power issues

Judges' power to pass judgment on the evidence presented to them by the parties at the trial is absolute and uncontested (although other legal professionals may have differing opinions regarding the correctness of their decisions). To facilitate this judges' training emphasizes autonomy. Autonomy in that context means the performance and embodiment of instrumental reason, the maintenance of physical and emotive-cognitive distance from distractions and affiliations, and self-assured structural security in one's professional position. Once permanently appointed, judges' autonomy is both manifested in and safeguarded by the security of their work position, both their symbolic and physical separation from the other professional and lay actors at court, and the principles of immediacy and orality that dispose judges to preside in court as if it was the first time the facts and narratives of the crime were given attention within the justice system. Although, in the civil-law system, judges do not make the law, they embody it. In this sense, the judge is power.

### *Power discomfort*

Put simply, judges must feel, or at least be able to display that they feel, that the power they exercise when passing judgment is indeed just and in accordance with the correct judicial procedure. To comfortably inhabit power is, however, not easy for all judges. Especially judges still in training can experience the imperative as quite uncomfortable:

> I think it's a bit ... scary anyway. If you think about it ... I think it's ... a bit unreal almost, that you – if I think about how much power I have, even after having worked just a couple of years, it's like "Who am I to sentence these people to jail?".... But it's not as if ... I go around at work, thinking "God, I'm so powerful". I don't think that'd be good.
>
> (Estelle, associate judge, 25+)

The feelings described by Estelle are those of discomfort – of fear, swaying self-confidence ("a bit unreal") – having to do with her newly acquired position of power as a judge. As pointed out in Chapter 1, power entails the possibility of guilt feelings for having misused one's power (Kemper, 2011). Doubt, fear, and failing self-confidence are emotions anticipating guilt, and the combination of these and similar emotions we label 'power discomfort'. Estelle also indirectly refers to an emotion management technique of hers, which she resorted to in order to deal with this discomfort: do not think about it too much. This echoes a common saying among judges: "forget the passed" (dömt är glömt), which they use to help them ward off doubt and remorse: what has been passed as a judgment belongs to the past and should be forgotten. Organizational pressure in the form of judges' increased workload tends to reinforce this strategy of backgrounding uncomfortable emotions of power. The emotive-cognitive judicial frame also provides emotional orientations, such as pride and security in judicial expertise, that silence any sense of power discomfort:

> I don't want my imaginary friend Charles, who always falls asleep in the bathtub when he's drunk, to be the pilot in a plane I am on, and I don't want to be judged by someone who sits at the same level as I do, someone who has the education that I have. Instead, I want a person who understands, someone who can see through it all and understands everything.
>
> (Jens, court clerk, 25+)

Jens's pilot analogy shows his way of justifying judicial power to be above all technical: judges, for him, should have their power because they know how to pass verdicts and sentences, just like pilots know how to fly. Being a clerk himself, he still seems to harbour the belief that judging is about exercising cognitive expert skills. Indeed, if it were that simple, sentencing people to prison would not give rise to doubt and discomfort. But even experienced judges in our material reported experiences of doubt. In the below quote, judge Bente both illustrates this doubt and displays yet another technique for managing power discomfort:

> If we were to sit and think about every single decision for one hundred years, then the parties will not get a decision. Especially in crime cases where the defendant denies having done it we need to come up with a decision relatively quickly, because it's not good [to let him wait]. But sure, sometimes it goes wrong. In fact, there've been cases where I've had to call one of the parties to let them know that I think they should appeal because my ruling was wrong [laughs]. I'm like [self-reproaching voice], "What was I thinking?" So once, for instance, I called the defence lawyer [when the appeal period was almost over and the defence had not appealed] and asked him, "Did you look at the sentence?" [...] adding "You know you have to appeal within three weeks".... I know some colleagues disapprove when I do that, but I can give them that. That particular time, the appeals court changed the sentence, so it was good that I made that call [laughs].
>
> (Bente, judge, 50+)

In the first part of this excerpt, Bente explains speedy decision-making as a service rendered to the defendant. Her concern for delivering a reasonably fast decision is thus motivated by a concern for the lay person's well-being. This can be seen as an extension of the good treatment policy, as Bente empathically imagines being in the limbo situation of the defendant. The good treatment policy can thus be used as a technique to overcome power discomfort, by putting aside doubt in the interest of a quick decision. But the empathic concern is also, and equally, about assuming the responsibility of power. In the second part of the excerpt, we see an extraordinary measure taken by Bente (calling up the defence lawyer and telling him to file an appeal), because she kept thinking about her decision even after the sentence was delivered: she did not apply the "forget the passed" maxim. Bente experienced guilt ("sometimes it goes wrong") and remorse ("what was I thinking?"). Guilt and remorse motivated her subsequent actions and revealed that she assumed responsibility for her mistake ("the appeals court changed the sentence"). At the same time, her whole reasoning revealed security in her status position at the court: first, through the fact that she admitted her mistake and, second, in the way she reasoned about her extraordinary action to correct it (she did not care becoming the target of collegial critique). The excerpt thus illustrates professional confidence and status deriving from experience and a secure position, which allows for power comfort even when decisions go wrong.

On a similar note, another experienced judge, Erik, below speaks rather easily about his power, but emphasizes the caring responsibility that comes with it:

> It's like in Pippi Longstocking: the one who has very much power also has to be very kind. [...] If [the defendant] is a regular and knows what to expect, that's one thing, but first-time offenders and ordinary people you have to handle with care.
>
> (Erik, judge, 50+)

A defendant should understand the rationale of the power exercise. If this is the case, and through care and gentle treatment, a judge may feel comfort in exercising power. Erik's reflection echoes Bente's account to the extent that it speaks about assuming the responsibility that comes with power. Comfort in power, we may therefore conclude, relies on awareness of power discomfort, because it keeps the judge attentive to the seriousness of possessing power and thereby opens up for critical reflexivity, empathy, and situated adaptation in the power exercise.

A different way to deal with power discomfort was represented by judges who did not associate their role with power at all:

> I don't see that I have any power, I cannot see how I could have any.... Well, I have the tools that I have – that I need, or which the legislators have provided for me, to implement my task.
>
> (Simon, judge, 60+)

Simon dissociates himself from the power invested in the role of the judge, which he sees merely as a function (tool) of someone else's (legislators') power. This is a bureaucratic approach to power (Arendt, 1977), and it is essentially a radical way to manage power discomfort, by denying personal responsibility. Reducing one's role to a cog in the machinery of law thus forecloses any discomfort of power. In a civil-law system, the bureaucratic approach to power lies ready at hand due to the idea that judicial power is about applying objective and stable laws. In line with this, even judges who assume responsibility still argue to some extent that they exercise power according to objective laws that they cannot influence or change, thus at least reducing the aura of power discretion surrounding their capacity as judges (cf. Remiche, 2015).

### *Personalizing or depersonalizing power?*

The aura of power – how power is perceived by the audience – is also subject to different opinions among judges about how power should be embodied. The positivist objectivity ideal – the God's eye perspective – pushes towards depersonalized power. This is to say that ideally any judge will exercise power in the exact same way, which reduces the importance of the person behind the stone face: "We are supposed to be a grey mass, and it shouldn't matter if it's Pia or Mia who's sitting there, it should be objective [laughs slightly]; that's the whole idea, not to be individuals" (Kristin, associate judge, 30+). The ceremonial elevation of the judges' bench, the stone faces, and the fact that they remain seated when people enter and until everyone has left accentuate depersonalized power. The earlier quoted court clerk Jens elaborated on how this ought to strengthen the court's legitimacy:

> You are sitting, literally looking down at the two parties. And I think that's a way to emphasize that it's the justice who decides. I don't know if I think that that's all wrong. In the Swedish culture, hierarchy is something ugly, but in some circumstances hierarchy is needed, and in court hierarchy is needed…. It's symbolic in a way. You don't want to be judged by – I don't know if you can say it like this – judged by your peers … you want them to be almost superhuman.
>
> (Jens, court clerk, 20+)

Interestingly, the notion of being judged by an elevated and superhuman God's eye disregards the presence of the lay judges, who actually represent being "judged by your peers". In this, we can sense a problem that the lay judge system poses to those professional judges who take judicial expertise to be the guarantee for the correct exercise of the power of law. Similarly, judges who embrace this depersonalized ideal tend to argue that a judge needs no instruments, or insights, other than legal expertise (Bladini, 2013). Knowledge about the world – particularly the world of the accused or the victim – would adventure the autonomy of the judge's decisions. The God's eye ideal, which likely but not necessarily overlaps with the bureaucratic power perspective, thus emphasizes the purity of the judge (cf. Abbott, 1981).

On the other side of the depersonalized vs. personalized power spectrum, representation of state authority is instead associated with being part of society, also as judge. Rather than the person disappearing behind the shield of the state, the state becomes embodied and gets a face through its association with a person. In the below quote, Sanna raises this point in connection with the much-discussed issue of whether also Swedish legal professionals should begin wearing gowns. Her points speak about the overlaps of personalized power with assuming responsibility for exercising power and the exercise of power empathically:

> There are many judges that are pushing this issue with gowns, and I can tell you right away that if that happens, and I've told them this, I will resign [slight laugh], though I'm probably quite alone in that. Because then you really distance yourself, you become a position. You become someone who's not participating, who's appointed by a celestial power [laughs]. We've had a lot of discussions about this, and for me, this all feels very strange. [...] Judges need to keep up with the society. We need to be able to talk to young people, we have to be able to talk to foreigners, to understand. Try to understand how they live and their way of life.
>
> (Sanna, chief judge, 50+)

Representation, according to Sanna, requires empathy for the people coming to court, the ability to tune in emotionally to them. Empathy in general is an ability that most respondents in our study, also the ones proclaiming distance, described as vital to their profession. Empathy in this general sense is a key term pertaining to the good treatment policy associated with the increased focus on procedural justice, which indicates that empathy's implications may not be interpreted in the same way by all judges. While all our participants embraced empathy, those advocating personalized representation, as demonstrated by Sanna, felt that they were alone in their belief, suggesting that depersonalized representation of state power still prevails as a legitimate ideal.

As we saw, the embodiment of power as a personal responsibility was geared towards empathy, as well as towards a personal responsibility for how the law is applied in the end. There seemed to be a continuity between comfortable power and personalized representation. Yet a bureaucratic understanding of power could also be consistent with personal representation emphasizing empathy; this would mean insisting on a mechanistic power-application with a personally empathic face when empathy meant taking care to properly inform lay people about the legal professionals and the procedure, and heed their particular needs (a break, a glass of water, napkins to wipe off tears). A bureaucratic understanding of power combined with this type of personal representation is common in other state bureaucracies (Wettergren, 2010).

Indeed, the policy of procedural justice was introduced to counteract the appearance of the courts as an impenetrable and unintelligible castle of juridical expertise. The fact that the courtroom is a front-stage interface between the people and the judiciary may once have induced respect in the people, but in complex modern societies it no longer does so in every case. Legitimacy for the court's exercise of power may have to be won rather than presumed. This puts judges in a tricky situation with regard to how far they can stretch their power in the courtroom.

### Limitations of power and low status: negotiating demeanour

While the decision-making power of judges is absolute, the actual power of the judge to preside in court in a procedurally correct manner presumes the ritual deference of the other legal professionals and the acquiescence of the particular lay people present. Defendants to whom justice has low legitimacy may have nothing to lose from literally obstructing the court's authority, as in the following case featuring a very angry defendant, kept in detention, accused of wife abuse and breaching a restraining order. In this case, not even his defence lawyer could calm the defendant, and it was merely due to the circumstance that the trial had been cancelled several times before, that the judge – on the request of the prosecutor – insisted on carrying through with it. The detention guards were present in the room and the judge had ordered them to release the defendant from his handcuffs. The general atmosphere was thus not threatening, but still tense:

> The accused howls: "This [whole justice system] is a catastrophe!" Judge: "[First and last name of the accused], now, really, you must!" [...] But the accused seems to be out of control, he continues shouting that this is a farce and a catastrophe and that none of his evidence has been included. In the end, he is howling, bending over the table and pointing his finger at the judge. The judge appears to be bracing his right elbow against the armrest of his chair, making him lean slightly towards his left, which is towards the side of the accused, as if he tries not to be blown away by the accused's shouting, while looking at the accused with an incredulous expression in his face.... Prosecutor: "But you know you have a restraining order against you?" Accused: "Yes, but that didn't stop *her* (meaning his wife) from coming to fuck with me, now did it?!" He says that he is keen on knowing "why you're carrying on with this witch hunt against me! You as a state office are a pure fucking joke!".... He turns to the judge again and shouts: "Are you a judge because you want to take notes for the protocol or because you want to find out what's right? *Justice*, man!!!"
> (Observation, abuse, judge John, 50+)

As we see in this excerpt, the defendant strongly disapproves of the way justice is pursued in his case. The legal system has no legitimacy in his eyes and he thereby refuses to subscribe to the feeling rules of the emotive-cognitive judicial frame; he is indeed shameless about breaking these rules. While the judge's voice remains calm and authoritative when speaking to the defendant, his body posture reveals substantial effort to uphold judicial demeanour and dignity. The prosecutor cooperates with the judge in this effort by attempting to examine the defendant. The hearing eventually had to be interrupted to remove the latter. In the break, the defence lawyer, the prosecutor, and the judge let go of their composure and laughed together, expressing relief. They then agreed to proceed with examining the witnesses without the defendant present. The example demonstrates the limitations of the judge's power in terms of punishing lay people who bluntly refuse to abide by the feeling and behavioural rules of the court. If defendants are misbehaving and interfere, the judge can put them in another room where they can follow the hearing through video link, but that is not possible when examining the defendant himself. If another person misbehaves, the court can adjudicate for contempt, but also that option is used with care due to the principle of public access to court hearings (CJP: Ch. 5).

Status relates to unwritten norms, that is, to the norm system of which the juridical professions are part. Connecting to this norm system means respecting the status of the other/the judge and the status of oneself in the courtroom (cf. Collins, 2004). In other words, if, in this case, the defendant does not acknowledge the norm system to which the juridical professions and their power belong, it implies that neither does he acknowledge the legitimacy of that system. He is there, he submits to it, merely because of its repressive power. Repressive power is illegitimate insofar as it requires violence or the threat of violence to be effective; it does not rely on people's compliance with the norms that, in turn, produce respect of the power holders' status (cf. Arendt, 1998). This, in essence, is why judges hesitate to venture outside the realm of their juridical power, putting not only their own status at risk of its being rejected, but even more so the legitimacy of the system, which they normatively embrace. Since it is important for the judges' image of themselves and the system that their power is legitimate, it is crucial to uphold the court ritual as if power were legitimate.

The illustration that several judges gave, demonstrating awareness of the limitations of their power, was whether or not to ask a person to take off their cap. If a judge tells a defendant to take off his or her cap, and the person refuses, the judges "put themselves in a position where they lose power" (Fred, chief judge, 50+), because they have no mandate to force the defendants. One of the judges in our material illustrated the ambivalence of this power limitation by being resolute in how he would deal with "the cap-situation" in his interview: "I would consider it really annoying if someone doesn't take off their cap when entering the courtroom…. Then we'll make them take it off [laughs]" (Asger, associate judge, 30+). Yet, when Asger actually encountered a defendant with a cap during a hearing, he did not mention it:

The defendant comes in; he wears something in between a cap and a hat, pulled deep down over his head. I expect the judge to say something but he ignores it. When the defendant's turn to speak has come, he curses a lot, often. The judge interrupts him: "Eh, try to think a bit about your language when here".... He flashes a forced smile at the defendant. The defendant does not stop cursing, though. The judge's face is turned slightly towards him when he talks, but with his mouth and chin covered by his hand. The defendant keeps the hat on throughout the entire trial.

(Observation, drug offence, associate judge Asger, 30+)

Judge Asger's decision to not make note of the cap and his failed attempt to tell the defendant to stop cursing both speak to the general limitation of the judge's power. Asger's forced smile is a poker-face strategy to cover up for his irritation, and his covered mouth signals embarrassment when the defendant ignores his request (cf. Bloch, 1996). To confront defendants on issues like dress or manner of behaviour or speech in the court, judges must rely on their status rather than their power. When their status is rejected, they are left with the option to resort to repressive power – such as cancelling the hearing – that would damage the legitimacy of justice in a broad sense and thus further reduce their professional status (cf. Abbott, 1981). Because the rule of law presumes public legitimacy, power thus ties in with status in the actual performance of justice in the courtroom. Meanwhile, some judges – for instance, Margareta in Chapter 4 (p. 107) – may comfortably allow the defendant to stray beyond conventional boundaries, demonstrating their secure power.

Yet, there are limits to how much deviation can be tolerated and there are solutions to "the cap dilemma". The judge can use the other legal professionals in the room, particularly the defence lawyer, to bridge the norm system of the court and the norm system of the defendant. In the following, an elderly and experienced judge recounts an episode where she anticipated that she, the professional judge, might be embarrassed by a defendant. She therefore takes the quick decision of changing her planned course of action. She cannot count on the defendant to obey her slightest command, but she can count on the legal professionals. Their deference to her authority is part of the court ritual:

The judge tells about a trial with a defendant who "kept chewing gum so hard that you could not hear what he said". As if that was not enough, when the prosecutor commented on this the defendant obnoxiously answered: "What? Got bad hearing?" The judge got angry and in her state of affect said "Well, I think it's time for the defendant to spit out that chewing gum!" She bent down to lift up the wastebasket, intending to walk over to the defendant to let him spit the gum in it. But the wastebasket was stuck to the floor! She had to pull it up real hard, and during the extra seconds she had time to stop and think about "What do I do if he refuses to spit it out?" So the moment she got the wastebasket off the floor she banged the basket on top of the desk and said: "And perhaps Mr [defence lawyer's name] can assist me with this!" The defence lawyer got up and fetched the wastebasket for his client, who, obediently, spat the chewing gum out.

(Fieldnotes, court)

The story, told during a casual conversation in the lunchroom, illustrates how the judge's authority in the courtroom is not necessarily given and how judges can be acutely aware of that. It further illustrates how the judge's successful performance in chairing the trial is partly constituted by the ritual deference of other legal professionals.

Maroney's study of American judges (2012) suggests a greater probability for American judges to extend their power to force compliance to legal rules of behaviour in the court. In the Swedish context, most judges would feel uncomfortable with (ab)using power that way, a feeling that is linked to the Swedish understanding that legitimate law means that it is just also in the eyes of the defendant. Abbott (1981) claims that judges lose status but gain power when they interfere in the ritual, but our example suggests that judges may also avoid interfering due to risk of exposing their lack of power, and thereby of losing legitimacy for the court. Abuse of power is a source of guilt (Kemper, 2011), and, as we have seen, judges avoid the risk of feeling guilt by either being 'kind' or conscientious or dissociating from the function of executing power.

We have argued that judicial power relies on the reproduction of autonomy, typically expressed by the judge's purification of messy reality and his or her capacity to embody pure (and isolated) reason. But we have also seen how, in the courtroom, the judges' power relies on the joint cooperation of the other legal professionals' ritual deference, which, in turn, derives from the norm system of the emotive-cognitive judicial frame that all the legal professionals share. Thus, even if the judge's personal professional status would be low in the eyes of the other legal professionals, it also lies in their interest to uphold the image of justice. But there is one situation where judges rely on their own capacity to negotiate status, while their power is limited: the deliberations with the lay judges.

### Power and status in deliberations

In deliberations, the emotive-cognitive judicial frame carried by the professional judge meets common sense and (since the lay judges are appointed by political parties) political ideology as represented by the lay judges (the latter is contested, but see Anwar et al., 2015). The norm systems may clash: although the lay judges should hold the legal system legitimate in principle, their political opinions may lead them to be critical. The appointments by political parties are traditionally geared towards elderly party members, and the relatively low remuneration for the time spent in court, which overlaps with ordinary working hours, makes serving as a lay judge a task most suitable for retired people. The fact that the lay judges have no legal education also makes them prone to express views and opinions deemed irrelevant by the emotive-cognitive judicial frame, thus causing feelings of embarrassment and irritation in the professional judges.

There is always at least a theoretical risk that three lay judges may turn against the professional judge. When this happens, the lay judges have the (three to one) upper hand in the democratic vote. In the deliberations, the professional judges thus find themselves in a rare situation of circumscribed autonomy: they formally depend on the lay judges for their legally based assessment to become the ruling of the court. This may then be another reason why the lay judge system causes some discomfort and irritation among professional judges. Even if lay judges usually do go along with the professional judge's juridical assessment, there are cases where the court's judgment turns out to be a "lay judgment" – a judgment in which the professional judge has expressed a dissenting opinion. Such judgments are virtually always appealed by the parties, assuming that they are juridically incorrect.

Consequently, professional judges had variously strong opinions about lay judges: while some thought that they are vital to the democratic system and also stressed that they appreciate the ability to "think together" with the lay judges about any opaque aspects of a case or a piece of evidence, a rather dominant pattern in our material was to consider lay judges legally irrelevant, although, nevertheless, an element of the legitimacy of the legal system that could not or should not be changed. In any case, judges agreed that the lay judges required strategic emotion management, particularly during the deliberations.

In uncomplicated trials with a short duration, it is common that the court deliberates and delivers its judgment at the end of the trial. Regardless, it usually deliberates, or at least begins its deliberations, directly after the end of a hearing. The code of judicial procedure demands that the professional judge – or, as part of their training and if invited to do so by the judge, the clerk – should give his or her legal evaluation of the evidence first. With this as their starting point, judges adopt different emotion management strategies. Below, we visit the deliberations of experienced judge Britta who directs the proceedings in a confidently pedagogical style, asking open questions and making sure that everyone agrees, yet holding a firm grip on the decision-making process. Britta opens the deliberations by giving the word to the clerk. Clerks are not allowed to vote but may be invited by the judge to present their juridical opinion. The case in question here is about theft:

> The judge moves her chair back so she can see everyone and encourages the clerk to do the same. Judge: "Let's do this in due order. Did [the accused] steal the money, [name of clerk]?" Clerk: "Yes, I think he did." The clerk develops her argument based on legal reasoning. Judge to the

lay judges: "Anyone wants to step in?" She looks around at the lay judges: "Does anyone think differently?" Lay judge 2 makes a comment and the judge nods: "But you still conclude that [the evidence] is convincing?" Lay judge 2 nods and the judge concludes that they then all agree. She turns to the clerk again and asks for the legal classification, develops the legal reasoning, and discusses the appropriate sanction with the clerk.

(Observation, theft, judge Britta, 45+)

Leaving the courtroom, Britta subsequently praised the clerk for her performance: she used the right gestures and was calm and steady. Accordingly, we see that the professional perspective includes a certain mastery of physical expressions, communicating security and confidence in explaining one's assessment to the lay judges. As we see in the excerpt, Britta then invites the lay judges to express their opinion, which is a way for her to acknowledge their status as lay judges. The recognition is an emotional gift that is likely to raise her own status and in return secure the lay judges' sympathetic support (cf. Clark, 1987). According to Kemper (2011), one is disposed to like those who accord status. The downwards according of status is a way to become appreciated in asymmetrical relationships that otherwise might cause resentment due to structural inequalities.

Jokes, humour, cheerfulness, and good temper are ways to prevent the lay judge's potential resentment of professional judges' higher status, and they represent variants of emotional gift giving. They are usually used in various combinations, and they tend to be backgrounded habituated strategies for the experienced judges, while associate judges and presiding clerks often need to reflect more on the best way to go about. Thus, in the above excerpt confident performance of status was part of judge Britta's strategy, in combination with her employment of an inviting and pedagogical style. The pedagogical approach might have been responded to differently had the judge been younger and less experienced, however, as it could have insulted the lay judges' status of age as well as their status as experienced lay judges, ending up evoking resentment instead (Kemper, 2011).

While the professional judges may be emotionally generous, they nevertheless maintain their expert role. In the above quote, Britta's "use" of the clerk to open the deliberations can be seen as a discretely intimidating way to strengthen the position of expert reasoning, a position that is formally represented only by the professional judge but here gets to be affirmed twice with also the clerk manifesting it. When professional judges feel the need to emphasize their expert position, emotional gift giving may be abandoned in favour of intimidating approaches. This strategy amounts to challenging the lay judge who expresses a dissenting opinion by using legalese, or by reading aloud from the code. For instance, during the deliberations in a drug offence case, one of the lay judges wanted to double the prison sentence being discussed, to which judge Ola, who did not agree, responded: "Then I think we need to look at the explanatory statements of the law, as I doubt that [such a long prison sentence] is established praxis". He then read aloud from the code in an articulated pedagogical manner. When asked about the situation in a follow-up interview, judge Ola said that he had had a similar incident with the same opposing lay judge the week before, with the result that the lay judges voted against him, and that he therefore decided to, this time, use "power language" on the lay judge. In the beginning of the quote, Ola refers to the first encounter with this lay judge:

> She persuaded the entire [lay judge] committee to side with her and they convicted a girl I thought should have been acquitted due to lack of evidence. That's how the legal rights of the individual are imperilled. I think it's rather upsetting actually. So then I decided that I needed to be more articulate. With [this lay judge] in particular, I need to make myself very clear. If she starts digressing and giving her opinions like "Well, well, this is how it should be" – without any real [legal] basis for it – then I think she's simply wrong. So, [reading the code] absolutely is about using power language, but I also think that it's important to do so. And although I don't think she gets it, [she needs] to understand that we can't [irritated voice] sentence people merely based on our opinions.
>
> (Ola, judge, 40+)

The example shows that resorting to the intimidating approach of "power language" in Ola's case was not necessarily an easy option for him to choose, and so it had to be used delicately. In Ola's case, it was chosen as a result of reflection and in correspondence with the correct procedure, given that the lay judge was legally wrong. Ola also remained calm and kind when interacting with the lay judge, in spite of the anger and irritation he expressed during his interview.

Careful and discrete emotion management, even when meant to intimidate, is common for professional judges in deliberations because they know that heads-on confrontations of opposing lay judges are likely to only worsen the problem of contentious lay judges. Indeed, it seems to be the case that argumentative lay judges often manage to convince entire committees. Judges in our material thus additionally opined that where possible, lay judge committees should not be allowed to discuss cases on their own, and that it would be good to have the deliberations towards the end of the day as by then the lay judges already long to go home and will thus be less inclined to have lengthy discussions.

To sum up, the judges' position as powerful embeds emotions of guilt, discomfort, confidence, and security. In a democratic system, especially in the Swedish system where a high degree of consensus represents a cultural good, the legitimacy of power ideally implies that the subject complies with the norms according to which he or she is rightfully submitted to a legal process. As we have seen, judges are either comfortable with having power but try to use it as "kindly" or responsibly as possible, or they are uneasy with it and choose to consider themselves as but a function of the system. Either way, "the cap story" serves to illustrate and help us reflect about the inherent insecurity of legitimate power: it is limited when clashing with different norm systems, and when its limit is reached, the judge's status as representative of a legitimate system may be undermined. Though judges nurture autonomy as their shared and sacred ideal, their performance of the legitimate rule of law rely upon the ritual deference of prosecutors and lawyers, as seen in the case of the gum-chewing defendant. Ritual deference as inscribed in the emotive-cognitive judicial frame embraced by all legal professionals ensures that the judge does not need to negotiate status in relation to other legal professionals. The situation is different with the lay judges, however: as we saw, judges need to engage in various status-enhancing emotion management strategies during deliberations with lay judges. Turning now to the prosecutors, such status-enhancing emotion management is a vital ingredient of their emotional profile, which is characterized by bounded independence.

## The independent prosecutor: status negotiations

In contrast to the ideally secluded autonomous work of the judge, prosecutors rely on an array of relations to other professionals who can either ease or obstruct their work, regardless of the formal juridical power relationship that puts the prosecutors in command. This makes the prosecutors' professional role distinct from that of the judges, in the sense that prosecutors continuously need to empathically imagine and thus anticipate others' reactions to the measures and decisions that they take in order to ensure efficient collaboration (cf. Wettergren and Bergman Blix, 2016). Paradoxically, as seen in Chapter 2, independence for a prosecutor denotes the capacity to distance oneself from, and be insensitive to, the emotions and reactions of others when that is called for by the objectivity ideal.

### *Prosecutors and the police*

According to the prosecutors in our material, in most cases collaboration with the police works fine but some officers may think that the prosecutors do not apply coercive measures extensively enough. Prosecutor Linus (40+) explains how he deals with that critique:

> Then you must tell them that this is my decision: I am the one who knows how the court works – if that knowledge wasn't needed, we wouldn't need any prosecutors. I decide, but I am not chief of the police, so … I can tell them *what* to do but not *how* and *when* they should do it.
>
> (Fieldnotes, prosecution office)

In the preliminary investigations – which in fact take most of the prosecutors' time – the prosecutors depend heavily on the competence and acquiescence of the police for their ability to do their job effectively.

The excerpt above illustrates the power divisions and conflicts between prosecutors and the police: the prosecutors decide about the coercive measures and whether to proceed with or close down the preliminary investigation, but the police are also an independent public authority and decide about how to do and organize their work. The prosecutors find it problematic that the police know too little about how the courts work, while the police consider the prosecutors too soft or too abstract in their reasoning:

> We are so narrow-mindedly focused on the evidence and, well, the requisites, what needs to be secured, the intent, and all that. [...] I know what I must be able to *demonstrate*, but in relation to the police it can be hard sometimes – because we close down cases – that they think like "come on, *this*, what's wrong with this, it's obvious that he's [the perpetrator]", and I can agree that right, he's probably the one who did it, but we can't *prove* it.... You have to show them each step, and try to pedagogically explain, but you don't always succeed, of course, because [the police] think we're way too abstract.
>
> (Elsa, prosecutor, 50+)

These conflicts reflect another aspect of the prosecutors' purifying work: the legal encoding and translations are performed by them, but the material – the facts and the narratives – are collected and provided by the police. The police are the paramount dirty workers (Ashforth and Kreiner, 1999) of the legal system in this sense, and the potential for mutual resentment is structurally embedded in the power relationship between the police and the prosecutors due to this status difference (Barbalet, 1998). The police who 'know', due to their immediate situatedness in the messy reality, what has happened are required by prosecutors to consider and organize their collection of evidence and witness stories so that these fit in the process of legal encoding. The squareness of this requirement "chafes, evokes emotional instability and cognitive dissonance" (Björk, 2014: 18, our translation) to the police. The quality of the evidence collected by the police needs to withstand judicial scrutiny to ensure that there is no overlooked evidence of alternative scenarios or other possible perpetrators – to "plug all the holes", as prosecutor August put it, and continuing:

> Many officers are geared more towards strengthening the aggravating evidence than considering alternative hypotheses, and then I see it as my role to guide them ... so initially I have many meetings with the police instead of merely giving them directives. [...] This is a sensitive issue because we cannot control the details. [...] I think about that a lot, how to, like, gain a good balance. It's very individual how much leadership they want; some want none at all although they need it.
>
> (August, prosecutor, 35+)

Police officers and prosecutors thus work in different organizations and with slightly different objectives. Most notably, police officers do not share the emotive-cognitive judicial frame and its orientation towards legal expertise. The police's sense of dignity and professionalism in their work is a sensitive matter, as stated by August above. As August also explained, rather than commanding the police ("giving them directives"), he tried to offer his "leadership" and "guidance" through meetings with them. Similar considerations were expressed in the previous excerpt by Elsa, who tried to "show them each step" and "pedagogically explain".

Similarly to judges with their circumscribed autonomy in the deliberations, prosecutors using their power to command police officers while failing to recognize the latter's status can prompt feelings of irritation and resentment among the police and lower the prosecutor's status (Kemper, 2011). The difference here is, however, that while professional judges can retain their professional pride by expressing a dissenting opinion in the judgment – resulting in a 'lay judgment' of low status among legal professionals, prosecutors cannot formally dissociate from police work. Loss of status in the eyes of the police does not only cause emotions of frustration for the prosecutors, but can obstruct prosecutors' power to effectively do their job.

Officers who dislike the prosecutor can delay the fulfilling of the latter's directives which, in turn, can affect the collection of evidence: an irritated police officer can cause the loss of important pieces of evidence such as CCTV films, erode the reliability of witness statements through sloppy protocols or important questions never asked, and so on. The police is generally known to struggle with work overload, so any neglect in fulfilling a directive can easily be explained away with reference to lack of time (Björk, 2014; Liederbach et al., 2011). The relationship to the police therefore needs to be continuously emotionally lubricated, ideally achieving a stable, mutually accorded status and trust. The following excerpt describes a lunch conversation between two prosecutors, who discuss ways to achieve just that:

> Prosecutor 1 says that when you meet police officers [the first time], they read you to find out what type you are and how they can approach you.... Prosecutors 1 and 2 keep talking about how to give directives in a nice manner, not forget to praise the police for a good piece of work, not just "do this and do that", and take their work for granted.
>
> (Fieldnotes, prosecution office)

The police's "reading" of the prosecutors noted in this excerpt reflects the police's subordinate position and can be compared to the way prosecutors and defence lawyers in our material tended to keep close track of the different judges they met in court (see below). Previous research suggests that the demands on emotion management for subordinate legal actors are higher than those for superiors (Francis, 2006; Lively, 2002; Pierce, 1999), which is in line with this 'upward reading'. But our data also suggest that in the case of prosecutors and police officers, the amount of emotion management depends on the degree of interdependence in the power relation. The prosecutors command the police during preliminary investigations and concerning coercive measures, but they also depend on the police for collecting the material they need for legal encoding. This dependency warrants prosecutors' emotion management in relation to the subordinate police. Prosecutors therefore also read the police: "You learn about individual officers that you work with, you know that 'OK, now it's that person, so I'll work like this', and you know how to get what you want out of [that relationship]" (Ursula, prosecutor, 30+). Prosecutors' dependence on collaboration with other professions such as the police thus brackets their actual power and directs attention to the mutual accordance of status that enables one to perform, in a position of superior and subordinate, in situations in which the superior depends on the acquiescence of the subordinate, but the actors belong to slightly different norm systems.

### Prosecutors and the judge

In court, prosecutors are independent players representing the state. However, they are also dependent on the other court professionals, without whom they cannot gain the situational status they need to do their job in court. They are also formally subordinated to the judge. The judge may affect prosecutors' performance in court, and in this sense, prosecutors, on the one hand, depend on the judges, as they do on the police. On the other hand, prosecutors may potentially resent their formal subordination, as the police may resent their subordination to the prosecutors. Differently from the relationship between police and prosecutor, however, prosecutors share the emotive-cognitive judicial frame with the superior judges, and ritual deference to the judge is deeply inscribed into that frame. This means that prosecutors must also comply with judges who obstruct, scold, or scorn their work. Judges are not as reluctant to exercise power over prosecutors and defence lawyers as they are over lay people, since all legal professionals by definition share the norms and values of the judicial system. In the broad perspective, as we argue throughout this book, they are "in it together": the legal professionals' group charisma depends on their joint performance of legitimate justice (see Elias and Scotson, 1994). Details of the situated interactions between prosecutor and judge in court will be discussed later in this chapter.

Since prosecutors depend on judges to give them space to perform in court, they – the same way that the police are attentive to the "type" of prosecutor – keep track of the "type" of judges, and adjust their performance to fit particular judges:

> When it's a new judge, you might ask your colleagues about what he or she is like, just so you can mentally prepare. What do I have to expect? If you're told that they have an uneven temper, then of course you become a bit more insecure.
>
> (Bror, prosecutor, 65+)

Prosecutors, however, also regulate their ritualistic strictness in terms of deferential displays depending on the judge:

> I went to the bench to let judge [name X] read the document. [...] I would never have dared to do that if judge [name Y] had been presiding, because then you have to ask for permission to approach the bench [laughs].
>
> (Josefin, prosecutor, 30+)

So far, we have shown that the prosecutor's role is shaped by complex power relations that in a number of ways make it distinct from the judge's role. In the juridical hierarchy, prosecutors are subordinate to judges, but superior to the police. They depend on both the police and the judges to do their work. First, while they formally have power over the police, the police represent a different institution with different norms and values attached to their specific (practical, action-oriented) professional pride, making many police officers predisposed to resent (the power of) prosecutors. Prosecutors thus need to develop emotion management skills that help them increase their status as well liked among the police. Second, the relationship to judges is collegial and they share the emotive-cognitive judicial frame. There is no norm or value conflict, nor can prosecutors escape the peer-evaluative eye of the judge in the courtroom.

### Prosecutors and lay people

Prosecutors exercise significant power over lay people, particularly during investigations in which they – through the police – subject them to coercive measures and police interrogations. In court, however, they must much more depend on their status as liked or disliked individuals to obtain results useful for their objectives. Prosecutors invest much strategic emotion management in examining defendants and plaintiffs, learning the art by trial and error. Insofar as the victim examinations are concerned, prosecutors may also have to perform emotion management to impact the trustworthiness of the victim in court, for instance, by making them more or less emotional (Wettergren and Bergman Blix, 2016).

The task of strategic emotion management becomes even more challenging when victims actively resist participation. During shadowing, prosecutor Klara (35+) recounted the example of a battered wife who had decided to no longer cooperate in the proceedings. In such cases, prosecutors embody the power that forces reluctant victims to submit to a hearing, relentlessly trying to make them talk against their will in court. Klara described the resentment directed at her by both the defendant and the victim at the trial, and the victim's evasive answers when she was faced with the evidence that her husband had actually injured her. Klara had to brace herself to stay calm and neutral, remaining "cunning, but not unkind". She continued: "Maybe I trick them, but I try to pretend that I don't. It's like playing a bit stupid and not understanding that they resent me". The victim here joins forces with the defendant and, as we see, the strategy adopted by the prosecutor is reminiscent of the one used by Faida in Chapter 1 (p. 20), habitually displaying neutrality in order to stay calm and focused. One difference here is, however, that the aim of the strategic emotion management in prosecutor Klara's case is not to reveal the defendant's inclination to violent behaviour but to reveal the victim's actual victimization.

### More distance – less personalized

The prosecutor sometimes struggles to uphold an aura of power and authority in relation to lay people in court (cf. Roach Anleu and Mack, 2017: 115–116 on the authority of magistrates). A wish to become more depersonalized was expressed by prosecutors in our material: "In Norway and Denmark, they wear gowns, and I would have wanted us to do that here as well, so you could de-identify as a person, become more of a public official" (Lara, prosecutor, 30+). By erasing bodily characteristics, it becomes possible to disassociate the representation of the state from the individual holding that position. The fact that prosecutors usually enter the court from the public area and meet and talk to the victim, and sometimes also the defendant in the hall, actualizes a wish for visible distinction:

> Actually it wouldn't be so bad if we had robes or something. [---] You wouldn't have to think so much about working clothes [...] and we would be immediately spotted, too, because that's not otherwise so easy today: when people come to court, they don't know who the prosecutor is.
>
> (Elsa, prosecutor, 50+)

Like judges, prosecutors represent the state, but unlike judges, they represent the state as a party in court, not – as is the case with the judge – justice per se with a fundamentally autonomous relation to the state. Prosecutors by definition serve as the personalized state: they exercise state power in leading investigations and in their decisions to pursue or close down cases. In all these instances, they represent the state in dealing with the victim; they may get frequent phone calls from victims who are angry, disappointed, and so forth. Furthermore, prosecutors take great pride in their professional requirement to conduct objective investigations, but as they switch to become a party in court, they still need to uphold distance to the victim(s). As seen in Chapter 4, contrary to judges, the issue for them is then not whether to give justice an empathic face; rather, it is about keeping distance and conveying the point that prosecutors do not represent the victim the same way defence lawyers represent defendants. This distance requires a habituated, tacit ability to move in and out of engagement depending on the objective needs of the victim. They also need to strategically manage the emotional expressions of victims as well as victims' expectations on the prosecutor. In relation to defendants, the prosecutors want to make sure that they understand that the prosecution against them is professional, not personal.

We have seen that due to a multitude of interdependent relationships, prosecutors need to negotiate power with emotion management strategies to gain status, which eases their work. At the same time they embody the exercise of power, sometimes against the expressed wishes or needs of the police and lay people. In this professionally habituated readiness to use power – in spite of becoming disliked, thwarted, and scorned – lies their profession-specific sacred value of independence. Independence is bounded by interdependent relationships and status negotiations, but proves its worth when prosecutors pursue their objective goals by the use of power, even if they lose status. In other words, prosecutors have both to be insensitive to the perspectives of others and empathically oriented towards them. This is also true in their relation to the judges, although in this relation, the prosecutors are structurally subordinated. In the last section, we will briefly elaborate on the power/status relationships between these two professional groups in court interactions.

## Judge and prosecutor: power and status challenges

The division of judicial skills between the professional parties constitutes one of the things that make the presiding judge de facto dependent on the other professional actors fulfilling their parts in a trial. Judges, who are general dealers, appreciate skilled prosecutors, and they can even draw on the expert competence of specialized prosecutors by asking them for advice. In contrast, prosecutors who leave gaps in the matter presented to the court put judges in a dilemma situation that evokes frustration and anger. Given that judges should be objective, they should not ask questions that "bring down the defendant" as described in the following quote. Whether a seemingly neutral question will have this effect is difficult to know before hearing the answer, and therefore judges hesitate to ask the questions a prosecutor has missed. Interventions can evoke feelings of power discomfort as they stretch the limits of judges' legitimate power.

> She [the prosecutor] never asked. It was never clear who [the defendant] bargained with, that was just implied, and it cannot be implied. I had to put those questions. And that is not my role. [...] When the prosecution doesn't function properly, isn't skilled, it's not good from a judge's point of view, because it undermines our objectivity. [...] I have investigative responsibility as well, but I won't go in and bring down the defendant.
> (Monika, judge, 45+)

Monika here did make sure the missing questions were asked, but, as we see, she resented the prosecutor ("doesn't function properly, isn't skilled") for putting her in this position. The reason why judges like Monika may nevertheless decide to venture into objectivity's grey zone is their distaste for waste of time and of taxpayers' money; if, instead of asking, they would issue a judgment to the effect that the case be dismissed due to lack of clarity, the prosecutor would appeal and an appeals court would presumably convict instead.

Feelings of resentment thus arise in judges when other parties fail to do their part. This said, judges' dependence on the other legal professionals in hearings does not warrant any status negotiations, as their power over defence lawyers and prosecutors normally goes uncontested. We have already discussed the mechanism behind this, which is ritual deference to the judge as a shared norm embedded in the emotive-cognitive judicial frame. Judges therefore do not need to work on their status in the eyes of other legal professionals: they do not (and autonomy postulates that they should not) need to be liked by them. Judges' dependence on other legal professionals instead disposes them to feelings of anger, an emotion associated with power. Their habituated position of autonomous power can thus make judges short-tempered:

> ...most people are very attentive to what ... you think up there, if I may say so, most people see that there is lots of power radiating from the bench and they do – yes, most people do as I want. Last time I roared at someone, it was actually a lawyer who wanted to make a statement at a point in the trial where he was not supposed to make any statements, to refer to circumstances that he was not supposed to refer to, [loud voice:] and then I had to roar that he was to be quiet [...] Well, then you must let it come forth, let the feeling come forth that I am not afraid to use the language of power.
>
> (Folke, judge, 60+)

This comfortable display of power depends on that the object of power (the defence lawyer) shares the judge's norm system. The lawyer in the excerpt might not have agreed that he did something wrong, but he would not openly challenge the judge's command.

Prosecutors in training may irritate judges for being slow and asking too many or too ineffective questions. Their impatience reflects the tension, managed by the judges, between staying on schedule and letting the parties have their say (Scarduzio, 2011). In the quote below, judge Hans becomes angry with a young assistant prosecutor. They have to cancel a grey trial because none of the parties have shown up for it and, as it turns out, the injured party is unlikely to participate at all since she has emigrated from Sweden. The judge advises the young assistant prosecutor to withdraw the case entirely:

> The judge to the prosecutor: "You have read the preliminary investigation, in which the evidence builds on the victim's story, so if she is not here maybe you should just drop the case." The prosecutor [with

a strained laugh]: "I will have to consider that." They have a short exchange about a previously cancelled hearing, and the prosecutor leans
back with her hands to her sides, as if showing that she thinks. The
room falls silent for a while and the judge looks at his papers, as if waiting for the prosecutor, who does not speak. Finally the judge speaks:
"So, we'll end the attempt to find the victim." Prosecutor: "Can I take a
short break to think this through?" Judge: "You can take a break until
our next trial." Prosecutor: "Good". She nods, stands up, and leaves the
courtroom.

(Observation, unlawful threat, judge Hans, 55+)

Typical of the kind of emotional toning pertinent to the front stage of the
courtroom (discussed in Chapter 4), the power contest between the prosecutor and the judge in this excerpt is subtle. The prosecutor's strained laugh
and body posture suggest that she is both humiliated and angry but unsure
how to proceed. Her hesitation to withdraw the charges and show deference
to the judge's opinion reinforces the judge's anger. From the prosecutor's
perspective, the lack of deference is an exercise of independence vital to
her profession, an attempt to stay in charge of a prosecutor's discretionary
space despite the pressure from the judge. In return, the judge overrules the
prosecutor's request to "think it through" by abruptly ending the trial, using
his power to show that she, the prosecutor, is not worthy of his respect. In his
follow-up interview, it became clear that judge Hans resented prosecutors in
general, for believing that they have power in these matters, and that the
interaction observed above was indeed meant to be a power manifestation:

[Condescending tone of voice] The prosecutor does not decide on anything, but some judges think they do. [...] The fact that the prosecutor
finds something important, in this case referring to [the victim's state-
ment], makes her completely forget about the nuisance it causes people
[when a case drags out for years], and then she doesn't abide to the law
the way it's intended [---]. And we pull together an entire court to decide
on this – that costs a lot of money for the taxpayers. There is no way that
we can make this victim come to the trial.

(Hans, judge, 55+)

Judge Hans belongs to a category of "aggressive" judges whom prosecutors generally dislike and some even fear, as they interfere with prosecutors'
independence in court. Such judges throw prosecutors off balance, making it hard for them to stay on their planned course of action during the
hearing. Novice prosecutors keep themselves particularly busy trying to get
all the procedural issues right and testing different examination strategies,
which sometimes means that they allow those examined to talk about things
deemed irrelevant by judges. Assistant prosecutor Magnus describes an aggressive judge:

I think [judge X] crosses the line sometimes for how much a judge can steer an examination, and how much he can cut in. He can tell a witness that he "should only talk about 'this', everything else is completely irrelevant".

(Magnus, assistant prosecutor, 30+)

The "cutting in" as described in this quote equals overruling the judgement of the prosecutor, the one to normally "steer" the examined person. When judges undermine novice prosecutors' professional status, they lower these prosecutors' self-confidence and security. As prosecutor Magnus continues to describe another such judge, he uses the word "painful" and blames his own lack of experience, indicating low self-feelings and shame (cf. Scheff, 1990):

Of course, if I have a full day with [judge Y] and she cuts in on *every* examination I hold, and kind of tells me "that's not interesting" or takes over the examination herself, *then* you can feel [dejected], it can be kind of painful. It has happened on some occasions, but, you know, being a beginner, I'm quite humble. I have a lot left to learn.

(Magnus, assistant prosecutor, 30+)

Judges' use of power this way may impact negatively on prosecutors' general performance, which, in turn, makes the judge more irritated, creating a vicious circle of an escalating shame-anger spiral consolidating feelings of insufficiency (Scheff, 1990). Interestingly, even experienced prosecutors can talk about and display feelings of discomfort and insecurity when about to enter trials with reputedly aggressive judges (see, e.g., p. 130).

As we have seen, prosecutors' independence requires insensitivity to criticism from both professionals and lay people. An ability to withstand patronizing assaults on their professional self by aggressive judges is also inherent to this necessary insensitivity, a skill they have to develop to pursue their goals. In the excerpt below, the earlier quoted judge Hans meets now instead an experienced male chief prosecutor who engages him in a status contest while upholding ritual deference as pure formality. The parties have just been called to begin the trial:

Walking in, the prosecutor says: "The defendant has not arrived". Without paying attention to the prosecutor, the judge looks at his papers and asks the clerk to check the database. Judge: "He has been served his indictment, stating that the case can be handled in his absence". Prosecutor: "Mm", leaning back with his arms crossed. The prosecutor then picks up his papers, reads for a few moments and turns to the judge: "I see that there is an incorrect date in the police report." The judge stares at his screen without acknowledging the prosecutor. Prosecutor: "I need to make an amendment and change the date to 31 January." The judge does not react. After a while the judge says: "When a case is handled in absence of the parties, it is not possible to..." The prosecutor quickly fills in: "...make amendments." The judge interrupts: "I was talking to the lay judges." Prosecutor: "Excuse me." Judge: "No problem," without looking at the prosecutor. When leaving, the prosecutor shakes his head, looks at the researcher, and smiles.

(Observation, drug offence, judge Hans, 55+)

In this excerpt, Judge Hans claims power and superior status through demonstrated indifference (Kemper 2011: 23), and emotional distance towards the prosecutor by not responding or even meeting the prosecutor's eye once during the short episode. Hans' insinuating that the chief prosecutor would not know that trials without the defendant present do not allow for amendments is a clear status withdrawal. In contrast to the young female prosecutor encountering judge Hans above, the male chief prosecutor, however, claims status by remaining confident, talking back to the judge to show his professional competence, and finally signalling that he finds the judge ridiculous by shaking his head and smiling on his way out. The prosecutor's filling in the judge's talk ("...make amendments") amounts to a verbal crossing of swords, revealing his keen defence of his status. Experienced and confident high status prosecutors may gain a reputation as such among judges and thereby claim more confident space of discretion in the court than other prosecutors claim. While there are judges, like judge Hans, who refuse to be impressed, it lies in the prosecutors' interest to not admit to being humiliated.

To sum up, even the autonomous judges depend on hierarchically subordinate other legal actors, but they do not need to negotiate status in these inter-professional relations. Whether those other legal actors like them or not, they are bound by the shared emotive-cognitive judicial frame to submit to the judges and show them respect and ritual deference. We have seen how this may result in judges who appear aggressive to prosecutors, which may cause emotional distress for the latter, especially the novice ones among them.

## Conclusion

In this chapter, we have focused on professional power and status relations. We have shown how judges and prosecutors are variously enmeshed in relations of dependence, while power and status work differently for the respective professions, resulting in different patterns of emotion management and emotion outcomes. Confidence and comfort of power are tied to the judge's performance of autonomy, but judges' position as powerful also embeds emotions of guilt, remorse, and discomfort. Some judges confidently habituate power by assuming personal responsibility that may go beyond their actual job description. Others reject the notion of their power and assume a bureaucratic approach, entirely denying responsibility. In order to be comfortably exercised in a democratic egalitarian society power also has to be legitimate. Bounded independence, requiring the mitigation of power by the continuous negotiation of status, characterizes prosecutors' power relations to a multitude of groups. Prosecutors therefore need to develop high empathic and emotion management skills. Yet, their independent, professionally required, pursuit of objectivity also propels them to be insensitive to others' emotions, as when they execute prosecutorial power over lay people or resist the tacit signals and emotional communication of the judge. These patterns contribute to the making of what we call different emotional profiles of judges and prosecutors within the emotive-cognitive judicial frame.

We have argued that judicial power relies on reproduction of autonomy, typically expressed by the judge's removal from messy reality and his or her capacity to embody pure reason. The emotional profile of the judges is characterized by a rather distinct absolute power that nevertheless requires a certain status of the rule of law in order to be comfortably exerted in relation to lay people who do not necessarily embrace the norms of the legal system and its legitimacy. When achieving legitimacy in court, judges thus rely on the ritual deference – inherent in the norms of the emotive-cognitive judicial frame – of the other legal professionals. Sharing the norms of the legal system, defence lawyers and prosecutors can bridge the norm gap between the judiciary and lay people. As we saw, status negotiations are necessary for judges primarily in relation to lay judges during deliberations. Given the good treatment policy, however, some judges attempt to work on their status through a more personalized approach in relation to lay people.

The emotional profile of the prosecutor is characterized by dependent power relations vis-à-vis both the police and the judges. Police officers who resent a prosecutor may not do as good a job in securing evidence fit for legal encoding as positively disposed officers do. Status negotiations in relation to the police are therefore vital in the preliminary investigations. Vis-à-vis judges, prosecutors may find their status undermined by aggressive judges, but to some extent, they also defend that status: even aggressive judges may be more tolerant of prosecutors they respect. Relations to lay people are more complex: here the prosecutor may exercise prosecutorial power against the wishes of the victim, thus putting up with the discomfort of both exercising absolute power and losing status (being disliked). Due to these complex power and status relations, the demands on prosecutors to flexibly manage and predict others' emotions and adapt relationally are considerably higher than those on judges.

We have seen examples of how resentment and anger among professionals can occur in court as the result of colliding professional agendas. Judges take pride in procedural correctness, in staying on schedule, in saving taxpayers' money, and, above all, in gaining lay people's recognition for the legitimacy of the law. Prosecutors share these values, but in court, their focus and pride lie in their capacity to steer the process forward according to the plan, presenting evidence and examining people. The different foci of judges and prosecutors give rise to different priorities. The judges may want clear and concise questions that generate the best substance for decision-making, while the prosecutors may want unwavering respect for a specific, strategic examination. In the court settings of interdependence and cooperation necessary to achieve shared sacred values of objective justice and professional pride, power and status become emotionally highly charged dimensions. Mutual respect and ritual deference become crucial for smooth professional relationships and, in the end, for the smooth working of justice.

# 6   Objectivity work as situated emotion management

> When the lay judges can identify with the accused, they put extremely high demands on the quality of the evidence; and when they can't, because it's some junkie, then they can convict that person more or less without any evidence at all. I've seen that over and over again. And quite often when they don't want to convict the defendant, even when I think there's really enough evidence, we end up having very weird discussions. I suppose, when I identify with someone, that's how it works for me as well. That's happened a few times and it's been rather unpleasant. [...] Now and then it happens that it's someone who could have been me, then it's hard. Because then I *feel* I'm less objective, and I think it's really very important to talk to someone, unload all that, so to speak, before you make your judgment. Because those feelings can make you judge, not necessarily milder at all ... but that I try to compensate for those feelings.
>
> (Tina, judge, 50+)

Tina in this excerpt speaks with unusual insight into the role of background emotions in judicial decision-making, an issue more visibly affecting lay judges who lack the tools and techniques of the emotive-cognitive judicial frame. From Tina's reflections on lay judges' contingent demands on the evidence, she infers similar processes in herself. Her view that judging sometimes should be preceded by "unloading" various emotional impressions in order to avoid unreflected influences on decision-making points to our argument in this book that while emotions can be rendered formally insignificant by the legal system, they will nonetheless still be present. The legal positivist notion of objectivity as something abstract, disembodied, and unemotional is therefore profoundly problematic (Bladini, 2013). In reality, as Tina seems to suggest above, the goal of objectivity might be better served by paying close attention to situated and contingent background emotional processes (Burkitt, 2012; Scheer, 2012).

In this chapter, we will show that judicial objectivity relies on situated emotion management and empathy. That is, rather than being static and universal, objectivity is a situated practice accomplished through "objectivity work" (Jacobsson, 2008: 46–47). We will also show how the positivist

objectivity ideal remains a chief organizing principle for legal professionals, sustained by the emotive-cognitive judicial frame and emotions of professional pride and shame. Lots of skilled emotion management goes into
upholding the positivist ideal itself and its appearance of unemotional detachment (Mack and Roach Anleu, 2010).

In practice, the different professional emotional profiles of prosecutors and
judges require different types of objectivity work. We begin with the judges
and their focus on the performative side of objectivity, consisting of an impartial demeanour (equal treatment) and an instrumental method of evaluating
legally encoded sections of complex and conflictual reality (evaluation). We
then proceed to analyse prosecutors' challenging task of being both partial
and objective, discussing the emotional agility required to balance emotions
of commitment and detachment. We look at this balancing act in relation to
preliminary investigations, which has not been given much attention earlier in
this book. Like the judges' method of evaluation, prosecutors have a method
of legal encoding that directs their focus when mediating between messy reality and the emotive-cognitive judicial frame. Finally, we analyse examples of
objectivity work as a collective achievement in court, which relies on intricate
and subtle inter-professional emotional communication and tacit signals.

## Objectivity and impartiality

Objectivity in legal practice is connected to impartiality, neutrality, and an
emphasis on facts. In our analysis, we found that empirically and theoretically distinguishing between impartiality and objectivity is helpful for understanding how prosecutors and judges adhere to the judicial objectivity
ideal in practice. According to the Oxford dictionary, being objective means
not being influenced "by personal feelings or opinions in considering and
representing facts", and objectivity means "the quality of being objective".
Being impartial means "treating rivals equally", not taking sides, and impartiality refers to "equal treatment" and "fairness".[1] Impartial and objective
can be synonyms, according to the Oxford dictionary, but, as we see, they
also stand for slightly different phenomena. It is, for instance, entirely possible to be objective but partial, which, we will argue, is the case with prosecutors when they appear as party in court on the basis of objective evidence.
It is also fully possible to appear impartial without being objective, treating
parties equally although one already has an opinion about the forthcom-
ing verdict. The latter is presumably not the case for judges – when asked,
they say that both objectivity and impartiality are equally important – but
front stage, impartiality is their primary focus. Arguably, impartiality is the
way for judges to demonstrate objectivity, whether or not they have begun
to think that objective facts speak in favour or against one of the parties. It
follows that impartiality can be seen as an external display, as interactional,
while objectivity is an emotive-cognitive process of the mind. If and when
the two coincide, impartiality is the external display of internal objectivity.

## Judges: justice must be seen to be done

Impartiality and independence are fundamental for the rule of law as put forth in the European Convention on Human Rights (ECHR: Art. 6.1) and the Swedish Code of Judicial Procedure (CJP: Ch. 3, Art. 13). These two legal frameworks deal with possible conflicts of interests, but the intentions of the laws are two-fold: to secure the fairness of a trial and public trust in the judicial system (Sandgren, 2014: 452). Both of these functions, fairness and trust, are represented in the below quote about "a good judge":

> Emphasizing impartiality, not that we stand above but – yes actually, that we stand above society's institutions, so to speak, in that we can assert the individual's right against society in general. And this is what characterizes a good judge: an ability to communicate that message.
>
> (Erik, judge, 50+)

In this quote, Erik emphasizes that judicial impartiality ultimately means safeguarding the rights of the individual against the state and its institutions ("society"). This implies that even though other institutions may present claims regarding the defendant's guilt or non-guilt, the defendant and the people in general can trust that the court stands above these institutions and makes an autonomous judgement. As also pointed out in the quote, a good judge can "communicate that message": in other words that "justice must not only be done but must manifestly and undoubtedly be seen to be done" (Hewart, 1924). In this section about judges' objectivity, we will show both how justice is done and how it is seen to be done, beginning with the latter: the presentation of an impartial demeanour. The way Swedish judges achieve "justice as seen to be done" is by not giving away any signs of sympathy (or antipathy) in any direction – that is, by upholding their stone face – or by expressing the same things in both directions – that is, by balancing their emotional expressions (cf. Roach Anleu and Mack, 2017).

### *Balancing emotional expressions*

An impartial demeanour is to communicate that no one is judged until everyone involved in the trial has been heard. It is essentially about balancing emotional expressions; whether this is achieved by a passive stone-faced attitude or some other means, the rule is to not intervene against one party more than the other. This often amounts, as explained by Folke in the following quote, to not showing any feelings at all, even if these feelings are related to the criminal act in question and not to the accused person:

> You have to be really careful with [feelings of] disgust. Just because you dislike rapists and those who abuse small children, I mean, they aren't [rapists] before they're proven guilty so to speak, so we're going to

examine if they really did it. So I don't know if it's a perpetrator sitting there; it's an accused sitting there. Whether or not he is a perpetrator, that is what I have to decide upon right, and until then the person is innocent. And that's – I believe we strive to live in line with that fiction.

(Folke, judge, 60+)

Folke's statement here indicates that impartiality can in fact hide strong opinions and feelings ("disgust") about what the accused may have done. In this sense, impartiality is surface acting with the stone face. On the other hand, the presumption that a person is innocent until proven guilty is fundamental to the principle of the rule of law, and it is therefore a sacred value of the emotive-cognitive judicial frame. This frame disciplines judges to actually feel proud when they succeed in keeping the accused separated from the criminal act, and thus in refraining from morally judging the accused beforehand ("they aren't rapists before proven guilty"). In this sense, impartiality is not surface acting but deep acting, using the emotive-cognitive judicial frame to actually neutralize any feelings for the accused (Hochschild, 1983). Equal treatment and an impartial demeanour is then connoted to actually feeling neutral towards the accused. Nevertheless, the ambivalence of this frame adherence comes through in Folke's last sentence: it is all "fiction" that judges "strive" to live by. In these words, we glimpse the usually overlooked gap between messy reality and the ideal order of the emotive-cognitive judicial frame.

Success in performing an impartial demeanour makes judges feel good and proud about doing their job well. As illustrated by chief judge Christer in the following quote, one way to know that you succeeded is from the (very rare) direct feedback from lay people. Christer had a murder case in which he sentenced the accused to forensic psychiatric care. The injured party called the clerk to ask about certain things after the trial, and then took the occasion to express her satisfaction:

She had been so nervous before the trial but now she was so satisfied; she felt that I had treated both [the accused] and her with such respect. And then I thought it was – then I felt really happy, actually, *really happy*. And I mean, she had no reason to tell me that if she – I mean, she had no – well, that's how she felt, anyway.

(Christer, chief judge, 50+)

Acknowledgement from a lay person is a great source of professional pride, a sign of legitimate exercise of power. In the quote, we see how Christer makes a point of emphasizing the fact that the victim had no reason to say any of this, stressing the view that she therefore truly must have meant it and – most importantly – that she did not try to influence the proceedings or the verdict. Christer felt free to express joy because doing so did not endanger his impartiality. Taking pride in the displayed fairness of the procedure is common to judges in our material and mirrors the ideas behind procedural

justice that there will be an enhanced acceptance of the legal judgment by
the accused and the victim if the trial is perceived as fair (Tyler and Bies,
1990). Displayed fairness thus increases the legitimacy of the rule of law.

Reversely, failure to adhere to the requirement of an impartial presentation leads to professional embarrassment. As chief judge Sanna explained,
recalling the time when she was working in an appellate court and – while
watching the recordings of the trial in court[2] – heard the district court judge
express unbalanced empathy for the victim:

> There was this [district court] judge who said [sighs, imitates compas-
> sionate tone of voice:] "Yes, I understand that this is really difficult
> for you, you have been subject to so much, poor you, you may take a
> break." [Normal voice:] Something like that, because the examination
> was getting emotional. And I felt like [hissing voice:] "Oh no! Good
> Lord! I mean, quiet, quiet, quiet!" [Normal voice:] Like, do not say one
> more word, it was so wrong. She didn't mean to, but what she said was
> so value laden, and I thought it was so unprofessional.
>
> (Sanna, chief judge, 50+)

Sanna's intensive shame in this quote is an effect of the district court judge's
open expression of compassion. Although judges' empathy may harbour
compassion,[3] it should be expressed in a by-the-way manner, as we saw in
Margareta's case in Chapter 4, or not at all. Sanna is ashamed on behalf
of the particular judge, but her shame is also related to judging in general:
judges transgressing professional values bring shame to the entire judiciary.

Insofar as the impartial demeanour is achieved using the stone face, it may
conflict with other aspects of procedural justice, such as expressions of empathy, required by the policy of good treatment. Almost all judges in our
material stressed the importance of empathy to manage emotions of others in
court, in the interest of a smooth procedure (see also Roach Anleu and Mack,
2017: 62–70). When being asked why he was a good judge, judge Fredrik replied "I can easily relate to people and attune to them, [in order to perceive]
how to proceed and make things work" (Fredrik, associate judge, 35). As
seen above, in the situation described by chief judge Sanna, also empathy
needs to be balanced in order not to adventure impartiality. In practice, this
means that the judges cannot respond empathically only to a victim's strong
expressions of pain and suffering. The solution to this dilemma may result in
the opposite of empathy. In one murder trial, the defendant gave a detailed
description of how he stabbed the victim multiple times with his knife:

> The defendant describes how the victim tries to wriggle out from under him
> and how he stabs her repeatedly in the neck with his knife. He repeats again
> and again that he did not want to hurt anyone, but still stabbed her every
> time she tried to move. No one in the room reacts as if he is talking about
> anything special. [...] The judge and lay judges are focused on taking notes.
>
> (Observation, murder, prosecutor Cecilia, 40+)

Arguably, keeping focus on the legal aspects is bound to be more difficult in horrific cases, and we know that judges feel things and even fail to hide their feelings sometimes. Indeed, keeping oneself busy with practical matters such as taking notes is a useful technique: apart from its function as a cognitive aid, judges and lay judges use note taking as a way to appear attentive and interested, to control boredom, and to shield off from emotional engagement.

Our observations repeatedly confirmed that the thicker the emotional atmosphere gets, or the stronger the emotional expressions of the lay people get, the more neutral and stone-faced the court appears. The reason may be that the stone face in these situations is no longer primarily directed at the audience front stage, but is really a habituated tool available for judges wanting to control also their internal states (foreground emotions).

The judges' concern for displaying an impartial demeanour, along with their concern for procedural justice and legitimate power, may influence their capacity to intervene even in cases where doing so would be appropriate (due to disturbance, for instance), sometimes resulting in awkward passivity. Judges' fear of risking the balance and going from observation to intervention (compare Moorhead, 2007) may indeed make them look like they favour the accused. As explicated by Judge Ola:

> I think it is important that the defence is allowed to ask the questions they want, in principle, in peace. [...] I usually let them ask a lot of questions and take breaks, so they can conduct the kind of examination they want [---] I might not even interfere when they go too far or when [their questions] are not entirely relevant. The reason is that I think that, beyond pleading their case, they should also have the feeling that they have been allowed to plead their case. I know [famous defence lawyer] once said that, in his experience, his clients rarely appeal when they feel that the court has listened to them [...] So I have [light laughter] taken that to heart; I think that's a rather important point.
>
> (Ola, judge, 40+)

In this excerpt, we see the implicit presumption that the defendant, rather than the victim, is the one most vulnerable of the two parties because he or she stands to be punished. Even if the defence lawyer goes too hard on the victim, and even if the lawyer's questions are irrelevant, they may be allowed for this reason. This presumption was widespread among judges in our material, although individual judges could be variously lenient with regard to the defence lawyers' examinations. As a rule, the more serious the crime and the more severe the sanction associated with it, the more space the accused was allowed.

The aim that the accused should ideally understand and comply with the sentence, however, also rests on the assumption that the accused will be convicted. As the legal system is built on the premise that prosecution should only take place if and when the prosecutor finds the objective evidence of the accused person's guilt to be sufficient, the accused is indeed likely to be convicted.[4] Yet, the impartiality of the judge, and the principles of orality and immediacy (see Chapter 1), still require the judge not to take this for granted. Eager to communicate this message, judges may overcompensate by giving the accused more space than they do for the victim. This compensatory behaviour may be implicit for the lay people, but it is rather explicit for the professional parties: the judge may appear and actually be stricter or harsher towards the prosecutor than towards the defence. In other words, the judges' concern to appear impartial may lead them to treat the prosecution with less concern for their feelings compared to how they treat the defence:

> A prosecutor described a trial where the judge had been unpleasant and tough. Afterwards the prosecutor and the judge spoke on the phone about the case and the judge asked: "Did you think I was unpleasant towards you?" The prosecutor said yes and the judge explained that he thought the case was so clear that, in order not to show that he had already made up his mind about it, he overcompensated by being tough [towards the prosecutor].
>
> (Fieldnotes, court)

The risk of overcompensating this way in cases where the accused is likely to be convicted shows that a concern for impartial demeanour does not necessarily coincide with an impartial state of mind: judges evaluate the evidence continuously while presiding. They may know where the trial is headed before it has reached its end; "all the time you sit there, not just listening but processing" (Kristin, judge, 30+). This should not lead us to question judges' objectivity, however: the judge merely considers the objective evidence to speak for the defendant's guilt before the trial has ended. If anything, given the inquisitorial preliminary investigation, the trial is tilted against the accused from the start, and, from this perspective, the judge's role is to compensate for that (Roach Anleu and Mack, 2017: 123). The fact that judges now and then also do acquit defendants demonstrates their actual autonomy and power. When that happens, their judgment has nothing to do with the truth, however, only with the quality of the evidence failing to meet the requirements. Turning our focus now onto how justice is done, let us take a closer look at the emotional foundations of the method of legal evaluation.

### Aesthetic pleasure, satisfaction, and confidence in legal evaluation

Interest in legal evaluation implies interest in law and its correct application. As we saw in Chapter 2, judges are often characterized by their inclination to ponder on legal issues – their intellectualism. During their training, judges are also encouraged to orient their interest towards the procedure and the legal meanings and value of the matter at hand. Clerk Jonna, in the following quote, describes her going from frustrated bewilderment to confidence when acquiring the juridical "method":

> Since I began attending hearings, my attitude has changed a lot, because in the beginning you were more ambivalent in these situations where you felt that both parties were rather convincing, and now you have a completely different method. And it's really about how you manage it in such a way that you have a method for evaluating people's statements. You have this attitude that you don't need to reach conclusions about the truth but you can reach conclusions about what's proven, and that's very – it releases lots of feelings of frustration you'd otherwise get from not being able to pinpoint who's lying. [...] I'd say that you use it a bit to protect you from the emotional [aspects] in a way.
>
> (Jonna, clerk, 25+)

Judges have no tools for establishing the truth, but they do have tools for deciding what has been proven, and when these tools help establishing a method, as Jonna describes, they orient focus and interest away from the "emotional sides" deemed irrelevant for evaluating the evidence. In the quote, we see Jonna's relief and even enthusiasm when discovering how she could apply this "method" instead of losing herself in bewilderment about "the truth". This method of legal evaluation is taught and habituated as if it were an objective one, uniform and clear and free of any interpretation (Bladini, 2013). It takes on an aesthetic character of coherency and consistency, similar to the way scientific models and theories appeal to researchers (cf. Barbalet, 2011). Mastering the method is a source of professional confidence and satisfaction (pride).

As professional background emotions, confidence, and satisfaction in the method of evaluating evidence delineate judges' focus and orient their interest towards the legal information of the case: "You look at [evidence] from a juridical perspective, if it falls within the criteria of a particular legal section" (Kerstin, judge 60+). This orientation is further strengthened by emotional trigger warnings, feelings of irritation, at irrelevant information:

> For the lay people involved, it is often the *before*, or even more often the *after* [an event], that is relevant. But for us, that is totally, *totally* uninteresting; or not uninteresting, but you understand what I'm saying.
>
> (Asger, associate judge, 30+)

In this quote, Asger indicates irritation ("*totally* uninteresting") at the mismatch between people's storytelling and the juridical focus of the trial. Irritation signals the risk of venturing into a different emotive-cognitive frame, one where judges' confidence in their method might be endangered.

The satisfaction judges derive from legal expertise can be quite intense, even enthusiastic. Judge Niklas (40+) below was shadowed during a long trial over tax fraud. During breaks, Niklas spoke with admiration of the skilled "terrier" prosecutor and also expressed his own moral indignation at the defendant, a wealthy person accused of massive tax evasion. The work of the prosecutor was indeed meticulous, and at the conclusion of the trial, the ruling seemed rather obvious. However, on the day of the deliberations with the lay judges, judge Niklas had worked through the case and the evidence thoroughly, consulting his books and a trusted senior colleague:

> When we enter the room where the lay judges are waiting, the judge pro-
> ceeds to declare that the defendant cannot be sentenced for tax fraud.
> "So we are forced to acquit," the judge says. The lay judges are stunned.
> "Really?" The judge now starts out on a lengthy explanation, step by
> step, involving both critique of the way the evidence was framed by the
> prosecutor and reading numerous previous court rulings out loud for
> the lay judges. Lay judge 2 admits that it seems they have to let the
> defendant go. The judge says: "This is of course not something we do
> happily but..." Lay judge 2 picks up: "...this is not about happiness or
> sorrow this is about the law!"
>
> (Fieldnotes, court)

As can be seen from the excerpt, Niklas' professional enthusiasm spread to the lay judges who were sceptical at first but then won over by the logics and consistency of the picture conveyed to them. According to Niklas, the gap in the law was easily overlooked, which was presumably the reason why an experienced prosecutor specialized in economic crime had also missed it. In a follow-up interview, Niklas said that the prosecutor was furious at him for the acquittal. It did not diminish his own pride and satisfaction, however; rather the opposite: he could be proud not only in his legal exper- tise, but also in having manifested his judicial autonomy and objectivity, by acquitting the suspect in a case in which a guilty verdict had seemed almost certain. In this sense, the method of legal evaluation – with its background emotions of professional pride, confidence, and even fascination – helped to create distance from background emotions of moral or private charac- ter that otherwise might have informed the decision-making. We suggest that Niklas' reflections on his moral background emotions, enabling their articulation (acquitting was "not something we do happily"), was a crucial element in this process of achieving objectivity in practice.

Leaving aside concerns about the truth or reality, the method of legal eval- uation emphasizes the separation of morality from legal practice (Chapter 1). Such a separation might be particularly pregnant in the Swedish legal cul- ture, with its high expectations of emotional reserve (Bergman Blix and Wettergren, 2016) and the idea of the judge as a civil servant rather than a moral guardian. In her article on "angry judges" in a North American context, Maroney has put forth the notion of "righteous anger", suggesting that judges' anger can function as a voice for society's moral principles. In our study, judges rather stressed the separation between (subjective) morality and (objective) law, seeing them as incompatible in all cases.[5] Morality thus pertains to the irrelevant aspects giving rise to background emotional trigger warnings:

> We have our method and we have our rules and in my opinion the important thing is – well, as you saw in the deliberations in the rifle case, we could have easily ventured into a general discussion along the lines of "was it wise of him to do this, right or wrong, blameworthy...?" The lay judges did do that, too, but my task as a judge is to evaluate the evidence according to the rules we have [...] and when you do that systematically, you may end up with something that you think – well, you might have preferred another outcome, but that's the way it is now.
>
> (Preben, judge, 45+)

Besides refuting moral judgement, this quote shows – similarly to the excerpt with Niklas – that discussions with lay judges during the deliberations may function as a way to articulate judges' own moral background emotions. "We could...", Preben says, and indicates that he, too, might have preferred a different outcome. Forming a "we-group" with the lay judges in this respect is rather rare, however, as in most cases the professional judges consider lay judges as an out-group. This enables them to distance their professional selves from the non-professional lay judges and thereby ascribe emotions only to the latter (see Chapter 5).

Experienced judges sometimes demonstrate a perceptual split between attuning to others' emotions, and recognizing their own emotions. On the one hand, they skilfully use emotional information to read the feelings of lay people in order to secure a correct and smooth procedure. On the other hand, they often completely silence their own emotions in relation to their judging. This is to say that they develop a tacit and implicit method for assessing and acting on the information brought by emotions of others when presiding and deliberating (managing the lay judges), but that this method to assess emotional information is rarely applied to judges' own emotions. The emotive-cognitive judicial frame does not readily offer conceptual access to judges' emotions.

Legal evaluation within the emotive-cognitive judicial frame is supposedly facts-based and straightforward; there is the evidence and there are the rules and procedures governing how to evaluate it in relation to the law. If the rules and procedures are followed, the verdict will be an objective fact, not the result of subjective, moral preferences or attitudes (which in this book we understand as emotive-cognitive positions). Morality is instead about taking a stance, a judgement based on involvement in a community, and thereby in a complex and messy reality far removed from the conceptual clarity of the law. Adhering to the method of legal evaluation thus allows judges to sustain belief and interest in the ideal of positivist objectivity (cf. Wettergren, 2010). Nevertheless, we argue, they can only do this because they *feel* the ideal as background (not conscious) emotional cues.

To summarize, we have seen that judges' professional interest as well as their feelings of confidence, satisfaction, and pride orient them towards mastery of the two main tools of judges' objectivity: (1) an impartial demeanour and (2) the method of legal evaluation (cf. Roach Anleu and Mack, 2017). The impartial demeanour is upheld by a balanced emotional display, in the form of either contained expression (passive stone face) or equal expressions towards both sides. Impartiality may contradict the policy of good treatment, because a passive stone face is not necessarily understood as neutral by distressed or upset lay people. In addition, the fact that the positivist notion of objectivity structures the entire set-up of the trial and the prosecution sometimes results in the impartial demeanour's seeming favouring of the accused. With the focus on the evidence and its legal weight and value, questions about truth and moral values are rendered irrelevant. Judges tend to put emotions in the same category as these two (truth and moral values), and thus assert that the method of legal evaluation is unemotional. However, as we have seen, background emotions are continuously present and necessary for judges' ability to identify relevant vs irrelevant information. Ultimately, when they succeed in judging according to the positivist objectivity ideal, they feel proud.

While judges are both physically and symbolically removed from the actual crime, prosecutors purify and translate messy reality into legal codes fitted for the method of legal evaluation. They stand with one foot on each side – messy reality and the neatly packaged legal reality. For this reason, their objectivity work is different.

## Prosecutors: partial objectivity

> It's kind of tricky that you are supposed to be objective, because of course we are, but ... I mean, we investigate for and against the accused [...] until we prosecute, and then we are still supposed to be objective, but when you prosecute, you only refer to the evidence.... Once you're sure that the overall evidence will hold, you only refer to the evidence that support a conviction; we don't call witnesses who appear unsure in this regard – that's up to the defence to do – so you are not entirely objective there....
>
> (Lara, prosecutor, 30+)

Prosecutor Lara pinpoints the contradiction and ambiguity at the core of the prosecutor's profession. Her description also reveals that she is not quite sure herself of how to deal with that contradiction and ambiguity, or how the legal system is set up to deal with it. The reliance on the adversarial procedure in the Swedish version of the civil-law system is based on the assumption that prosecutors can be both objective investigators of a crime and a party (partial) in court. In other words, prosecutors serve justice and the state based on a dual loyalty/commitment: to maintaining the objectivity and fairness of the law, on the one hand, and to pursuing and punishing those guilty, on the other hand (Bandes, 2006; Kjelby, 2015). There is no one solution for all prosecutors faced by this dilemma – some do not even see it as a dilemma – but we suggest that the demand for being objective in the investigation phase (inquisitorial) and partial but still objective in court (accusatorial) leads prosecutors to explore the difference in practice between impartiality and objectivity. In this section, we analyse how they go about doing this by balancing commitment and detachment, and guided by confidence and satisfaction in legal encoding. During preliminary investigations, the prosecutor's focus lies on objectivity work and thereby on the purification, translation, and preparation work that precedes the prosecutor's appearance in court.

### Balancing emotions of commitment and detachment

In contrast to judges, prosecutors safeguard a sense of moral righteousness inherent in the requirement to be committed to their work. This is not to say that they see the law and morality as one; they are just as keen as judges to keep these concepts separate in theory. In Chapter 2, we began discussing the particularly contradictive requirement on prosecutors to keep switching between commitment and detachment in order to be able to adhere to the objectivity ideal. In Chapter 4, we saw an example of how prosecutors try to maintain a detached relationship to victims, yet remain prepared to become flexibly engaged when victims need assistance.

Similar flexible detachment and engagement of prosecutors is required during the investigation phase, when objectivity demands neutral gathering of evidence while the police may be pressuring for a more partisan approach (see Chapter 5). In larger-scale investigations, prosecutors may be drawn into the excitement of the detective work, and the satisfaction coming from the growing evidence against the suspect (Bandes, 2006). Shadowing prosecutors in large investigations, we observed how they remained neutral and sceptical during the early investigation phase, before knowing which direction the investigation would take. When the evidence against a suspect grew and the case against him or her became stronger, prosecutors' engagement in the case grew correspondingly and they could display intensive emotional involvement. Moral emotions and the feeling rules of the emotive-cognitive judicial frame merged to fuel each other.

The following excerpt describes a meeting during the investigation conducted in a fraud case. In it, Linus the prosecutor and two police officers are listening to a series of wiretapped calls made by one of the suspects. The suspect had telephoned his target/victim – a retired man – several times, each time pretending to be a different person while trying to find out as much as possible about the old man's whereabouts.

On the recording, the suspect asks the victim: "Are you home alone and all?" Prosecutor Linus comments [angry voice]: "What an asshole – Are you home alone!" He discusses with the police officers and concludes: "[The suspect] is fishing around, trying to find out how [the victim] lives his life!" During the next call, made at the time of the crime in question, the recorded suspect suddenly says to someone "Go now!" Prosecutor Linus repeats that phrase asking the police officers what it might mean. One of the officers points out that there is also the sound of something like a car door slammed shut on the recording. They re-play this particular part of the recording a couple of times, and eventually everyone clearly hears the sound of the door slamming shut:

LINUS [EXCITED]: "Then they are two suspects, one in the car and one at the crime scene! Have we got both of their mobile phones on the same mobile tower?!"

POLICE OFFICER: "This is pure gold. [...] This is damn good!!"

LINUS: "This is really great! This is so much better than just having the story of an old man [the victim] describing their shrewdness!"
(Observation, fraud investigation, Linus, prosecutor, 40+)

The sound of the door slamming shut and the suspect saying "Go now!" meant that they could prove that the two suspects were at the criminal scene just before the crime took place. Based on the telephones being connected to the same mobile tower and other pieces of evidence, the investigation team could infer that the suspect commanded his accomplice to go knocking on the victim's door to commit the crime. After the meeting, Linus described feeling good and happy about the wiretapping's having paid off so well. Wiretapping requires lots of resources and it was his responsibility as a prosecutor to "hit the brakes" as he said, balancing the costs against the pay-off, asking questions like: "In which ways can this huge amount of material be used for prosecution and how can it support a verdict?"

This example with Linus' fraud investigation tells of the density of the emotional atmosphere in investigations, in which the police and the prosecutor work closely together and meet regularly to discuss new evidence and next steps. As we saw, Linus did not refrain from moral judgements and emotions, and he rejoiced with the police regarding the quality of the evidence gathered through wiretapping. We also see that Linus' professional detachment does not relate to the guilt of the suspect, of which he is convinced. When asked about his feelings for the suspect, he exclaimed: "A bloody asshole he is; he makes me mad!" Linus' detached concern is rather related to his duty as a state employee to ensure cost efficiency. While the costs of producing evidence must always be weighed against the severity of the crime, thinking about the costs may also be a technique for creating the detachment needed to manage and contain growing emotions of involvement.

At any rate, growing commitment is likely to orient one's interest, away from responsiveness to new information that does not conform to the direction in which an investigation is proceeding. Instead, such new information becomes wrapped in feelings of irritation, sensitized as "irrelevant" information. The moment the prosecutor eventually makes the decision to prosecute, commitment is rather solid and his or her focus narrows on the presentation of the evidence with the clearly defined aim of obtaining conviction. "If I decide to prosecute, I think, based on the investigation I have, that 'this will be convicted'" (Dagur, prosecutor, 35+).

During the trial, prosecutors' commitment may be further fuelled by their interaction with the victim(s), the behaviour of the defendant(s), and, notably, the defence lawyer's enactment of antagonism, which can be either fine-tuned or more openly aggressive. In one murder case, in which we shadowed prosecutor Charlotte, all these elements of reinforcement were present. The investigation had been complicated, demanding lots of resources over several years, but yielding also a lot of "good" evidence. As a result, Charlotte was strongly committed to get the defendant convicted. The moral dimension of her commitment was fuelled by a meeting she had with the victim's mother:

> We walk to the waiting room where the mother is sitting, and prosecutor Charlotte and she talk for a long time, even a while after the parties have been called to the courtroom. Charlotte, with tears in her eyes, silently listens to the mother's despair and grief, as well as to her thoughts about both the accused and her [deceased] son.
>
> (Observation, murder, Charlotte, prosecutor, 40+)

As seen in this excerpt, closeness between the victim and the prosecutor can prompt feelings of empathy for the victim, which are likely to reinforce the prosecutor's moral emotions and thereby commitment. In Chapter 4, we discussed this moral reinforcement in terms of dramaturgical stress – realizing the real suffering and need for justice behind the dry legal aspects of a case.

The defendant in the above case had confessed to murder, but argued self-defence, and had a generally soft appearance, which irritated Charlotte. During the trial, which lasted for several days, her irritation was sometimes expressed as moral outrage at the defendant for his lack of stamina and his attempts to appear as a victim himself, instead of assuming responsibility for what he had done. The defence lawyer wholeheartedly sided with his client and – in a rather aggressive manner – suggested that the prosecution was reluctant to see things that spoke to the defendant's advantage, which made Charlotte even angrier. In effect, the defence accused the prosecution for not being objective – a sure way to upset prosecutors.

This said, some prosecutors may well maintain a clear emotional distance and display only strategic empathy, in the interest of being able to work better with the victim in the case. It is, furthermore, not impossible for experienced prosecutors to actually remain sensitive to incoming new information in spite of emotional investment: both Charlotte and Linus expressed doubts regarding their case every now and then throughout the entire trial. During breaks and lunch hours, Charlotte reflected extensively on every piece of new information or argument brought up by the defence. Thus, while the antagonism between the prosecution and the defence in court may reinforce partiality and counteract prosecutors' objectivity, the emotive-cognitive judicial frame orients prosecutors to at least give the possible objections and new evidence a good thought before dismissing them. This is because there is also emotional investment in the emotive-cognitive judicial frame and the professional pride of sustaining it, which means that prosecutors must be at least theoretically prepared to bite the bullet and forgo commitment for the case for the higher purpose of commitment to the professional ideal:

> If you can't manage to [secure enough supporting evidence], then you must be honest and fair, because in that lies the objectivity. [...] I mean, I have no prestige and to me the issue is not whether I win or lose; that's not what you do as a prosecutor. The most important thing is to make the right decision, so you don't cause innocent people to be convicted. [...] You must rather let ten guilty people walk free than wrongfully convict one innocent person.
>
> (Henrik, prosecutor, 50+)

Henrik's statement represents a standard official response to the question on commitment vs detachment. Yet it also reflects how the manoeuvre to maintain detachment is done in terms of emotion management: through the decoupling of guilt in a moral sense and guilt in the sense of law. There is intense professional pride in the capacity to let "ten guilty people walk free rather than wrongfully convict one innocent person", reinforced by the shame-warning trigger that convicting innocent people would undermine the ideal of objective investigations. Yet, in our material, there were also prosecutors who, like Klara (35+), solved the commitment/detachment dilemma by interpreting the objectivity ideal in a practical rather than idealistic manner:

> On the issue of objectivity, Klara says she doesn't think that prosecutors always need to be objective. "If the accused has no defence lawyer, I ask defence questions, too, obviously, but if the accused has a lawyer it's not my job to be objective." She says this with emphasis: "That's how I look at it."
>
> (Fieldnotes, prosecution office)

To Klara, her objectivity in court depended on the situation of the counterparty rather than the circumstances of the crime: if there was a defence lawyer, it was no longer her role to highlight evidence speaking to the defendant's favour, whether such existed or not. Few prosecutors were as explicit about this as Klara, but our observations generally confirmed prosecutors' commitment to being partial in court to be stronger when defence lawyers were present (for more on this, see the last section in this chapter).

Moral emotions are quite visible in prosecutors' work, both during investigations and in court. In fact, moral judgements may help achieve professional detachment, as indicated by Henrik in the quote above, since moral judgements become an emotional outlet for prosecutors' potential frustration of having to withdraw charges. Thus, moral grounds for judging are not to be confused with legal grounds, but when the two converge, they reinforce each other and allow for emotional involvement in the particular case. When the moral and the legal diverge, commitment to the professional goal of objectivity overrides involvement, and detachment takes its place. Thereby, pride and satisfaction in commitment may remain intact, but the primary goal of commitment (to achieve either the objectivity ideal in principle, or to achieve justice in the particular case) shifts depending on the circumstances.

### *Aesthetic pleasure, satisfaction, and interest in legal encoding*

In line with judges' aesthetic pleasure and confidence in legal evaluation, prosecutors find satisfaction and interest in legal encoding. Legal encoding, as we have seen in this book, is one of the main functions of the prosecutor's profession, positioned as they are between messy reality and the reduced complexity of the legal world. The background emotions of pleasure and satisfaction in the expertise of legal encoding orient and sustain professional emotive-cognitive values of detachment, and of the objectivity ideal. Legal encoding determines whether a case can proceed to court or has to be dropped (and moral judgement and legal judgment diverge). Legal encoding provides the professional interest and pleasure that spur a minimum level of commitment even in routine investigations and grey trials.

Perhaps most importantly, legal encoding creates detachment in terms of emotional distance as prosecutors approach real crimes with a tunnel vision, protecting them from an emotional involvement that might disrupt their professionalism. As prosecutor Karen explains, reading the police interrogations of a case is "like a special kind of detailed dissection", explaining also how she approaches a testimony with an interested "focus on the prerequisites: How can I prove this?". Karen continues by giving the example of a domestic abuse case:

> You read a story in a very different way than a reader who's not a lawyer. If you read the defendant's statement, you know there will be standard objections like "it was self-defence". [...] So, OK, you read very closely until to the description of the first hit [Imitates internal dialogue:] "Did she do anything then? Did she shove him or...? No. OK". And then he began: Bam! Then he hit her. And you continue reading that way [detailing the abuse]. The rest of the story is less important.
>
> (Karen, prosecutor, 30+)

In this excerpt, Karen's strong professional focus is conveyed by the contrast between, on the one hand, the dry interest and focus on the prerequisites and evidence of the abuse, and, on the other hand, the underlying narrative as such, which contains vivid emotional cues ("Bam!") that are left uncommented. A man hits his girlfriend or wife, unprovoked. Karen approaches the story with an interest in legal encoding, and her description of how this works conveys satisfaction at finding the prerequisites for an abuse and not a self-defence ("did she shove him?"), and thereafter a sense of disinterest ("the rest is less important"). This satisfaction and Karen's subsequent waning interest illustrate prosecutors' aesthetic pleasure in terms of logics and consistency in building a case.

The emotional processes surrounding the selection and presentation of a case in court, once the decision to prosecute has been made, are similarly oriented by aesthetic feelings of consistency and logic. Evidence has been deemed sufficient for conviction, but there is usually a lot more evidence than can be presented. Deciding what kind of evidence to include and what to leave out is therefore another vital part of the legal encoding, as shown when prosecutor Cecilia (35+) prepares for an upcoming trial:

> She shows me a statement where a witness has said that it was not like a stab, but that he rather dug into her with the knife – "that gives a sense of intent, not just a temporary rage". She has highlighted that sentence and written "good" on a sticky note next to it.
>
> (Fieldnotes, prosecution office)

The excerpt speaks of both the judicial emotive-cognitive orientation with the associated emotional distance and the commitment to the case at hand ("good" evidence). When prosecutors decide to prosecute, they prepare their cases with an eye to convincing the court, and although they may be increasingly morally committed and emotionally involved, they also maintain an emotional distance necessary for their ability to do their work.

We see that the emotive-cognitive judicial frame orients prosecutors' approach to criminal events through their interest in legal encoding and the pleasure they derive from the beauty of finding new evidence that fits the picture. At the same time, this emotive-cognitive orientation almost automatically forecloses any emotional distractions, achieving emotional distance. Although, as we saw in the previous section, empathetic emotions may bring prosecutors close to the victim during the trial, and although moral and professional impetus of commitment intersect through this, prosecutors' prioritized orientation is professional, and professional goals may be variously motivated and oriented by background emotions of detachment and moral involvement.

In terms of commitment vs detachment, it should be clear that emotional distance is not the same as detachment. As we have seen, commitment to the case develops during the course of an investigation. Commitment can thus be entirely professional until prosecutors go to court and begin to interact with the victim. It is at that point that their commitment can also be reinforced by empathic perspective-taking of the victim, and in some cases – as discussed in Chapter 4 (p. 111ff) – dramaturgical stress makes it hard to uphold emotional distance. In the next and last section of this chapter, we combine the orientations of the different legal professionals to analyse the collaborative elements of performing objective justice in court.

## Objectivity work as collective achievement

In court, the different legal professionals with their different emotional profiles meet and interact. Judges' focus on impartiality and legal evaluation and prosecutors' focus on partial objectivity and legal encoding collaborate there, (ideally) achieving the objective rule of law. For this to happen, the tools of tacit signals and emotional communication (Chapter 4) need to be in place and mutually understood, and the power and status relations between the legal professionals (Chapter 5) must be respected.

Empathic perspective-taking belongs to judges' emotion management tools intended to not only help achieve a smooth procedure, but also attain the goal of the trial: correct procedure and good treatment. As we saw in the section on judges' impartiality above in this chapter, the balanced display of emotional expressions, crucial to impartial demeanour, becomes endangered if there is more need for empathic engagement on the part of one side. Other legal professionals may then step in to prevent the possible disturbance of the court ritual:

> I had a victim – it was a sexual offence – and she was literally shaking [...] and then it became a kind of teamwork between the victim's counsel and me. Because it's important that it's primarily the victim's counsel who is the one caring for her client. It's about the court's independence, that you don't [...] end up in a situation where the defendant feels that "they only care about the victim, I'm probably screwed already".
>
> (Naomi, chief judge, 50+)

Naomi is concerned about the emotionally upset victim because it may cause disturbance to the smooth procedure. Although only implied in the quote, by keeping her focus on impartial demeanour Naomi made sure through emotional communication that the victim's counsel would take necessary precautions to comfort her client.

The system with victim counsels was introduced in order to strengthen the legal position of victims, but it has also had the consequence of supporting (emotional) distance between the prosecutor and the victim and thus of preventing any confusion about the fact that the prosecutor represents the state and not the victim. Yet, our data shows that as parties in court, prosecutors generally consider empathic engagement with the victim to be part of their tasks, and they rarely trust victim counsels to fulfil this function alone. For good reasons, as it often turns out:

The hall outside of the courtroom is full of people on this first day of the murder trial. The murder victim's husband approaches and the prosecutor sits down with him on a sofa. [...] She gives him all her attention and takes time to listen to his worries about the trial. The injured party's counsel stands silently by their side for a short while and then leaves to chitchat and laugh with another lawyer a few feet away.

(Observation, murder, Cecilia, prosecutor, 35+)

Unlike this counsel, good victim counsels not only relieve the prosecutor – and the judge – of some of their emotion management burden vis-à-vis the victim, but, if they are skilled, also complement and sometimes improve prosecutors' examinations and closing statements with their own contributions.

Defence lawyers, of course, play a crucial role in the collaborative performance of objectivity work in court. The right to a defence is a cornerstone of the rule-of-law system, and both judges and prosecutors appreciate defence lawyers for this reason. However, in minor offences the defendant is usually unrepresented and both the prosecutor and the judge endeavour to support the defendant, thus substituting for the absence of a legal counsel:

If they don't have [a defence lawyer], then I have to think a bit about asking questions that illuminate the case from different perspectives. [...] And then the judge can also take the defence's role and ask questions that should be asked from the accused person's perspective.

(Elsa, prosecutor, 50+)

Here Elsa describes how she has to engage in empathic perspective-taking beyond the goal of pursuing her case against the accused, in order to also imagine the perspective of the defence (Wettergren and Bergman Blix, 2016). For prosecutors, these occasions to perform their objective role may not only bring professional pride, but they also demand a "double consciousness" (Goffman, 1990) that may be difficult to uphold.

If the role of the defence lawyer in the tripartite performance of objective justice is obvious when there are no defence lawyers assigned, it is a great source of prosecutorial irritation when lawyers fulfil their roles badly. Bad lawyers, from the perspective of prosecutors, are those who make too big a case – perhaps a show, even – of defending their client. Lawyers who make reasonable objections and grasp the quality of the evidence presented against their client are instead well liked for their part in performing the collaborative objectivity work. As explained by Valdemar:

PROSECUTOR VALDEMAR: There is this very skilled elderly defence lawyer who, if [he sees that] his client is done for, gets them to confess nine times out of ten and instead focuses on the sanction part. Then there are lawyers who are the exact opposite, lawyers who, in spite of overwhelming evidence, keep shouting about this and that, who keep complicating things and keep calling witnesses who might even be committing perjury. That's not something a good defence lawyer does; it just delays the process and makes it more costly, and sometimes it also puts the client in a worse position.

RESEARCHER: And still the same outcome.

VALDEMAR: Yes, although through a much more cumbersome process that costs more and brings more unnecessary suffering for everyone involved.

(Valdemar, assistant prosecutor, 30+)

As indicated in this quote, following the emotive-cognitive judicial frame, the evidence put forward by the prosecutor are objective. Lawyers that accept this claim also acknowledge the status of prosecutors as objective in the preliminary investigation, evoking emotions of mutual respect and recognition. Nevertheless, as we saw earlier in this chapter, even lawyers who insist on the point of their client's innocence when the evidence is overwhelming may force the prosecutors to rethink something of relevance. In relation to the overall goal of achieving objectivity, they are therefore considered better collaborators compared to passive or disinterested lawyers.

We have seen that prosecutors take pride in their capacity to withdraw charges if new information undermines their case in court. However, in actual practice, this capacity is often circumscribed. They are only allowed to change another prosecutor's decision to prosecute if there are new evidence. Furthermore, to openly dismiss or disapprove of a colleague's decision to prosecute goes against the team spirit and solidarity of prosecutors. As we have seen, unlike judges, prosecutors have quite a lot of respect and tolerance for collegial mistakes, given their workload and the frequent change of prosecutors in primarily minor cases. As part of their bounded independence, they are also careful not to evoke resentment among the investigating police officers by openly dismissing their work.

The most common thing to do is instead to signal one's wish to withdraw a case by tacit signals to the judge. For instance, one can steer the examinations in a way that calls attention to inconsistencies in the evidence (if a defence lawyer is absent or bad). In one case, a man was accused of threatening a security guard at a pub, but in the examination of the witness, serious doubts were cast on the security guard's/victim's story. It appeared that the guard had kicked the defendant's girlfriend and the defendant then told the guard that he "won't get away with that". At the trial, the prosecutor probed into this version of the story, thereby highlighting the doubts regarding the victim to the judge. After the trial, the researcher met the prosecutor Bertil (45+):

When I meet the prosecutor on my way home, he says that sometimes he wonders what has actually happened. "I don't want to be a part of someone being convicted on faulty grounds. Sometimes with security guards, you wonder if it's not the defendant who actually is the victim."

(Fieldnotes, prosecution office)

In this case, prosecutor Bertil afterwards admitted having felt unsure about the case, and yet he did not withdraw the charges but instead made sure to bring to light all the questionable aspects involved in the victim's story (the court acquitted the defendant). In a similar fashion, phrases like "I will leave it to the justice to decide" in prosecutors' closing statements serve as indications of the weakness of the case. Judges normally register such signals:

> I've had prosecutors who are really sincere and say, "There's a lot that speaks against the case, so I'll leave it to the justice to decide". [They say this] because many have ... well, they can't go against a colleague's decision to prosecute, for instance, so they can't tell the court to acquit, and they can't withdraw the charges, but they can formulate it like "I'll leave it to the justice to decide, whether this has been proven or not".
>
> (Ellinor, judge, 35+)

Tacit signals and emotional communication are important for the collaborative achievement of objectivity in court. Because they are tacit and build on silent knowledge acquired through experience, and because some signals may require understanding of other legal professionals' way of communicating, these signals are not always picked up, nor understood, and sometimes they miss the target. This is particularly the case for judges who do not want to risk sounding partial and instead become too subtle. In our observations, judges' tacit communication was often difficult for prosecutors to detect, as corroborated by those among them who had formally been judges. They spoke of having the advantage of "sort of knowing how judges think" (Lovisa, prosecutor, 40+) and of needing to often explain those signals to their colleagues. Lovisa continues:

> [When I was a judge] I didn't want to say it openly, because you didn't want to help the prosecutor to the extent that you became partial. That's hard, and it can become really strange, because the judge is hinting something and the prosecutor doesn't understand the hint at all.
>
> (Lovisa, prosecutor, 40+)

If and when judges decide to be explicit, it may go wrong. During our data collection at one court, a judge in a fraud trial in another court had to resign from a case after having been seen giving the prosecutors a note outside of the hearing, instructing them to adjust the charges of the criminal act (Malmö District Court, case B 645-13). Following the objectivity ideal, the prosecutors reported the judge for conflict of interest. The event became a topic of conversation among the judges in the courts where we collected data:

> The chief prosecutor says he is ashamed on behalf of the judiciary: "It's abominable for a judge to act like that; it undermines public trust and the legitimacy of the legal system". The story circulates as a joke, and is repeatedly referred to during coffee breaks.
>
> (Fieldnotes, court)

Disgust ("it is abominable") here is a moral emotional evaluation deriving from another person's claim to undue status (Kemper, 2011). Together with the way that this incident was discussed, it was clear that judges in our court felt ashamed on behalf of their colleague who, undermining the trust in the entire legal system, had proved unworthy of the status of the judge.

While judges and prosecutors share the same emotive-cognitive judicial frame, they realize its ideals – and particularly the ideal of objectivity – in different ways. The mutual collegial tolerance among prosecutors can be seen as a way to avoid shaming one another in a professional context where one is consistently subject to routine shaming and where demonstrated insensitivity is a means of gaining professional confidence. It stands in stark contrast to the poignant sensitivity of judges to their colleagues' professional transgressions and mistakes.

## Conclusion

Objectivity work in practice is emotionally loaded and requires skilled emotion management as well as sensitivity to tacit signals and emotional communication. The emotive-cognitive frame provides background orienting emotions, notably professional pride and shame, to help sustain the ideal of positivist objectivity. Meanwhile the feeling rules of the frame foreclose emotional reflexivity regarding background emotions influencing judicial decision-making.

Judges' objectivity work is focused on impartial demeanour, whereas prosecutors' objectivity work is contingent and shifting, depending on developments during the preliminary investigation and in court. Prosecutors continuously balance between commitment and detachment, striving to solve the dilemma of being partial yet objective. The emotive-cognitive judicial frame shared by judges and prosecutors does not allow law and morality to be confounded. Yet, prosecutors can comment on issues they find morally reprehensive, even when they need to mark that their moral evaluation is distinct from their professional decision-making. For judges, morality is above all associated with lay judges' emotional opinions and misunderstanding of the rule of law. The method of legal evaluation should be free from any moral judgement.

As translators (into the legal code), prosecutors need to manage emotions of involvement and commitment regarding the moral aspects of the cases they investigate and take to court. Their closeness to real events and the suffering involved makes dramaturgical stress a bigger issue for them than for judges. At the same time, prosecutors' method of legal encoding is vital for their ability to maintain emotional distance. Legal encoding provides the interest and orientation prosecutors need to follow their professional duty to dismiss cases that lack enough evidence to show a crime was committed, regardless of their level of (moral) involvement. By separating guilt in the moral sense from guilt in the legal sense, they can retain their pride in professional integrity.

Even if the method of legal evaluation also helps judges to keep an emotional distance and orient their interest away from issues of truth, they rarely face the question of emotional involvement as urgently as prosecutors do. The higher one gets in the legal hierarchy and the further the case proceeds, the more taboo it becomes to express moral emotions. This dissociation between morality and legal interpretation can be linked to the aesthetic dimension. The more removed from messy reality the case is, the more it becomes adjusted to legal interpretation. It is thus easier for judges to focus on the form, while prosecutors remain closer to the content.

## Notes

1 https://en.oxforddictionaries.com. Search words were "objective", "objectivity", "impartial", and "impartiality".
2 The appeal court trials do not include new examinations and cross-examinations, but instead the court reviews the video-recorded examinations from the district court.
3 Interestingly, Roach Anleu and Mack found that compassion was valued as important (and for men even more important) as empathy by Australian magistrates (cf. Roach Anleu and Mack, 2017: 69).
4 In 2014, 92% of the prosecuted cases lead to a guilty verdict in court (Nordén, 2015).
5 Interestingly, the only exception here were trials involving young offenders, at the end of which judges sometimes did express moral judgements, voicing moral concerns of a caring adult world in the hopes of persuading the offender(s) to thereafter stay away from a life of crime.

# 7   Concluding discussion

One key contribution of this book, we argue, is its detailed demonstration of how the emotive-cognitive judicial frame systematically silences emotions. In our data, even participants who willingly spoke about professional emotions and emotional processes had trouble articulating these. The emotive-cognitive judicial frame has no workable concepts, no distinct language for disentangling, ordering, or evaluating emotional information (see also Maroney, 2011). Evidently, the emotive-cognitive frame has a self-disciplining and performative function (Foucault, 1995; Reddy, 2001). "Emotion talk" does not need to be explicitly prohibited for the legal professionals to realize that it does not belong to the professional arena. Reversely, emotions are associated with the private, or, more exactly, the weak and failing private self. Nevertheless, by demonstrating how background emotions are part and parcel of the emotive-cognitive frame's silencing of emotions, in the various dimensions of legal practice, we have come closer to an understanding of how emotional processes are fundamental to professional life at large. In the following, we will first summarize the chapters and then expound upon some central themes in this book.

## Summary

Prosecutors and judges share the same background in legal education and, in Sweden, also in having served as a clerk in a court before entering into their separate legal specializations. This shared training entails adherence to 'the emotive-cognitive judicial frame'. The emotive-cognitive judicial frame provides the context within which legal professionals interpret their everyday work and interactions as essentially dispassionate or non-emotional, thus silencing the impact that emotions nevertheless have. Furthermore, the judicial frame is sustained and reproduced by emotions as implicated by the concept of 'group charisma' (Elias and Scotson, 1994). Group charisma adds the dimensions of collectivity and social status group, to Collins' (2004) interaction ritual theory. It is not only social bonds (solidarity) and emotional energy (individual emotional resources) that are generated in interaction rituals, but, depending on each group's social status, group charisma. The concept of group charisma refers directly to the fact that not all groups in society (whether professional or other) are capable of generating the same amount of solidarity and emotional energy. To be a member of the community of legal professionals promotes confidence, pride, and security (emotional energy). Individual members will therefore submit to the hardships and potential suffering involved in upholding the group's core values and ideals, oriented by pride in living up to the ideals and shame when failing to do so.

Although all legal professionals adhere to the judicial frame, their different work tasks and organizational settings lead them to develop different 'emotional profiles' consisting of everyday background emotional processes and emotion management strategies. Judges are at the top of the status hierarchy among the legal professions, as emphasized by the selection process into the judge profession and its continuous evaluation over several years to secure juridical excellence and "good judgement". Judges embody impartiality and independent pursuit of justice through their autonomous position. Their habituation and performance of autonomy are central for the legitimacy of the legal system as a whole and they proudly embody that system. Paradoxically, the judges' performance of autonomy depends on the prosecutors' ability to perform their role to purify, mediate, and encode messy reality into ordered matter to which the judges can apply their method of legal evaluation.

Prosecutors take pride in their purifying and translating role, but they are also exposed to critique and pressure due to their mediating position. The continuous attacks on their professional selves from lay people such as victims and defendants, as well as from other professionals such as police, defence lawyers, and judges, accentuate what we regard as their 'bounded independence': a constant pull between holding strong judicial power, on the one hand, and dependence on others to perform their work, on the other hand. In contrast to the constitutional loneliness of judges, prosecutors rely on their strong sense of solidarity with other prosecutors and their relatively high degree of tolerance for collegial mistakes. While judges embrace the ideal of positivist objectivity in their strict focus on evaluating evidence, prosecutors' objectivity work implies a navigation between positivist objectivity and embedded truth-seeking, as shown in their responsibility to present objective evidence in court, yet be alert to heed potential counterclaims. Prosecutors take pride in their flexible capacity to balance detachment and commitment. The division of labour and the distinct emotional profiles of prosecutors and judges are vital for the emotive-cognitive judicial frame's systematic silencing of emotions, and thus for sustaining the core ideal of positivist objectivity.

The organizational settings of the courts and prosecution offices also shape the emotional profiles of the respective professions. For judges, work is fundamentally organized around time as a tool; they take pride in contemplation and reflection. Prosecutors' work, on the other hand, is organized around time as a challenge; they take pride in their capacity to make quick decisions and to let go. These different relations to time support the orientation towards autonomy for judges as well as the bounded independence and teamwork for prosecutors.

Both professions are influenced by New Public Management ideals such as an increased focus on measuring outcomes, more administration, and digitalization, all leading to tighter time frames and a faster work pace. These features provide emotion management tools in themselves by organizing work in an assembly line structure, in effect pushing for emotional detachment. The call for time efficiency has also put more focus on "good treatment policies" to counteract the effects of an augmented mechanization. This focus, in contrast, leads to higher demands on judges in particular to develop deliberate emotion management strategies, including empathy, when meeting lay people in court.

The only articulated emotion in the court and prosecution organizations is fear related to threats. The growing attention to threats and focus on security alert the legal professionals to potential experiences of fear in their work. The feeling of fear, however, can be seen as an anomaly to a fair and legitimate legal system; increased control and security undermines trust and transparency in legal institutions. The legal professionals are therefore reluctant to give way to fear since fear undermines their professional self-confidence as well as confidence in the legitimacy of the legal system.

The disconnection between emotions and a belief in the legitimacy of the legal system safeguards the silencing of emotions implied in the emotive-cognitive judicial frame and promotes a 'teflon culture', assuming that emotions do not stick to legal professionals. The teflon culture undermines professional mechanisms for deliberate emotion management and renders emotions insignificant through techniques of 'othering', associating emotional distress with specified or unspecified others rather than themselves, and with 'ventriloquism', talking about emotions in indirect ways. A professional, it seems, endures emotional hardships, work pressure, and stress because they "don't have any emotions". The ability to manage emotions is explained by innate personality traits; traits that fit or do not fit with being a professional. As a result, even when management offers debriefing at the workplace, there is a general reluctance to use these resources. Submission to, and endurance of, hardships further accentuate group charisma and the recognition of belonging accorded to the individuals who possess the required personality traits.

To uncover the implicit background emotions and emotion management necessary for everyday legal work, it is efficient to approach the court as a theatre, including a stage (the courtroom), a script (the code of judicial procedure), and an appropriate language (the legal code). In order to perform the drama (moving a hearing forward in a procedurally correct manner), the legal professionals all need to play their parts, and emotionally tune in and communicate both openly, with lay people, and tacitly, with each other. They need to cooperate around challenges and obstacles, and produce the emotional authenticity needed for the lay audience's trust in the performance of justice.

Open communication directed at lay people is primarily made with the use of the two professional masks: 'stone face' and 'poker face' accompanied by subtle bodily gestures. Stone face is the primary judge mask communicating impartial listening, while poker face primarily is employed by prosecutors (and defence lawyers) to perform their adversarial parts in court. Both masks demand emotional toning – amplifying or attenuating emotional display depending on role requirements. 'Tacit signals' are used in inter-professional communication, primarily through looks and subtle gestures, such as the judge putting down her/his pen to communicate irritation. The legal professionals closely follow the procedural script, but the presence of lay people and the potentially dramatic content of the cases often demand improvisation. The professional actors employ 'situated adaptation' and 'strategic empathy' to better anticipate and avert potential obstacles for a smooth and procedurally correct hearing. The emotive-cognitive judicial frame embraces all these performing tools, but lay people's expectations on justice nevertheless entail potential ruptures of the frame, producing professional 'dramaturgical stress', such as when bureaucratic mishaps increase lay peoples' suffering.

The court ritual as well as the backstage legal work also rest on relations of dependence. Judges and prosecutors both belong to the powerful group that incarnates the state's monopoly of violence. Representing state agency equals power and power is an ambivalent "thing" to possess. Both judges and prosecutors balance power and status in order to avoid the naked face of repressive power. Power in a democratic context needs to be legitimate and legitimacy is associated with status; a person's judgment and deliberations will be heeded if the person is respected. The way power is mitigated by status follows the same logic for institutions, which is essentially the idea with procedural justice. The objectivity (impartiality and fairness) of power is also crucial for legitimacy. This said, prosecutors and judges approach their power and status as state representatives in different ways. Prosecutors' bounded independence and judges' autonomy produce different power and status relations, adding to the different emotional profiles of judges and prosecutors within the emotive-cognitive judicial frame. The role of the judge is tied not only to confidence and comfort of being in power, but also to conceivable emotions of guilt and remorse if their power is misused. Some judges habituate power by integrating its performance into their self-perception, accepting personal responsibility for their decisions. Others take a bureaucratic approach. They deny being in a position of power declaring that they merely apply the law. In court, the judge depends on ritual deference from the other professional actors to achieve legitimacy for the procedure. During deliberations, the judge engages in strategic emotion management to secure status and produce legitimate decisions.

The role of the prosecutor is tied to high empathic and emotion manage-ment skills, due to their bounded independence. Their power is mitigated by continuous negotiation of status to secure good relations to a multitude of actors such as police and judges. However, prosecutors' empathic skills are also combined with an insensitivity to others' emotions in order to secure their objective power, such as when they lose status by forcing victims to carry through with charges they want to withdraw. This complex web of sta-tus and power relations makes it a crucial capacity for prosecutors to flex-ibly manage and predict others' emotions and adapt relationally to them.

Judges' objectivity work is primarily oriented towards impartiality – the way justice is seen to be done in an objective way. They also focus on the method of legal evaluation to ensure that they do not concern themselves with moral judgement or beliefs about the truth. Prosecutors' objectivity work in-stead balances requirements of commitment and detachment, and becomes particularly precarious when they assume their role as a party in court.

In court, ideally, legal professionals engage in joint objectivity work, prem-ised by their different roles and emotional profiles, in order to secure the per-formance of objective justice. While failure to fulfil one's role causes discomfort and irritation for the other legal professionals, inter-professional power and status challenges, for the sake of manifesting one's professional self, also occur. Professional pride, power, and status are highly charged dimensions for legal professionals. Meanwhile, the smooth working of a hearing presumes mutual respect and ritual deference. Successful cooperation in this regard is often seen when the defendant is a first-time offender, young, insecure, and regretful, or in other ways intimidated by the sheer fact of (having to) being in court.

The emotive-cognitive judicial frame positions morality on the 'other' – irrelevant – side along with the emotions. We argue, to the contrary, that the rule of law rests on institutionalized collective moral consciousness and that the emotive-cognitive judicial frame is a moral compass in its own right, al-beit concerning good or bad ways to pursue the rule of law. As we have seen, common sense morality and perceptions of justice are closer to, and more readily expressed by, prosecutors who in their purifying work straddle the boundary between the messy reality and the legal code.

## The emotive-cognitive judicial frame and the self

The emotive-cognitive judicial frame shared and habituated by judges and prosecutors (perhaps lawyers in general) renders, we suggest, powerful group charisma, shaping the respective professional selves. Group charisma conceptualizes the simultaneous and ongoing subjectivation to, and habit-uation of, group norms and values, including the "right" and "wrong" ways to feel and think about one-self and about the world (cf. Johnson, 2010).

Group charisma (Elias and Scotson, 1994) furthermore explains the magic spell of sacred values that have become the tacit nodal points of a group's self-image, values that are thus both persistent and irritable. Sacred values become habituated by training. They become what Monique Scheer (2012) calls "emotions as practice". To submit these values to scrutiny is therefore associated with discomfort for the individual. The intensity of the felt discomfort varies individually, but some level of discomfort is bound to be felt.

The way that the emotive-cognitive judicial frame thus influences professional performance is bound to affect also the private self. As we have seen, when we discussed habituation of power in the case of judges (Chapter 2), professional subjectivation is aligned with the construction of one's sense of self. This means that part of the 'ontological security' of legal professionals' construction of 'self' relies on the values and ideals of the emotive-cognitive judicial frame. An interesting point about the concept of 'dramaturgical stress' (discussed in Chapter 4) is that it highlights the investment of the self in the professional role. When the professional sense of legitimate justice, as incorporated within the judicial frame, is threatened by the "realness" of the situation, as when prosecutor Henrik felt an overwhelming responsibility for the father's ordeal during the murder trial of a young girl, a crack in the frame occurs. The resulting dramaturgical stress signals an impending disconnection between the performance of justice according to the emotive-cognitive frame and the performance of justice according to lay people's expectations. But it also signals an impending crack between self and the professional role that threatens the status of both; their ontological security is destabilized. Peter Freund links dramaturgical stress to vulnerable, low-status groups, arguing that threats to ontological security derives from being in a vulnerable position, lacking a status shield, while having to be "open to the world" (1998: 285). However, as we have shown, high-status professionals in court whose power and independence to some extent is depending on the performance and deference of other professionals, along with a continuous demand for 'situated adaption', also need to be "open to the world", and thus vulnerable to threats to their definition of the situation within the emotive-cognitive judicial frame.

Nonetheless, the investment of self in the emotive-cognitive judicial frame makes the frame persistent and enduring in line with Elias' reasoning that "affective experiences and fantasies of individual people are not arbitrary" (1994: xxxvi) – they are created by and closely linked to the group and therefore likely to be strongly defended both individually and by the group. While "the elasticity of the bonds linking a person's self-regulation to the regulating pressures of a we-group" can vary on the individual level, it "has no zero-point" (Ibid: xii). This is to say that – because the individual sense of worth derives from group-relations – there is no such thing as an autonomous individual who can entirely escape the self-regulation imposed by the group's sacred values.

As implied by judge Christer (vignette, Chapter 5), in his argument about judges needing to habituate comfort in power, while remaining humble, the legitimacy of the powerful positions of legal professionals necessitates a continuous sensitivity to cracks, in effect to being vulnerable. Judges and prosecutors need to balance their comfort and pride, on the one hand, and humbleness and potential guilt, on the other hand. If taken too far, the aesthetic pleasure and pride in procedural correctness and legal encoding can become a way to tail away reality while trying to fit it with the model, in this case the law. Reality is never perfectly compatible with the legal frame, it is chaotic and unruly. The court needs to find a balance between the exactness and perfection of the legal frame and the chaotic reality represented by the laypeople whose narratives are heard in court. This can be paralleled to Weber's concerns about the iron cage of bureaucracy (Weber, 1995). The legal system's exactness and repeatability representing the ultimate iron cage rub against the chaos of reality. This creates an inbuilt tension in the hearings, a tension that is vital to preserve in order for justice to be just – if the law gets too much latitude we get the iron cage, if reality gets too much latitude we get chaos. In the same way, researchers can become so beguiled by their theoretical models that they lose sight of what the model is supposed to explain. Reality can become a disturbance rather than a foundation for the model.

On a more general note, we can see that in a frame that expects emotionlessness, we do not get less emotion, but rather a toning down of emotional display. The toning down in the Swedish court is extreme to the extent that subtly putting down a pen can signal a strong emotion. This implies that only professionals who themselves are part of the frame detect the ongoing emotional interaction, but also that to communicate, the legal professionals need to become very sensitive to emotions. An allegedly emotion-free rational environment thus raises emotional sensitivity.

### Refuges of the emotive-cognitive judicial frame

As we have seen, some of the hardships that submission to the group charisma of lawyers requires are associated with the inconsistencies and strain of the feeling rules of the emotive-cognitive judicial frame. In Reddy's words, submission to an emotional regime always causes some degree of emotional suffering, and the extent to which this suffering is alleviated has to do with the access to "emotional refuges" (Reddy, 2001). The use of the concept of frame (Goffman, 1974) makes it possible to distinguish different ways of managing emotions within different frames – the front-stage professional expressions are subject to distinct rules of subtle expressivity, which interestingly does not block backstage vivid expressions when recounting and/ or ventilating the front-stage experiences. The norms of non-emotionality and the focus on moving the procedure forward further a "letting go" of interactional emotional sparks, parking them out of the way until the coffee break or the ride home from work. In this way, the emotive-cognitive judicial frame can become habituated and thus be performed without deliberate or conscious strain, yet remain one of several frames within which the legal actors perform. The strictness and elaborate rules of the professional court performance demand meticulous emotion management training and habituation, but the evident front-stage rituality also paves the way for alternative frames in adjacent settings.

The emotional experience of performing objectivity and professionalism is largely the same in both back- and front-stage presentations. As described by judge Ruth in Chapter 1, her seriousness is an enduring and important emotion for her continuing after her retirement. Just like priests cannot believe a little less in God on their days off, judges cannot embrace objectivity a little less in the office than in a trial. Their emotional display, or how they express their emotions, however, is differentiated between the two arenas. The front-stage presentation is both restricted by the ritual (the code of judicial procedure), and by the ideal of non-emotional objectivity. The backstage, as described, shares the same "objective experience" as the front stage, but the presentation can be less conscientious and more relaxed. Judges, for example, never express any preliminary judgment, when the lay judges are present, and clearly distance themselves from any values that the lay judges sometimes express in breaks, but when the door closes and they are alone with the clerk, they can discuss where it leans, etc.; they both know that they are objective. The prosecutors can easily switch from the backstage joking about a type of defendant to the front-stage stearn demeanour: they know that all legal professionals backstage are objective. When we as researchers came to the courts and prosecution offices, this switch could almost happen midsentence; start out with the front-stage demeanour, and then relax back to the "sloppy" presentation when we became trusted.

### *Emotional profiles*

The concept of emotional profile pertains to how emotional reflexivity and emotion management are differently shaped for judges and prosecutors. Their different power and status relations, their different types of objectivity work, and their different types of organizations (courts vs prosecution offices) generate different emotional profiles for the professionals working there, even though both professions share the same basic legal training and work in the same courts (Table 7.1).

In terms of the script of judicial dispassion, identified by a number of previous studies on emotions in court (Maroney and Gross, 2014), it can be argued that the different emotional profiles are also shaped by the need to reproduce and sustain the illusion that emotions are irrelevant in legal professional work. In fact, the judges' lower dependency on others' acquiescence and collaboration makes the division between emotion and rationality more readily reproduced by them at a discursive level. In contrast, prosecutors more readily recognize and speak of the emotion management skills needed in interactions with police, lay people, and other court professionals. Given these insights, judges are less likely to tolerate ruptures in the presentation of objective justice and are more sensitive to critique against the legal system, than are prosecutors.

*Table 7.1* Professional emotional profiles of judging and prosecution

| The emotive-cognitive judicial frame | Judges | Prosecutors |
| --- | --- | --- |
| Status | Purity, removed from messy reality | Dirty work, straddling messy reality and the judicial code |
| Positivist objectivity | Impartiality; stone face or balanced emotional display | 'Be' objective; poker face, balance detachment and commitment, reflexivity |
| Time | Work tool; intellectual contemplation | Challenge; quick decision-making, multitasking |
| Power | Bureaucratic, responsible | Status as power resource |
| Independence | Autonomy, seclusion | Bounded independence |
| Work relations | Isolation, a trusted few | Team work, solidarity, and trust |
| Identification with the legal system (pride and shame) | Justice; low shame threshold | The prosecution office; high shame threshold |

Furthermore, legal work is evaluated along the lines of pure reason (Abbott, 1981), making it necessary to link inter-professional hierarchy of status to the court work's distance to concrete human matters, including foreground emotions. Prosecutors' transformation and purification of lay peoples' narratives into judicial codes for the judge to decide on thereby function as an inter-professional status marker. Prosecutors are closer to the "dirty" reality than are judges. This implies that the group charisma binding judges to the high held ideals of objective justice as devoid of emotion, including the belief that the legitimacy of the justice system relies on this ideal, is stronger for judges than for prosecutors. Meanwhile, judges can enjoy their higher status as closer to the ideal of pure reason merely because prosecutors prepare and serve them with a neatly encoded case. Judges' higher status relies on prosecutors' dirty work. The court ritual itself contributes to purification for the benefit of the judge, through procedural regulation and architecture; as we have seen, the design of the courtroom sets a physical distance between judge and the parties accentuated by the elevation of the judge's bench.

Judges' conformist autonomy, with its high expectations for procedural correctness and sound judgement, makes them sensitive to shaming if they make professional mistakes. Prosecutors' bounded independence, with its continuous exposure to criticism, promotes collegial solidarity and high tolerance for mistakes, effectively forming a shield against shaming (Wettergren and Bergman Blix, 2016).

Just like field observations of judges give the impression of a high degree of individualism, self-assurance, and identification with the legal system, field observations of prosecutors give the impression of solidarity within the profession, collective emotion management similar to what Olsson (2008) labels "emotional harbouring", and identification with the "office". This sense of community and collective emotion management functions as a shame shield supporting their professional exposure to status challenges.

## *Background emotions in the legal system – further reflections*

The theoretical approach taken by us in this book refutes the idea of pure rationality as unemotional. The notion of background emotions is a way to conceptualize that there are situations in which emotion functions to inform and orient action without being the focus of attention. The focus of attention we imply here is primarily the subject's own, because there are certainly situations where a perfectly rational professional is visibly (to others) fuelled by emotion. In Chapter 6, we saw how judge Niklas was enthusiastic about the conclusion of his legal evaluation. He never reflected on this enthusiasm because to him it was not disruptive to his rational goal, rather the opposite. This suggests that emotions can be backgrounded in experience but foregrounded in expression as long as it is in line with the feeling rules of the emotive-cognitive judicial frame (such as being enthusiastic about legal evaluation). Other emotional expressions may similarly escape the silencing of emotions: prosecutors' excitement about the progress of a tricky investigation; judges' anger about legal professionals' bad or inappropriate behaviour in court; prosecutors' expression of compassion for victims in court; and prosecutors' or defence lawyers' aggressive cross-examinations. This means that background emotions need not be characterized by low visibility, as suggested by Barbalet (2011) – they are merely "invisible" to the emoting subject.

The fact that background emotions and rational action are connected does not mean that foreground emotions necessarily disrupt goal-oriented action. Consider, for instance, the situation when a judge engages in strategic emotion management to induce interest and curiosity both in herself and in the lay judges prior to the hearing of grey trial (see Chapter 4, p. 107). At this point, emotion becomes foregrounded as an object of attention, but with the purpose to evoke the emotion needed to perform a desired action. Interest is indeed quite often an emotion consciously summoned by "emotives" ("this will be fun") when one is faced with a boring work task (Reddy, 2001). In this book, we have also seen that foreground emotion can have low, or close to no, visibility, particularly in a context like the emotive-cognitive judicial frame. Foreground emotions are toned down to the extent that it may be very difficult for anyone, but the legal professionals to see that the judge, for instance, is struggling with intensely experienced anger. Again, the foreground emotion becomes disruptive because of the feeling rules, and it is the effort to adapt to these rules that causes the subject's split focus. This suggests that when emotion is summoned to perform a desired action it is likely not experienced as disruptive.

That said, background emotions which are conducive to desired actions, in line with the feeling rules of the emotive-cognitive judicial frame, often have low visibility and pass below the radar of the self's experience of emotion. Legal professionals, particularly judges, may indeed believe that they have "no emotions" when they work. This brings us to the notion of "irrational" background emotions. Even if they are in line with the feeling rules and conducive to the action of performing justice, background emotions in legal practice may indeed lead to both good and bad, objective and biased, decisions. The reason for this is twofold. First, the discussion above regarding the self and group charisma suggested that the private and the professional selves cannot be as clearly separated as the emotive-cognitive frame implies. Instead, the memory bank of wisdom, intuition, and experience that are brought to us by emotion pertain to both the professional and private spheres. In other words, the background emotion regarding a victim's trustworthiness, or a defendant's fate were he to be convicted, may skew judgement. In the vignette to Chapter 6 in this book, judge Tina reflects on the possibility that she, like the lay judges, may be affected in her decisions when she recognizes herself in a defendant or victim. This brings us to the second reason: Within the emotive-cognitive frame, it is more or less impossible to reflect on, and to assess, the information brought by background emotions. As mentioned in the opening of this concluding chapter, "emotion talk" is automatically marked as unprofessional and this means that it will be associated with shame-warning triggers for the legal professionals. There is, as of yet, no way for a legal professional to reflect on the emotions that inform their decisions without running the risk of excluding themselves from those seen "fit" to do the job. When judge Tina ventures to do this anyway, and when all the participants in our project reflected on their emotions with us, it is because the research project created a safe space, and provided the theoretical tools, to do so.

Tina's example is inspiring because apart from actually reflecting on how background emotion may bias her decisions, she suggests two ways of dealing with this problem. One is "to go somewhere" and "unload" herself, implying some organized reflection on background emotions. The other is reflection initiated by the interaction between her-self and the lay judges. Instead of exclusively being embarrassed by them as being an out-group of disturbingly unprofessional legal actors, she uses their manner of deliberating as an entry to critical self-reflection.

If we are to propose any practical implications for the courts and prosecution offices based on our results from this book, it would be along these lines of critical reflections. At an early stage in our research we decided to be clear about one thing in relation to our participants: we would not promise them a five-step list entitled "How to learn to reflect about the quality of the information brought to you by emotion". Such a list would just turn into a standardized policy that would lose its meaning, and provide an additional source of stress and irritation. What we suggest instead is that the legal system opens up for critical reflection about the role of emotions in legal work, both at the structural and at the personal level. Courses and training providing tools and language to reflect on emotions can be useful, but there has to be an organizationally embedded tolerance of emotion talk and extended knowledge in the first place. By that we mean, of course, talk about both foreground and background emotions. The social space (promoting interpersonal trust) and conceptual tools created by us when we did our fieldwork serve as good examples. In fact, the project inspired processes of raised levels of reflection that many of our participants appreciated and found valuable for their work. If this would leave a mark on the prosecution and court organizations, it would imply freedom between colleagues to continue these mutual and continuous dialogues and discussions about emotions.

# Appendix
## The Swedish judicial procedure

While Scandinavian law adheres to the civil-law tradition with its base in legal codes, it is nonetheless regarded as distinct from other continental European law, in not being directly founded upon Roman law and in using case law to some degree. In Sweden, the law of today represents a revival of the country's unified Civil Code of 1734. The structure of the Code of 1734 remains, but the substantial parts are replaced, such as the Code of Judicial Procedure (from here on CJP). CJP was revised in 1942 (effectuated in 1948), turning the originally inquisitorial process with an active court to an adversarial process in which the judge functions as a passive arbitrator. Nevertheless, the Swedish criminal procedural system has elements of both inquisitorial and adversarial practices (Eser, 1996: 343; Forsgren, 2014: 219ff.); the pretrial features are in many ways inquisitorial, while the trial itself is adversarial. As Zila has noted:

> Unlike from a typical continental procedure, the Swedish criminal process has a distinctive adversial character. The judges are considerably less active during trial than [...] in a number of the European continental countries. In this respect, Swedish criminal procedure resembles the criminal procedure known in the common law countries more closely.
>
> (Zila, 2006: 287)

In their position, judges are to restrain from interpretations of their own, adhering, instead, to the written laws, along with its sources. This is in contrast to the more dynamic procedure in common-law contexts, in which judges actively shape the law through case law. This understanding of the legal procedure can also be traced in the CJP, as evidenced by its lack of elaborate rules of evidence – "what the judge finds relevant can be introduced as evidence" – and lenient rules on examination and cross-examination (Gomard, 1961: 37). Swedish courts can seem rather informal in that neither lawyers, nor prosecutors, nor judges wear robes or wigs: an ordinary suit is the costume in court, and prosecutors can appear even more informal wearing just a jacket and a pair of jeans. At the same time, however, the language used in court is normally impersonal and formal, avoiding first-person pronouns and rife with legal-bureaucratic terminology (Bladini, 2013). The Swedish legislation in general is significantly open and transparent (Wergens, 2002), with the legal procedure as well as all the documents pertaining to the procedure open for the public to access (CJP: Ch. 5, Art. 1).

All the legal professions in Sweden require a law degree, which is four and a half years long. Law school graduates hoping to become judges, prosecutors, or lawyers most commonly apply to serve as legal clerks in the lower courts (district or administrative courts). The position of a court clerk is a training position that involves taking clerk courses, preparing cases, taking notes in court in all matters, and writing draft judgments for the judge. The clerk does not have a vote in connection with the court's deliberations, but depending on the judge and the clerk's seniority, they may still be able to do what in Swedish is termed *votera*, which is to present their interpretation of the case and suggest a decision during deliberations. Eventually, they also get to preside in court in minor matters such as those involving traffic offences and shoplifting. The selection for the court clerk's position is based on grades from the law school programme, which is one reason why law school in Sweden is so commonly experienced as highly competitive and often stressful. An appointment to a court clerk position is considered a sign of recognition of one's excellence as a student and an opportunity to gain valuable work experience. Clerks serve for two years, after which many of them leave the courts. Following clerk service, the training is divided into separate tracks for prosecutors and judges.

## Prosecution and the prosecutor

After initial tests and interviews, the future prosecutors begin their training by working as a prosecutor trainee for a period of nine months. For the first eight weeks, they shadow an experienced prosecutor, followed by four weeks of shadowing different police units. The trainee programme also includes one month spent at another prosecutor's office and one week spent at the office of the Prosecutor-General. After the trainee period, the candidates are tried for a permanent position, embarking, if they receive a positive evaluation, on a two-year period as an assistant prosecutor. During this period, they take a total of 15 weeks worth of coursework. Upon its completion, the candidates become public prosecutors. Positions for specialized prosecutors can be found at the national centres and international offices, but, at the general prosecution offices, prosecutors may also specialize in certain types of crime such as domestic violence or youth offences. Prosecutors have a relatively secure steady employment. All in all, there are approximately 950 prosecutors working in Sweden. In 2016, 60% of them were women (Åklagarmyndigheten, 2017).

Prosecutors lead the preliminary investigations of suspected offences. In less serious cases, the investigation can be conducted by the police with the case then handed over to the prosecutor who summons those suspected to the trial. Prosecutors are required to remain impartial during the preliminary investigations: they have to investigate circumstances both incriminating and exonerating for the defendant (CJP: Ch. 23, Art. 4). The questioning of suspects and witnesses is performed by the police, often as instructed by the prosecutor.

During the preliminary investigation stage, the prosecutor also decides on coercive measures, such as arrest and searching warrants. When a person has been arrested, the prosecutor has three days to send to the court a request for the suspect to be detained. The court then decides on the matter in a *detention hearing*. For a detention decision, the person must be suspected with a probable cause along with a statutory penalty of a minimum one-year imprisonment for the suspected crime. In addition, there needs to be a risk that the suspect might flee prosecution or punishment, continue his or her criminal activity (*recidivism*), or obstruct the investigation (*collusion*). If the statutory penalty is a minimum of two years of imprisonment, the suspect is to be detained unless there is clear and established reason not to (CJP: Ch. 24, Art. 1–2). The prosecutor can also order restrictions to the detained person's contact with the outside world, including their access to newspapers, visits they may receive, or telephone calls they can make. Sweden has recurrently been criticized by the European Committee for the Prevention of Torture and Inhuman or Degrading Treatment or Punishment for the length of detention in isolation in the country, particularly on the part of youth suspects (SOU, 2016: 52: 75ff).

At the end of the preliminary investigation, the prosecutor decides whether to prosecute or close down the case. If there is enough evidence, prosecution is mandatory in most cases (Wergens, 2002). Closing the case is an option when the cost of conducting the investigation is likely to be greater than the significance of the matter, or when the interest of the state is low, such as in cases like theft within the family (CJP: Ch. 20, Art. 4a). The crime victims are not to influence the decision, and it is not possible to 'drop the charges'. Moreover, plea bargains are not permitted in Sweden[1]; if the prosecutor decides to pursue the case, a trial is the only possible outcome (Åklagarmyndigheten, 2017).

Compared to other European countries, prosecutors in Sweden possess considerable judicial power (Zila, 2006: 287). If the prosecutor finds that there is sufficient evidence, the suspect has admitted to the criminal act, and the alleged offence carries a conditional sentence or a fine, he or she can order a summary punishment (such as, e.g., when the case is of a traffic offence, shoplifting, or theft).[2] In cases where concurrent sentences are passed or the offenders are young (15–18 years), the prosecutor can also grant a waiver of prosecution or initiate mediation (when the defendant is 15–21 years old). In 2016, 22% of the decisions by the prosecution authorities led to a notification in the criminal records registry without a court being involved (Åklagarmyndigheten, 2017). In relatively trivial matters ('grey trials'), it is common that the preliminary investigation and the trial are handled by different prosecutors, but in more serious or complicated matters the prosecutor can decide to handle the matter all the way from preliminary investigation to the end of the trial and potential appeal process.

Sweden has a relatively low level of incarceration. In 2016, there were 53 persons imprisoned for every 100,000 persons in the national population, while in the US, which scored the highest in the world, the corresponding figure was 666 (World Prison Brief, 2017). Such differences are partly explained by the facts that Sweden traditionally adheres to norms of restorative rather than retributive justice and the correctional institutions are all state owned.

In criminal matters, the prosecutor initiates the prosecution by sending the court a written application for a summon against the person to be charged. The application has to contain a classification and a description of the offence. The prosecution cannot be changed, but it can be extended, adding new alleged acts or new circumstances. The prosecutor can also decide to change the legal qualification of the act at the trial, or even withdraw the prosecution, if new evidence is presented to the court before judgment has been delivered (CJP: Ch. 20, Art. 9). In court, the prosecutors take the role of the accusing/state party, although they still need to remain objective. New or unexpected circumstances coming to light during the trial will have to be considered regardless of whether they are incriminating or exonerating for the defendant (CJP: Ch. 45, Art. 3a).

In contrast to common-law practices, the injured party has a strong position and is included in the proceedings (Zila, 2006). "The Swedish word for injured party literally means 'he (sic!) who owns the case'" (Wergens, 2002: 270). In cases where the victim has died, the family represents the injured party. A hearing involving a victim includes an examination of the injured party (CJP: Ch. 46, Art. 6). In murder cases, the bereaved family can thus sit right next to the prosecutor during the entire trial.

## The court and the judge

The general courts in Sweden deal with both criminal and civil cases. There are 48 district courts representing the first instance of the general courts. In addition, there are six appellate courts. The court of last instance is the supreme court, which reviews cases from the appellate courts upon their decision to grant a review permit (CJP: Ch. 54, Art. 10).

All in all, there are approximately 2,300 judges working in Sweden. In 2016, 1,225 of them had a permanent position, 52% of them were women and 6% were first- or second-generation immigrants. 753 judges served on district courts (Domstolsverket, 2017). As there are no specialized courts and no specialization in the general courts in Sweden, all judges handle all types of cases, both criminal and civil. Presiding in most district court trials are one professional judge and three lay judges. In the appellate courts, the proportion is reversed, with the courts composed of three professional judges and two lay judges. Lay judges have no formal legal education; they are selected from the political parties, their appointment is for four years, and they can be re-elected. The mean age of lay judges in the country is 58 years (Domstolsverket, 2015).

Judge is a career profession in Sweden, with an extensive training required before appointment. To begin with, one can apply to the judge programme only after having worked for two years as a court clerk. Admittance requires excellent grades from the law school and excellent credentials from clerk service. The training starts in a high court (a general or an administrative court of appeal), where the future judges prepare cases for decision. After a year, the judge candidates move to a lower court where they serve for two years as associate judges. As associate judges, they are in principle allowed to preside in all matters, although in reality there is a gradual progression in terms of the severity of the matter they can decide in. Following the two years, the judge candidates spend another year in the high court, this time as an acting member of the court. The training also includes ten weeks worth of coursework, spread out over the programme years. Upon the completion of the training programme, the judge candidates are awarded the title of assessor and can, in principle at least, now apply for permanent positions. However, it is common for the graduates to first serve at the ministry of justice or the Supreme Court for some years and also take substitute positions as a judge while waiting for an opportunity to apply for a permanent position. The common practice for assessors to work in the justice ministry for some time on legislative matters before seeking appointment as a judge, has been argued to reinforce "a civil service mentality" among them (Sundberg, 1969: 203). Another alternative is to become appointed as a judge based on work experience, for instance, as a prosecutor, a lawyer, or a law professor. This, however, only became possible in 2007, and thus does not represent a very common path; still, there were a few examples of it in our study.

During the judges' training and before their actual appointment, there are high demands for conformity: trainees are evaluated by the other judges sitting in the court, while the Chief Judge gathers information from the chief prosecutor of the associated prosecution office. The mean age of first-time judge appointees in the country is 44 years; the permanent appointments are made by the government. In order to protect the judicial independence of judges, their security of tenure is stronger than any other position in Sweden (Regeringsformen: Ch. 11, Art. 7).[3]

## Lawyers

Public defence lawyers are ordinarily members of the Swedish Bar Association and are assigned to a case by the court. The court has a list of lawyers available in the region, from which, when the defendant does not wish to engage any particular individual, it picks one in the order they are given. Lawyers who decline court assignments without a valid reason are eventually removed from the list (field notes).

The defendant has the right to have a defence lawyer if she is detained or if the crime in question carries a mandatory minimum sentence of six months imprisonment. Legal representation should also be assigned to defendants should they require it during the preliminary investigation, when the possible mandatory sentence is ambiguous, or when there are particular reasons for it owing to the nature of the case or the defendant's personal circumstances (CJP: Ch. 21, Art. 3a). In one case in this study, the defendant was intellectually disabled, for which reason the judge cancelled the trial in order to appoint a defence lawyer, explaining that the court doubted the defendant's ability to make his case. Defence lawyer's fees are reviewed and ruled on by the court, with the costs paid by the state when the defendant lacks the means to do so (CJP: Ch. 31, Art. 1).

The suspect or his or her lawyer can suggest certain particular investigative measures, but it is always the prosecutor who decides on the measures to be taken. Upon the completion of the investigation, the suspect (and his or her lawyer) is informed of its content, and if the decision is made to prosecute the case, the defence lawyer will receive a copy of the investigation protocol (CJP: Ch. 23, Art. 21).

During the 1980s and 1990s, several legislative changes were implemented to further protect the rights of the injured party in criminal proceedings. This meant, among other things, the introduction of an expanded right to legal representation in court, especially in cases involving violence (Enarsson, 2013; Wergens, 2002). Unlike defence lawyers, the legal advisor of the victim does not have to be a member of the Bar Association. In practice, victims are often represented by freshly minted lawyers looking for work experience in order to be able to enter the Bar Association. The assignment tends to be of lower status than working as a defence lawyer.

### The trial

The two main principles governing the trial proceedings in Sweden are those of *orality* (CJP: Ch. 46, Art. 5) and *immediacy* (CJP: Ch. 30, Art. 2). They imply that the evidence should be presented orally; the parties should, in general, talk freely; and the judgment should be based on the facts presented during the trial. In the following, the ritual of the trial will be presented.

In the district courts, the professional judge chairs the sessions and is the only representative of the court to speak during the trial. If the lay judges have questions, they forward them on a note to the presiding chair. The chair verifies the presence of all those required in the room and that there are no impediments for the hearing to take place; witnesses are usually not allowed in the room before their examination. The chair then asks the prosecutor to present his or her claims. If the injured party claims compensation for damages but is unrepresented, the prosecutor also makes a claim for compensation. After that, the chairperson asks the defendant (or the defence lawyer) about his or her plea to the charges and to the claim for damages.

The prosecutor develops the particulars of the claim, describing the circumstances and presenting the written evidence. Written evidence can either be read aloud or merely referred to (if granted permission by the other party and the court). When the prosecutor has developed his or her claims, the defence is given an opportunity to present its version of the matter (CJP: Ch. 46).

The examinations in court begin with the injured party. In some cases, the examination of victims and witnesses can take place without the defendant's presence in the room, in which case the latter will sit in another room and follow the proceedings through a video link. In most cases, the prosecutor first asks the victim to provide a full account of the events before probing into details. The defence then cross-examines the victim. If the statement given in court differs from the statement given to the police during preliminary investigation, the prosecutor and the defence lawyer may obtain the court's permission to also read aloud extracts from the police examination record.[4] There is a principle according to which crime victims must not be "unduly subjected to inconveniences in the proceedings" (Wergens, 2002: 259) although judges often find it difficult to interfere in court examinations in this regard (Heuman, 2007: 224). The presiding judge can ask clarifying questions during all examinations, but should refrain from asking questions that result in the defendant being convicted. After the examination of the victim, the judge asks the defendant to give his or her description of the events. Should the defendant not want to make a full statement or has difficulty providing the description, the judge can leave the questioning to the prosecutor. That it is the judge who first addresses the defendant in this regard is to provide the latter with an opportunity to give his or her account in full without being interrupted by questions. Following the examination by the prosecutor, the defence lawyer can ask complementary questions to the defendant.

Once the examination of the victim and the defendant is over, witnesses are called in one at a time. If they are not related to the defendant, they must first take the oath, with the court chair informing them about the consequences of perjury. The one calling the witness – the prosecutor or the defence lawyer – will begin the questioning (CJP: Ch. 36, Art. 11).

When all examinations have been concluded, the court chair reviews the defendant's personal circumstances, including prior criminal history and any reports from the non-custodial authority (the unit at the country's prison and probation authority that handles probation matters). The chair then asks questions directly from the defendant concerning his or her financial status. In some cases, also guardians or other relatives are asked to describe the defendant's living conditions at this point. The last part of the public phase of the trial consists of the closing statements by the prosecutor and the defence lawyer, summing up their arguments including their demand for any sanction.

If the trial is of short duration, the chair and the lay judges often begin their deliberations immediately afterwards, staying behind in the courtroom behind closed doors. The deliberations are closed to outsiders and the discussions remain confidential even after the judgment has been delivered. During the deliberations, the chair is the first to present her arguments, referring to the applicable sections of the law (CJP: Ch. 30, Art. 7). Then each lay judge's opinion is heard. Sometimes, as part of the court clerk training, the court clerk is asked to speak first, while still having no vote in the verdict. The verdict and the sentence are decided through a simple majority vote by the professional judge and the lay judges. If the vote is not unanimous, it should be stated in the judgment, and if it is a tie the most lenient vote determines the verdict (CJP: Ch. 29). The professional judge delivers the judgment, sometimes orally in direct relation to the trial, but always in a written form as well, sent to the parties by mail.

Both the prosecutor, the defendant, and the victim can appeal the verdict to an appellate court, but, in some circumstances (as in minor matters), a review permit is required (CJP: Ch. 20, Art. 2). From 2008 onward, only entirely new evidence or complementary examinations have been allowed in appellate courts. As a rule, the district court examinations are to be presented to the appeal court by video (The Ministry of Justice, 2015), as a result of which the procedure in the appellate courts in practice, to a large extent, consists of watching video recordings from the country's district courts.

## Notes

1 Zila has argued that

> [i]t doesn't exist any kind of simplified criminal proceedings in court according to the Swedish law. Once the prosecution in court has been instituted, the proceedings follow the rules mentioned above. However, the fact whether the suspect has confessed to the offence or not, influences presentation of evidence. If the defendant has confessed the offence, the presentation of evidence will be simplified, but it is a matter of fact, not a question of different rules.
>
> (2006: 292)

2 In most cases, the prosecutors will order a summary punishment when possible, but the decision to do so remains theirs. When asked about how prosecutors deal with child pornography cases, one prosecutor stated that one way was to always force them to actually show up in court (i.e. not to order a summary punishment), so that the offender will have to bear the shame of a trial.

3 Permanent judges can only be removed from office if they have committed a "criminal act or through gross or repeated neglect of his or her official duties" shown themselves to be unfit for their office, or when they have reached retirement age or lost their working capacity for a protracted time (Regeringsformen: Ch. 11, Art. 7).

4 There are two types of interrogation records produced by the Swedish police: "dialogue interrogation reports", which are verbatim transcripts of the police interrogation carried out, and "summary interrogation reports", which present a summary of the interrogation carried out by the police. A common complaint by defendants, witnesses, and also judges is that the summary reports are not nearly always accurate.

# References

Abbott Andrew (1981) Status and Status Strain in the Professions. *American Journal of Sociology* 86: 819–835.

Abrams Kathryn (2010) Empathy and Experience in the Sotomayor Hearings. *Ohio North University Law Review* 36: 263–286.

Agar Michael (1986) *Speaking of Ethnography*. London: SAGE.

Alvesson Mats and Sköldberg Kaj (2009) *Reflexive Methodology: New Vistas for Qualitative Research*. London: SAGE.

Anwar Shamena, Bayer Patrick and Hjalmarsson Randi (2015) Politics in the Courtroom: Political Ideology and Jury Decision Making. Working paper No 622: National Bureau of Economic Research.

Arendt Hannah (1977) *Eichmann in Jerusalem: A Report on the Banality of Evil*. New York, NY: Penguin Books.

Arendt Hannah (1998) *The Human Condition*. Chicago, IL: University of Chicago Press.

Ashforth Blake E. and Kreiner Glen E. (1999) "How Can You Do It?" Dirty Work and the Challenge of Constructing a Positive Identity. *Academy of Management Review* 24: 413–434.

Asplund Johan (1992) *Det sociala livets elementära former (The Elementary Forms of Social Life)*. Göteborg: Korpen.

Bandes Susan A. (1996) Empathy, Narrative, and Victim Impact Statements. *The University of Chicago Law Review* 63: 361–412.

Bandes Susan A. (1999) *The Passions of Law*. New York, NY: New York University Press.

Bandes Susan A. (2006) Loyalty to One's Convictions: The Prosecutor and Tunnel Vision. *Howard Law Journal* 49: 475–494.

Bandes Susan A. (2009) Empathetic Judging and the Rule of Law. *Cardozo Law Review De Novo* 133–148.

Barbalet Jack (1998) *Emotion, Social Theory, and Social Structure – A Macrosociological Approach*. Cambridge: Cambridge University Press.

Barbalet Jack (2011) Emotions beyond Regulation: Backgrounded Emotions in Science and Trust. *Emotion Review* 3: 36–43.

Bergman Blix Stina (2009) Emotional Participation – The Use of the Observer's Emotions as a Methodological Tool When Studying Professional Stage Actors Rehearsing a Role for the Stage. *Nordic Theatre Studies* 21: 29–38.

Bergman Blix Stina (2015) Professional Emotion Management as a Rehearsal Process. *Professions and Professionalism* 5: 1–15.

184    *References*

Bergman Blix Stina and Wettergren Åsa (2016) A Sociological Perspective on Emotions in the Judiciary. *Emotion Review* 8: 32–37.

Bergman Blix Stina and Wettergren Åsa (2018) Humour in the Swedish Court: Managing Emotions, Status and Power. In: Milner Davis Jessica and Roach Anleu Sharyn (eds) *Judges, Judging and Humour*. London: Palgrave Macmillan, 179–209.

Björk Micael (2014) Polisens brottsutredningar: Problem, förklaringar, utvägar. (The Crime Investigations of the Police: Problems, Explanations and Ways Out). https://polisen.se/PageFiles/506240/polisens_brottsutredningar.pdf.

Bladini Moa (2013) *I objektivitetens sken: en kritisk granskning av objektivitetsideal, objektivitetsanspråk och legitimeringsstrategier i diskurser om dömande i brottmål (In the Semblance of Objectivity – A Critical Review of Objectivity Claims and Legitimation Strategies in Criminal Trial Discourses)*. Göteborg: Makadam förlag.

Bloch Charlotte (1996) Emotions and Discourse. *Text* 16: 323–341.

Bloch Charlotte (2016) *Passion and Paranoia: Emotions and the Culture of Emotion in Academia*. London: Routledge.

Booth Tracey (2012) 'Cooling Out' Victims of Crime: Managing Victim Participation in the Sentencing Process in a Superior Sentencing Court. *Australian & New Zealand Journal of Criminology* 45: 214–230.

Bourdieu Pierre (1999) *Distinction – A Social Critique of the Judgement of Taste*. London: Routledge.

Bowen Deirdre M. (2009) Calling Your Bluff: How Prosecutors and Defense Attorneys Adapt Plea Bargaining Strategies to Increased Formalization. *Justice Quarterly* 26: 2–29.

Brannigan Augustine and Lynch Michael (1987) Credibility as an Interactional Accomplishment. *Journal of Contemporary Ethnography* 16: 115–146.

Brennan Jr William J. (1988) Reason, Passion, and the Progress of the Law. *Cardozo Law Review* 10: 3–23.

Burkitt Ian (2012) Emotional Reflexivity: Feeling, Emotion and Imagination in Reflexive Dialogues. *Sociology* 46: 458–472.

CJP. The Swedish Code of Judicial Procedure (Rättegångsbalken) 1942.

Clark Candace (1987) Sympathy Biography and Sympathy Margin. *The American Journal of Sociology* 93: 290–321.

Clark Candace (1997) *Misery and Company. Sympathy in Everyday Life*. Chicago, IL: University of Chicago Press.

Collins Randall (1981) On the Microfoundations of Macrosociology. *The American Journal of Sociology* 86: 984–1014.

Collins Randall (1988) Theoretical Continuities in Goffman's Work. In: Drew Paul and Wootton Anthony (eds) *Erving Goffman – Exploring the Interaction Order*. Cambridge: Polity Press, 41–63.

Collins Randall (2004) *Interaction Ritual Chains*. Princeton, NJ: Princeton University Press.

Dahlberg Leif (2009) Emotional Tropes in the Courtroom: On Representation of Affect and Emotion in Legal Court Proceedings. *Nordic Theatre Studies* 21: 129–152.

Damasio Antonio R. (2003) *Descartes misstag: känsla, förnuft och den mänskliga hjärnan (Descartes' Error: Emotion, Reason and the Human Brain)*. Stockholm: Natur och kultur.

Damasio Antonio (2009) When Emotions Make Better Decisions – Antonio Damasio. www.youtube.com/watch?v=1wup_K2WN0I.

Darbyshire Penny (2011) *Sitting in Judgment: The Working Lives of Judges*. Oxford: Hart Publishing Ltd.

Daun Åke (1996) *The Swedish Mentality*. University Park, PA: The Pennsylvania State University Press.

Diesen Christian (2015) *Bevis: Bevisprövning i brottmål (Evidence: Evaluation of Evidence in Criminal Trials)*. Stockholm: Norstedts juridik.

Domstolsverket (2015) Uppdrag till Domstolsverket att genomföra särskilda informationsinsatser inför nämndemannavalet 2014 Slutrapport (The Swedish National Courts Administration). www.domstol.se/upload/Slutrapport%20upp drag%20informationsinsatser%20n%C3%A4mndemannaval%202014%20 Ju2014_2894_DOM.pdf.

Domstolsverket (2017) The Swedish National Courts Administration Annual Report. www.domstol.se/Ladda-ner--bestall/Verksamhetsstyrning/Arsredovisning/ Arsredovisning-2016/.

Du Gay Paul (2008) 'Without Affection or Enthusiasm' Problems of Involvement and Attachment in 'Responsive' Public Management. *Organization* 15: 335–353.

Durkheim Emile (2008) *The Elementary Forms of Religious Life*. Oxford: Oxford Paperbacks.

ECHR. European Convention on Human Rights 2010.

Ekelöf Per Olof, Edelstam Henrik and Heuman Lars (2009) *Rättegång IV (The Trial, Part 4)*. Stockholm: Nordstedts Juridik.

Elias Norbert and Scotson John L. (1994) *The Established and the Outsiders*. London: SAGE.

Enander Viveka (2010) "A Fool to Keep Staying": Battered Women Labeling Themselves Stupid as an Expression of Gendered Shame. *Violence Against Women* 16: 5–31.

Enarsson Therese (2009) Acknowledging Victims. The Implementation of Victims' Rights in National Justice Systems. In: Granström Görel and Hjertstedt Mattias (eds) *Lagstiftning i teori och praktik*. Department of Law. Umeå: Umeå University, 33–44.

Enarsson Therese (2013) *Brottsoffer i rättskedjan: en rättsvetenskaplig studie av förhållandet mellan brottsoffers rättigheter och rättsväsendets skyldigheter (Victims of Crime in the Judicial System – A Legal Study of the Relationship Between Victims' Rights and the Responsibilities of Actors in the Judicial Process)*. Uppsala: Iustus förlag.

Eser Albin (1996) Acceleration of Criminal Proceedings and the Rights of the Accused: Comparative Observations as to the Reform of Criminal Procedure in Europe. *Maastricht Journal of European and Comparative Law* 3: 341–370.

Feldman Barrett Lisa (2013) Psychological Construction: The Darwinian Approach to the Science of Emotion. *Emotion Review* 5: 379–389.

Fineman Stephen (1995) Stress, Emotion and Intervention. In: Newton Tim (ed) *'Managing' Stress: Emotion and Power at Work*. London: SAGE, 120–135.

Fisher Stanley Z. (1987) In Search of the Virtuous Prosecutor: A Conceptual Framework. *American Journal of Criminal Law* 15: 197–261.

Flower Lisa (2014) The (Un)emotional Law Student. *International Journal of Work Organisation and Emotion* 6: 295–309.

Flower Lisa (2018) Doing Loyalty: Defense Lawyers' Subtle Dramas in the Courtroom. *Journal of Contemporary Ethnography* 47: 226–254.

Forsgren Mikael (2014) Opartiska domare och effektiv resurshantering (Impartial Judges and an Efficent Use of Resources). *Svensk Juristtidning (Swedish Law Journal)* 217–225.

Foucault Michel (1995) *Discipline and Punish: The Birth of the Prison.* New York, NY: Random House.

Francis Andrew (2006) 'I'm Not One of Those Women's Libber Type People but…': Gender, Class and Professional Power within the Third Branch of the English Legal Profession. *Social & Legal Studies* 15: 475–493.

Freund Peter ES. (1998) Social Performances and Their Discontents – The Biopsychosocial Aspects of Dramaturgical Stress. In: Bendelow Gillian and Williams Simon J. (eds) *Emotions in Social Life.* London: Routledge, 268–294.

Goffman Erving (1956) Embarrassment and Social Organization. *The American Journal of Sociology* 62: 264–271.

Goffman Erving (1959) *The Presentation of Self in Everyday Life.* Garden City, NY: Doubleday.

Goffman Erving (1961) *Encounters: Two Studies in the Sociology of Interaction.* Indianapolis, IN: The Bobbs-Merrill Company, Inc.

Goffman Erving (1967) *Interaction Ritual. Essays on Face-to-Face Behavior.* Garden City, NY: Pantheon Books.

Goffman Erving (1974) *Frame Analysis: An Essay on the Organization of Experience.* Boston, MA: Northeastern University Press.

Goffman Erving (1990) *Stigma: Notes on the Management of Spoiled Identity.* Harmondsworth: Penguin.

Gomard Bernhard (1961) Civil Law, Common Law and Scandinavian Law. *Scandinavian Studies in Law* 5: 27–38.

Goodrum Sarah (2013) Bridging the Gap between Prosecutors' Cases and Victims' Biographies in the Criminal Justice System through Shared Emotions. *Law and Social Inquiry* 38: 257–287.

Granhag Pär Anders, Strömwall Leif A and Hartwig Maria (2005) Granting Asylum or Not? Migration Board Personnel's Beliefs about Deception. *Journal of Ethnic and Migration Studies* 31: 29–50.

Halkier Bente (2011) Methodological Practicalities in Analytical Generalization. *Qualitative Inquiry* 17: 787–797.

Harris Lloyd C. (2002) The Emotional Labour of Barristers: An Exploration of Emotional Labour by Status Professionals. *Journal of Management Studies* 39: 553–584.

Henderson Lynne (1987) Legality and Empathy. *Michigan Law Review* 85: 1574–1655.

Herzog-Evans Martine (2014) *French Reentry Courts and Rehabilitation: Mister Jourdain of Desistance.* Paris: Editions L'Harmattan.

Heuman Lars (2007) Objectivity in Swedish Criminal Proceedings. *Scandinavian Studies in Law* 51: 213–228.

Hewart Lord Chief Justice (1924) R y Sussex Justices. *Ex parte McCarthy ([1924] 1 KB 256, [1923] All ER233).*

Hochschild Arlie Russell (1983) *The Managed Heart – Commercialization of Human Feeling.* Berkeley, LA: University of California Press.

Holt Fanny (2015) The Balancing Act: The Emotion Work Produced by Attorneys in Their Everyday Work Life. *Department of Sociology and Work Life Science.* University of Gothenburg.

Hunter Rosemary (2005) Styles of Judging: How Magistrates Deal with Applications for Intervention Orders. *Alternative Law Journal* 30: 231–246.

Jacobsson Katarina (2008) "We Can't Just Do It Any Which Way": Objectivity Work among Swedish Prosecutors. *Qualitative Sociology Review* IV: 46–68.

Johnson Carol (2010) The Politics of Affective Citizenship: From Blair to Obama. *Citizenship Studies* 14: 495–509.

Kahan Dan M. (1999) The Progressive Appropriation of Disgust. In: Bandes Susan A. (ed) *The Passions of Law.* New York, NY: New York University Press, 63–79.

Keltner Dacher, Gruenfeld Deborah H. and Anderson Cameron (2003) Power, Approach, and Inhibition. *Psychological Review* 110: 265–284.

Kemper Theodore D. (2011) *Status, Power and Ritual Interaction – A Relational Reading of Durkheim, Goffman and Collins.* Farnham and Surrey: Ashgate Publishing Limited.

Kjelby Gert Johan (2015) Some Aspects of and Perspectives on the Public Prosecutor's Objectivity According to ECtHR Case-Law. *Bergen Journal of Criminal Law and Criminal Justice* 3: 61–83.

Kleres Jochen and Wettergren Åsa (2017) Fear, Hope, Anger, and Guilt in Climate Activism. *Social Movement Studies* 16: 507–519.

Kvale Steinar and Brinkmann Svend (2014) *Interviews. Learning the Craft of Qualitative Research Interviewing.* London: SAGE.

Landström Sara, Ask Karl, Sommar Charlotte, Willén, Rebecca (2015) Children's Testimony and the Emotional Victim Effect. *Legal and Criminological Psychology* 20: 365–383.

Lange Bettina (2002) The Emotional Dimension in Legal Regulation. *Journal of Law and Society* 29: 197–225.

Liederbach John, Fritsch Eric J. and Womack Charissa L. (2011) Detective Workload and Opportunities for Increased Productivity in Criminal Investigation. *Police Practice and Research* 12: 50–65.

Lively Kathryn J. (2002) Client Contact and Emotional Labor. *Work and Occupations* 29: 198–225.

Lukes Steven (2005) *Power: A Radical View.* Houndmills and Basingstoke: Palgrave Macmillan.

Mack Kathy and Roach Anleu Sharyn (2007) 'Getting through the List': Judgecraft and Legitimacy in the Lower Courts. *Social & Legal Studies* 16: 341–361.

Mack Kathy and Roach Anleu Sharyn (2010) Performing Impartiality: Judicial Demeanor and Legitimacy. *Law and Social Inquiry-Journal of the American Bar Foundation* 35: 137–173.

Maroney Terry A. (2011) The Persistent Cultural Script of Judicial Dispassion. *California Law Review* 99: 629–681.

Maroney Terry A. (2012) Angry Judges. *Vanderbilt Law Review* 65: 1207–1286.

Maroney Terry A. and Gross James J. (2014) The Ideal of the Dispassionate Judge: An Emotion Regulation Perspective. *Emotion Review* 6: 142–151.

McDonald Seonaidh (2005) Studying Actions in Context: A Qualitative Shadowing Method for Organizational Research. *Qualitative Research* 5: 455–473.

Mellqvist Mikael (2013) Om empatisk rättstillämpning (On Empathic Application of Law). *Svensk Juristtidning (Swedish Law Journal).* 494–501.

Moorhead Richard (2007) The Passive Arbiter: Litigants in Person and the Challenge To Neutrality. *Social & Legal Studies* 16: 405–424.

Morton Adam (2013) *Emotion and Imagination*. Cambridge: Polity Press.

Murphy Jeffrie G. (1999) Moral Epistemology, the Retributive Emotions, and the "Clumsy Moral Philosophy" of Jesus Christ. In: Bandes Susan A (ed) *The Passions of Law*. New York, NY: New York University Press, 149–167.

NJA. (2009:44) Nytt Juridiskt Arkiv: 447.

NJA. (2010:17) Nytt Juridiskt Arkiv: 671.

Nordén Elisabeth (2015) Utvecklingen av personuppklarade misstankar och bifallna åtal 2004–2014 (The Development of the Number of Offences Brought to Justice and Number of Approved Prosecutions 2004–2014). Brottsförebyggande rådet, BRÅ.

Nordh Roberth (2013) Det mest betydelsefulla verktyget vid bevisvärdering är trots allt domarens intuition (The Most Valuable Tool for Judges' Evaluation of Evidence Is Nevertheless Intuition). *Dagens juridik.* (accessed 25 September 2017).

Nussbaum Martha C. (1996) Emotion in the Language of Judging. *St. John's Law Review* 70: 23–30.

Nussbaum Martha C. (1999) "The Sewers of Vice": Disgust, Bodies, and the Law. In: Bandes Susan A. (ed) *The Passions of Law*. New York, NY: New York University Press, 17–62.

Olsson Eva (2008) Emotioner i arbete (Emotions at Work). *Department of Social Studies*. Karlstad: Karlstad University.

Pierce Jennifer L. (1999) Emotional Labor among Paralegals. *The ANNALS of the American Academy of Political and Social Science* 561: 127–142.

Posner Richard A. (1999) Emotion Versus Emotionalism in Law. In: Bandes Susan A. (ed) *The Passions of Law*. New York, NY: New York University Press, 309–329.

Ptacek James (1999) *Battered Women in the Courtroom: The Power of Judicial Responses*. Boston, MA: Northeastern University Press.

Rampling Martina (2015) Emotionsarbete som professionell praktik: Advokaten som klientens guide genom brottmålsprocessen. *Department of Sociology*. Stockholm University.

Reddy William (2001) *The Navigation of Feeling – A Framework for the History of Emotions*. Cambridge: Cambridge University Press.

Regeringsformen. The instrument of government 1974, amended 2010.

Remiche Adélaïde (2015) When Judging Is Power: A Gendered Perspective on the French and American Judiciaries. *Journal of Law and Courts* 3: 95–113.

Roach Anleu Sharyn and Mack Kathy (2005) Magistrates' Everyday Work and Emotional Labour. *Journal of Law and Society* 32: 590–614.

Roach Anleu Sharyn and Mack Kathy (2013) Judicial Authority and Emotion Work. *Judicial Review: Selected Conference Papers: Journal of the Judicial Commission of New South Wales* 11: 329–347.

Roach Anleu Sharyn and Mack Kathy (2017) *Performing Judicial Authority in the Lower Courts*. London: Palgrave Socio-Legal Studies.

Roeser Sabine (2012) Risk Communication. Public Engagement, and Climate Change: A Role for Emotions. *Risk Analysis* 32: 1033–1040.

Rosenbaum Thane (2005) *The Myth of Moral Justice: Why Our Legal System Fails to Do What's Right*. New York, NY: Harper Collins Publishers.

Rothstein Bo and Stolle Dietland (2008) The State and Social Capital: An Institutional Theory of Generalized Trust. *Comparative Politics* 40: 441–459.

Sandgren Claes (2014) Jäv mot domare, särskilt nämndeman (Conflict of Interest by Judges, in Particular Lay Judges). *Svensk Juristtidning (Swedish Law Journal)* 446–463.

Scarduzio Jennifer A. (2011) Maintaining Order through Deviance? The Emotional Deviance, Power, and Professional Work of Municipal Court Judges. *Management Communication Quarterly* 25: 283–310.

Scarduzio Jennifer A. and Tracy Sarah J. (2015) Sensegiving and Sensebreaking via Emotion Cycles and Emotional Buffering: How Collective Communication Creates Order in the Courtroom. *Management Communication Quarterly* 29: 331–357.

Scheer Monique (2012) Are Emotions a Kind of Practice (And Is That What Makes Them Have a History)? A Bourdieuan Approach to Understanding Emotions. *History and Theory* 51: 193–220.

Scheff Thomas J. (1990) *Microsociology. Discourse, Emotion, and Social Structure.* Chicago, IL: The University of Chicago Press.

Scheffer Thomas, Hannken-Illjes Kati and Kozin Alexander (2010) *Criminal Defence and Procedure: Comparative Ethnographies in the United Kingdom, Germany, and the United States.* Basingstoke: Palgrave Macmillan.

Schuster Mary L. and Propen Amy (2010) Degrees of Emotion: Judicial Responses to Victim Impact Statements. *Law, Culture and the Humanities* 6: 75–104.

Sieben Barbara and Wettergren Åsa (2010) *Emotionalizing Organizations and Organizing Emotions.* London: Palgrave MacMillan.

Siemsen Cynthia (2004) *Emotional Trials: The Moral Dilemmas of Women Criminal Defense Attorneys.* Boston, MA: Northeastern University Press.

Solomon Robert C. (1999) Justice v. Vengeance: On Law and the Satisfaction of Emotion. In: Bandes Susan A (ed) *The Passions of Law.* New York, NY: New York University Press, 121–148

SOU. (2016:52) Färre i häkte och minskad isolering (Less People in Detention and with Restrictions). Statens offentliga utredningar.

Strömwall Leif A. and Granhag Pär Anders (2003) How to Detect Deception? Arresting the Beliefs of Police Officers, Prosecutors and Judges. *Psychology, Crime & Law* 9: 19–36.

Sundberg Jakob (1969) Civil Law, Common Law, and the Scandinavians. *Scandinavian Studies in Law* 13: 179–205.

Svensson Petra (2018) *Cross-Sector Strategists. Dedicated Bureaucrats in Local Government Administration.* Gothenburg: University of Gothenburg.

The Ministry of Justice. (2015) *En modernare rättegång II (A Modern Trial II).* www.regeringen.se/rattsdokument/lagradsremiss/2015/05/en-modernare-rattegang-ii/.

Thoits Peggy A. (1989) The Sociology of Emotions. *Annual Review of Sociology* 15: 317–342.

Tilly Charles (2008) *Why?* Princeton, NJ: Princeton University Press.

Törnqvist Nina (2017) Att göra rätt. En studie om professionell respektabilitet, emotioner och narrativa linjer bland relationsvåldsspecialiserade åklagare (Doing just right: A Study on Professional Respectability, Emotions and Narrative Lines Among Prosecutors Specialised in Relationship Violence). *Department of Criminology.* Stockholm University.

Tyler Tom R. (2003) Procedural Justice, Legitimacy, and the Effective Rule of Law. *Crime and Justice* 30: 283–357.

Tyler Tom R. (2006) *Why People Obey the Law.* Princeton, NJ: Princeton University Press.

Tyler Tom R. and Bies Robert J. (1990) Beyond Formal Procedures: The Interpersonal Context of Procedural Justice. *Applied Social Psychology and Organizational Settings* 77: 98.

von Wright Georg Henrik (1986) *Vetenskapen och förnuftet (Science and Reason)*. Stockholm: Bonnier.

Vrij Aldert, Granhag Pär Anders and Porter Stephen (2010) Pitfalls and Opportunities in Nonverbal and Verbal Lie Detection. *Psychological Science in the Public Interest* 11: 89–121.

Weber Max (1948) Bureaucracy. In: Gerth Hans H. and Mills C. Wright (eds) *From Max Weber: Essays in Sociology*. New York, NY: Routledge, 196–244.

Weber Max (1978) *Economy and Society*. Berkeley, CA: University of California Press.

Weber Max (1995) *Den protestantiska etiken och kapitalismens anda (The Protestant Ethic and the Spirit of Capitalism)*. Lund: Argos.

Wergens Anna (2002) The Role and Standing of the Victim in the Face of Criminal Procedure in Sweden. *Revue internationale de droit pénal* 73: 259–300.

Wettergren Åsa (2009) Fun and Laughter: Culture Jamming and the Emotional Regime of Late Capitalism. *Social Movement Studies* 8: 1–16.

Wettergren Åsa (2010) Managing Unlawful Feelings: The Emotional Regime of the Swedish Migration Board. *International Journal for Work, Organisation and Emotion* 3: 400–419.

Wettergren Åsa (2013) *Emotionssociologi*. Malmö: Gleerups.

Wettergren Åsa (2015) How Do We Know What They Feel? In: Flam Helena and Kleres Jochen (eds) *Methods of Exploring Emotions*. London: Routledge, 115–124.

Wettergren Åsa and Bergman Blix Stina (2016) Empathy and Objectivity in the Legal Process: The Case of Swedish Prosecutors. *Journal of Scandinavian Studies in Criminology and Crime Prevention* 17: 19–35.

Wettergren Åsa and Bergman Blix Stina (2018) Judges' Professional Emotion Management: Contrasting Civil Case Mediation with Criminal Case Presiding. *Sharing and Regulating Emotions in Legal Spaces: Mediation, Restoration, and Reconciliation*. Oñati International Institute for the Sociology of Law.

World Prison Brief. (2017) http://prisonstudies.org/world-prison-brief-data.

Zaki Jamil (2014) Empathy: A Motivated Account. *Psychological Bulletin* 140: 1608–1647.

Zila Josef (2006) The Prosecution Service Function within the Swedish Criminal Justice System. In: Jehle Jörg-Martin and Wade Marianne (eds) *Coping with Overloaded Criminal Justice Systems*. Berlin and Heidelberg: Springer, 285–311.

Åklagarmyndigheten. (2017) The Swedish Prosecution Authority Annual Report. https://www.aklagare.se/globalassets/dokument/planering-och-uppfoljning/arsredovisningar/arsredovisning_2016.pdf.

# Index